Cobras in the Rough

Cobras in the Rough

Grant Gordon

Constable · London

Constable & Robinson Ltd
55–56 Russell Square
London WC1B 4HP
www.constablerobinson.com

First published in the UK by Constable,
an imprint of Constable & Robinson Ltd, 2012

A copy of the British Library Cataloguing in Publication Data is available from the British Library

ISBN: 978-1-84901-721-3 (hardback)
ISBN: 978-1-78033-512-4 (ebook)

Printed and bound in the UK

1 3 5 7 9 10 8 6 4 2

CATG-PEFC-052
www.pefc.org

For Tony Gordon, 1927–2009

Contents

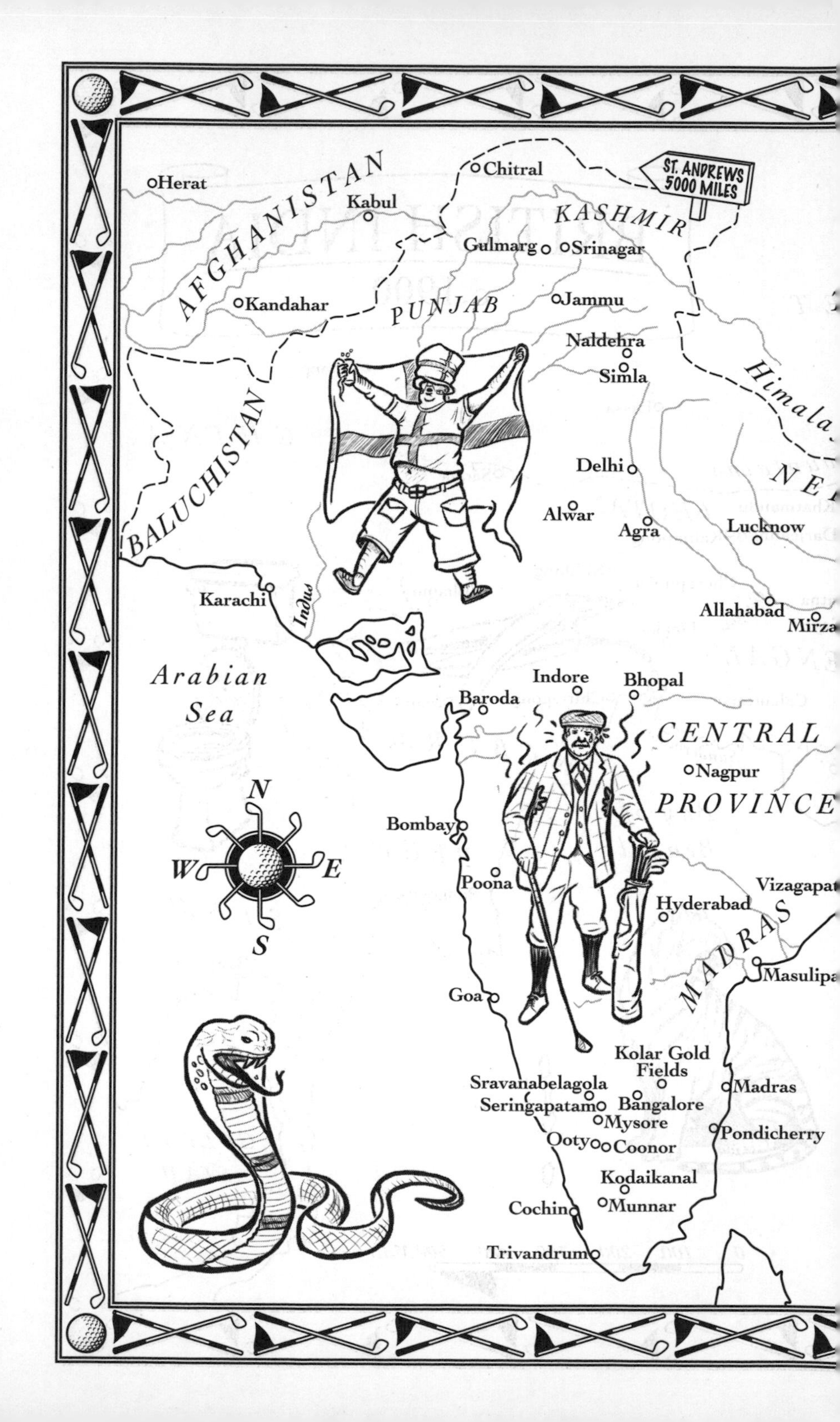

ST. ANDREWS 5000 MILES
Herat
AFGHANISTAN
Kabul
Chitral
KASHMIR
Gulmarg
Srinagar
Kandahar
PUNJAB
Jammu
Naldehra
Simla
Himala
BALUCHISTAN
Delhi
NE
Alwar
Agra
Lucknow
Karachi
Indus
Allahabad
Mirza
Arabian Sea
Indore
Bhopal
Baroda
CENTRAL
Nagpur
PROVINCE
N
Bombay
W
E
Poona
S
Hyderabad
Vizagapat
MADRAS
Masulipa
Goa
Kolar Gold Fields
Sravanabelagola
Seringapatam
Bangalore
Madras
Mysore
Pondicherry
Ooty
Coonor
Kodaikanal
Cochin
Munnar
Trivandrum

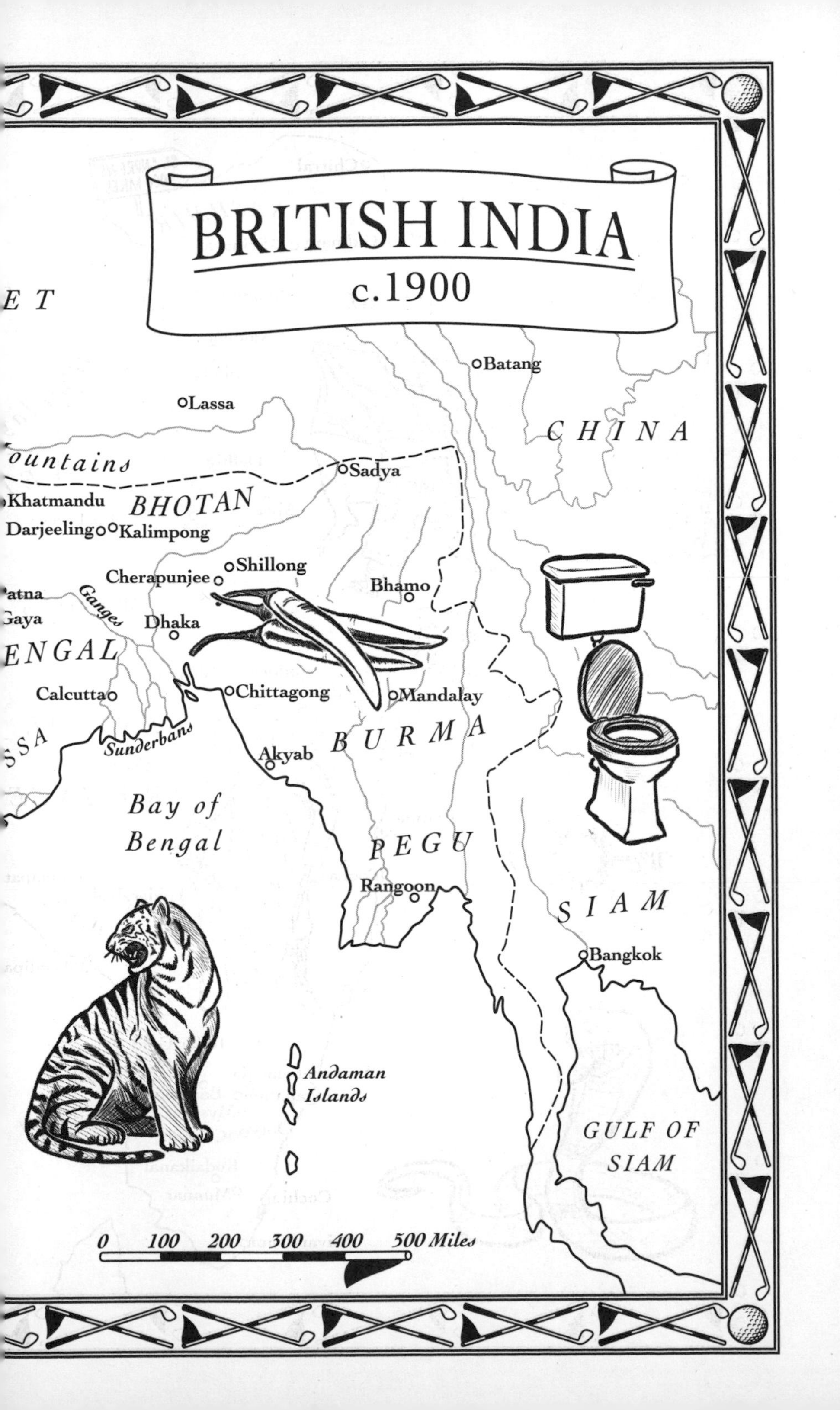
BRITISH INDIA
c.1900
E T
Batang
Lassa
C H I N A
ountains
Sadya
Khatmandu
BHOTAN
Darjeeling
Kalimpong
Shillong
Cherapunjee
Bhamo
atna
Ganges
Gaya
Dhaka
ENGAL
Calcutta
Chittagong
Mandalay
B U R M A
SSA
Sunderbans
Akyab
Bay of
Bengal
PEGU
Rangoon
S I A M
Bangkok
Andaman
Islands
GULF OF
SIAM
0
100
200
300
400
500 Miles

He will do more than any other man in history to change the course of humanity . . . he is the Chosen One. He'll have the power to impact nations. Not people. Nations. The world is just getting a taste of his power.

Earl Woods on his son, Tiger (1996)

1

Kashmir – Golf in Paradise

[illegible]

Rudyard Kipling, *Plain Tales from the Hills* (1888)

Cobra-headed driver in hand, I am taking the last golf lesson of my life on the world's highest golf course. I am hitting due north-west. Forty miles away is the disputed border beyond which lies blood-soaked land that Pakistan has claimed since 1947 as rightfully its own. A hundred miles further west is the city of Peshawar and the Khyber Pass, the ancient northern route into Afghanistan, and a vital military and trade artery in and out of British India for 200 years. I am surrounded by magnificent snow-

1

Kashmir – Golf in Paradise

This Boy came out. He was pretty and was petted. He took the pettings seriously and fretted over women not worth saddling a pony to call upon. He found his new free life in India very good. It does look attractive in the beginning, from a subaltern's point of view – all ponies, partners, dancing and so on.

Rudyard Kipling, *Plain Tales from the Hills* (1888)

Cobra-headed driver in hand, I am having the best golf lesson of my life on the world's highest golf course. I am hitting directly due west. Forty miles away is the disputed border beyond which lies blood-soaked land that Pakistan has claimed since 1947 as rightfully its own. A hundred miles further west is the city of Peshawar, and the Khyber Pass, the ancient northern route into Afghanistan, and a vital military and trade artery in and out of British India for 200 years. I am surrounded by magnificent, snowy, grey mountains; I gasp, breathless after every shot as the altitude tricks my lungs into hyperventilating. The sky is a perfect blue, there is a crisp alpine bite to the air and yet I am sweating as I would in Delhi traffic at noon. There is utter Himalayan silence except for the thwack-whoosh of my strikes and the gentle purr in my ear of my instructor Dinmohd suggesting changes to my swing, the balance of weight between my feet or the catwalk-model swivel of my hips, as I caress ball after ball off the tee towards the guns of Pakistan. For a few blissful hours high up in this beautiful war zone I forget what has driven me here, and am delighted to be playing high-altitude golf, just as the British had done a hundred years ago.

The hill station of Gulmarg lies a two-hour drive northwest from Kashmir's capital Srinagar. It is India's leading ski resort in the winter and, amazingly, there, 8,960 feet above sea level, the British built a golf course, which is used as dry ski slopes in winter. As in other places in India, the British picked the best views for their golf courses.

Srinagar feels like Belfast in the 1980s, except that it's in a beautiful valley and surrounded by gargantuan mountains. Soldiers are everywhere, mostly just lounging around at crossroads, their guns lazily pointing at the ground, their gait slouched and bored, cheap cigarettes and beedis dangling from the corners of lips. At the main road junctions there are armoured trucks with manned gun turrets pointing at shoppers. At the entrance to our hotel's small road, a soldier is huddled in a den of sandbags, with a machine gun pointing out at the street. I always say 'Hello' to him and smile, and he seems to like this.

We had chosen one of the best hotels in town, not really knowing what to expect of the city. I stayed in Sarajevo shortly after the end of the Bosnian war in 1996, and I half wondered if Srinagar would resemble that Balkan capital – bullet holes everywhere, bombed-out buildings, minefields to be avoided, with our hotel perhaps a Kashmiri version of the famous Holiday Inn in Sarajevo, which absorbed the blast of many Serb shells as the Western journalists staying there cowered and fired off their frontline reports.

In fact, the Broadway resembles a slightly tropical Hilton. With a nice swimming pool. That is bizarrely closed 'due to swine flu'. Maybe the residents of this town have been so much under attack recently that they see lethal insurgents everywhere, even in the shape of this al-Qaeda of viruses. The longer we stay, the more we modify our hotel comparison: in fact, it calls to mind the hotel in *The Shining* – vast, utterly deserted, slightly spooky and with bored, unpredictable staff popping up in odd places to startle you.

Srinagar had been the leading British holiday spot for the north-west region, and there are two Raj-era golf courses here to discover. Opposite the hotel is the old British polo ground, now converted into a running track that Tom, my trusted wingman who I had pushed into travelling with me on this Indian adventure, thought he'd go jogging on, though later he wondered if he'd be deemed a security risk and changed his mind. As in Northern Ireland, the British have been partly responsible for the problems here. In the 1840s the British handed control of this Muslim-dominated area to a Hindu dynasty, which in turn gave rise to the violence and discord there has been between Pakistan and India ever since Partition. Kashmir is now trying to woo tourists back, but it remains somewhat ironic that the British called the region 'Paradise on Earth'.

From the moment we arrived we'd told everyone what we were doing in order to be as transparent as possible. We are going to Gulmarg, we said, the highest golf course in the world, to play some golf. Everyone thought this was a splendid idea – cabbies, Hotel Broadway receptionists, waiters, the smart travelling salesmen with whom we drank too much rough Indian Royal Stag whisky, the barmen who were themselves from Gulmarg – and they were clearly delighted we were going there, telling us how beautiful it was. It all sounded great.

But no one mentioned that Gulmarg golf club had been shut for a year.

***

One of my most nervous moments in the UK was when I passed from the Irish Republic into Northern Ireland when touring as the drummer of a rock band during the Troubles. It was the middle of the night, and I was in a battered van with three Ulstermen and three Englishman. Two of us (I was one) had left our passports at home in London by mistake. On the way in, we had managed to sneak past the lazy immigration officers at Dun Laoghaire port in Dublin, but I thought this was going to be the real test. We drove slowly through the surreal barbed wired half-mile of no-man's-land that in those days (the early 1990s) separated the two countries. It felt like a Cold War thriller. We were aware of the gun turrets and cameras all around us. I was terrified. Finally, we came to a barrier. 'STOP YOUR VEHICLE NOW AND TURN OFF YOUR ENGINE!' ordered the sign. We did. The second the engine was off, an intensely bright beam gushed through our van from a spotlight on the hill opposite, blinding us. We knew then that our faces were being scrutinised by some young English squaddie. I thought I'd probably spend the night in an RUC cell or worse. But eventually, the light went out, the barrier lifted and we were back in the UK.

I had expected similar checkpoints and hassle on the road to Gulmarg out of Srinagar, but in fact there was none of this. Just one very long, very straight, very bumpy road across the valley floor towards the mountains.

After two hours we reached a village and pulled up at a small wooden hut. 'You have to pay a toll here,' our driver said, though for what I wasn't sure. I could see him tell the men at this questionable toll booth that we were here to play golf. Golf? They were all shaking their heads. Then one who spoke English got into the car and said: 'No golf in Gulmarg, not since a year ago; they are repairing the course, I am guide – I will show you other things in Gulmarg, it is very beautiful town.'

We thanked him for the advice, persuaded him out of the vehicle and then considered what he'd said. Surely someone would have told us before? If the golf course – one of the area's oldest and most famous attractions – had been shut for a whole year, wouldn't someone in Srinagar have known?

Mohan, our driver, was therefore surprised we still wanted to ascend, but we insisted. Slowly we climbed up the winding mountain roads, the views of the Kashmir Valley below becoming more and more astounding. At the top we passed two police checkpoints. Both times it was clear that the cop was saying 'Why do these idiots dressed in their silly golf gear want to go to the golf club? It has been shut for a year.' But we kept insisting and finally, after passing through the town we came to a large plateau, fringed by huge grey-brown mountains, and with a mass of links-type heath grass in the middle. 'Golf course,' said Mohan.

Hmm. No players, no flags, nothing. It certainly looked like a golf course, but a very shut one. Blast. Still, it was worth a look and it was certainly a beautiful Swiss-type spot.

We drove to the clubhouse and were delighted to see a putting green, with numbered little flags, like at the sea-front in Bexhill-on-Sea – signs of golf life. I met the care-taker who showed us around the ghostly place. The golf club was founded in 1901, and at one time was one of the most famous and prestigious in India. It boasts several slightly dubious records, including being the highest course in the world and the second oldest golf club in India (not true – Mumbai, Bangalore and Shillong clubs are all older). But it also claims, more plausibly, to be the longest course in India (6,805 yards) and to possess the longest hole – the mighty 600-yard eighth. It has six par-five holes in total.

When the British built hill stations, they built sports facilities. With exceptions, the type of Brit who ended up as a servant of the Raj tended not to be too interested in intellectual or artistic pursuits; these were outdoor people, tough and competitive, who had grown up with games. Indeed, in the public schools like Haileybury (specially set up in 1809 by the East India Company to train young men to rule India) the culture of sporting excellence was engrained in the psyches of these young rulers-to-be. The sports of Empire – cricket, rugby, polo, tennis (and anything involving chasing and killing rare exotic animals) – grew in popularity and importance in the time when British colonial domination of the world was being established, and became engrained in the culture of imperial rule.

Sports clubs – called gymkhanas – were built at every hill station. Sometimes – as in Ooty, Jorhat and Madras – they were centred on a racecourse, and offered a range of sports and pastimes to the relaxing Raj.

One other sport of Empire that was becoming popular during this period was golf. The Royal Calcutta Golf Club was founded in 1829 and is proud to this day of being the first club in the world established outside of Britain. So what would be more natural than for the British decamped haut-bourgeoisie in Kashmir to build a golf course here amongst the mountains and dream of St Andrews?

The current clubhouse dates from 1953 after a fire destroyed the original British one, but it has been decorated and furnished in late Raj style. In the two main rooms of the new building, there are winners' boards from 1901 onwards when a certain Captain John Hill of the 15th Sikh Regiment won the men's championship and Mrs R. C. Plowden the ladies prize, and various pictures of British men and women enjoying the links. There is also a full-size snooker table there (100 rupees an hour for us), but that's about it. We were just about to have a token few putts on the putting green and then disappointedly head back down to Srinagar, when a thirty-something, short, scrawny figure in the brightest, stripiest jumper appeared. 'This is golf pro,' said the caretaker. We were sceptical, but Dinmohd soon won us over with his calmness and golf sincerity. There was no hard sell here, he just suggested we maybe use the 'driving range'. OK we said, sounds good. Er . . . where is it?

'Over there,' said Dinmohd pointing at a bit of the under-repair course. 'I will position my caddies out on the course, and they will pick up the balls. I will watch you hit, and make suggestions.'

'Well, why not?' we thought. It was all so weird anyway, why not hit a few balls on the highest golf course in the world?

Dinmohd had been the pro here for seven years, taking the job over from his father when he retired. He placed his caddies 100 yards away and told me to hit a pitching wedge so he could see my swing. He seemed pleased with what he saw, but urged me to follow through more, which was good advice. However, I know I can pitch decently. If this was to be a lesson, I wanted to work on things I couldn't do so well. So I reached for my hybrid and told Dinmohd to make this work for me. First, he yelled at his boys to move back to 150 yards. Like bored sulky teenagers having to hang out with their parents, they complied. With his help, I started hitting perfect rescue club shots one after another, following my bespoke four-step mantra – ball to heel, slow backswing, full follow-through and above all, head down. It felt great, but I noticed I couldn't actually breathe. This was not like the asthma of my childhood; it was as though there just wasn't any air to breathe any more.

'You are at high altitude,' reassured Dinmohd. 'Take your time, you will be fine.'

He was right, and I noticed that the ball seemed to go further and faster at this altitude and also made a strange, zippy, ping sound on being struck, as though it was carving its path through the air. Finally, I got out the driver that recently I had started to hate. Dinmohd moved his boys well back and I started smacking balls to every area of the plateau. One horrific slice I'm sure landed in the Pakistani border zone and would have been considered incoming hostile fire.

His most helpful comment with this club was 'Why are you using a 9.5 degree clubface? You should use 11 degrees. This is a very hard club.' Even so, he got me hitting over 50 per cent straightish, which was some improvement on my recent woeful form off the tee, so I was pleased. He spent the same patient time with Tom, and then had a look at our putting and chipping. As ever in India, it's hard to practise putting on such bumpy and unmown turf, but Dinmohd passed on some good tips. We gave him 500 rupees (about £8) for his forty-five minutes with us, which, as a caddie receives 100 rupees (plus tip) for an eighteen-hole round, we thought might be the going rate. I felt sorry for him – a talented sportsman, a great teacher and a passionate man of golf, with a ghost golf club to watch over. Hopefully the state tourism people will get their act together and reopen Gulmarg soon – it's such a shame this beautiful course is mothballed.

We gave Dinmohd a lift down the hill, during which he quizzed me vigorously about golf in Britain . . . what the courses were like and how much everything cost. He seemed shocked that it costs £5 to hit 100 balls at a driving range in the UK. This is about 400 rupees. In India this could get you five very decent restaurant meals, or pay for a fifty-mile taxi ride. I told him we had just played at Naldehra, and he had a business competitor's interest in what that course was like. How rough were the fairways? How well kept were the greens? How annoying was the sharing of the fairways?

We dropped him off at a bleak-looking crossroads, and I watched as he started walking up a rather desolate hill. We headed back down into the valley.

***

The next day we walked the length of a long par-four hole from our machine-gunner-in-sandbags-protected five-star hotel to the Kashmir Golf Club (KGC) down the road. Dressed in gaudy golf gear, with clubs on our backs in the harsh lunchtime sun, we felt utterly incongruous. Apart from at the airport we felt we were the only Westerners in Srinagar, and we were without doubt the only Western golfers in town.

At first I thought we couldn't look more ridiculous nor at risk had we marched down the Falls Road in Belfast wearing nothing but Union Jack boxer shorts, whistling 'Rule Britannia'. Gradually, though, I realized that no one seemed at all bothered by us: we received barely any inquisitive looks, let alone hassle, and when we stopped at the petrol station to stock up on Pepsi and snacks for the round, we were welcomed heartily. I began to think that tourism is still strongly in the Kashmiri DNA, and the quirky needs and behaviour of tourists are perhaps just accepted.

As we entered the golf club we were surrounded by the usual phalanx of caddies pitching their shoulders for hire. But whereas usually the caddies behave like pushy taxi-drivers at Delhi airport, heckling for business, out-shouting each other, urging you into hiring them, these guys didn't seem to quite know what to do, so surprised were they to see us. It was as if deep down they were remembering that they ought to be pushy towards us but they couldn't quite remember how to do it. The babble of caddy opinion on what we needed to do to get started was irritating, so we headed into the clubhouse to find some members, pay our respects and hopefully grab some tea.

There are two buildings at the KGC. The old wing, where the Starter's office and pro shop are situated, dates from the course's foundation a century ago. It's low and wooden, like a prep school's cricket pavilion. There are honours boards on the walls, going back to the 1920s – all British names until the 1950s. There is a hole-in-one board there too, with the name of everyone who's had to buy the whole clubhouse a drink for the last eighty-five years. It was from these timbered huts that emerged the great Ghulam Mohammad, India's first ever golf professional in 1930. The new building is modern, architecturally brutalist and has the feel of a 1960s car park perched on London's South Bank. The balcony, however, is very pleasant, and several old members were having coffee while watching the action on the first tee and eighteenth green. All the members of the KGC seemed old. Apart from the caddies, we were the youngest people there by a considerable margin. The members were very welcoming, asked us the usual check'em out questions – what's your handicap, why are you here, have you got clubs, where have you played – and then invited us to join them. The mood was languid, torporific and a little wistful.

The old members told us that we had to see the Starter,

but he was at prayers, so why not have some tea? We were placed inside the clubhouse in a discreet corner where we wouldn't annoy anyone, and managed to persuade the terse, Methuselah-like waiter (who seemed like he'd been there since before Independence) to bring us some toast and jam, too. This consumed, I wandered down to the old buildings to see if the Starter was back from prayers. Seventy-five per cent of Kashmir is Muslim. On the previous night, we were watching England v Australia cricket on TV in a bar. I was trying to engage the bar staff in chat about the Indian cricket team, and was receiving some unusually short, polite but disinterested replies. I retired drunk early that night. The next morning Tom told me that the bar guys had said to him that they knew I was just trying to be polite, but as Muslims they all support Pakistan at cricket, and always want the Indian team to lose. I reflected on why they couldn't have told me that, but could tell Tom. Perhaps it's my intimidating patrician air . . .

The Starter was back from prayers but boy, was he pissed off. I hovered at the doorway while he blasted a helper about something. This finished, he looked up at me sharply, stared me aggressively in the eye and said 'Yes?' He gave a Basil Fawlty-like air of being someone far too busy to have to deal with the irritating needs of customers, even though I was the only person demanding his attention.

'Hello, we'd like to play a round please, may we?' I said.

'No, sorry, that is not possible. Course is closed, please come back tomorrow,' he said.

'Oh, that's a shame. We are from England, and we are on a golf tour of the courses the British built in northern India, we'd heard so much about the Kashmir Golf Club and . . .' This was all being met by averted, irritable eyes, much negative shaking of the head and the general vibe that I was ruining his day. I persevered. '. . . We went up to

Gulmarg, and would love to play a quick nine if that's not too much trouble?'

The Starter fixed me with an intense stare from wide, cataract-y eyes and sent the torpedo he thought would sink me: 'Do you have your own clubs?' He looked triumphant, thinking he had found a good reason to refuse admission.

'Yes we do,' I said. Suddenly his whole manner and countenance changed, and he was very welcoming, as though I'd somehow passed some golf initiation test: that if we were silly enough to drag our own clubs into this valley then we must be serious golfers. Having our own clubs was much appreciated on all the courses we played; I think it showed that we weren't just tourists on a jolly. Actually, we were serious. It's just that often we weren't very good.

I was issued with a caddy, Younis. He was the only caddy I had in India who was younger than me. He was also the only person I saw in our whole trip that was taller than me. He was also the worst caddy by far. Teeing off on the first, I felt the eyes and breath of the old members on the clubhouse balcony fixed on my back. Younis was pressing me to take a driver on this 425-yard hole, but I insisted on him giving me my five-iron. I just wanted to get this away and not look like an idiot. I hit a good tee shot, as did Tom. Huge relief, followed by that energy-filled 'We're off!' march down the first fairway.

I then took the five-iron again, and hit a pretty decent positional shot through a tree-fringed fairway bottleneck to leave a wedge on to the green. This pitch I hit well, and thought it would land on the green, but it wavered slightly right, and plopped into one of the ring of greenside bunkers. Shit. I hate bunkers. And I hadn't brought a sand wedge.

Kashmir Golf Club is a pleasant course. Situated in this huge valley, it is absolutely flat and fringed by mountains to the east. The fairways are mostly wide and it would be really quite an easy course were it not for the epidemic of dark grey sandtraps that stain every hole like psoriasis. Wherever you want to naturally hit the ball, there is a bunker to negotiate. Each green is like a high citadel, ringed by a moat of sandtraps. It's tough. And it destroyed my round. I took three to get out of the bunker on the first, then two-putted for an eight. If my pitch had landed a foot to the left, I was putting for par. Instead I get a bloody eight.

In fury I grabbed the driver from my bag (even though Younis handed me the five-iron, thinking he'd sussed me), and teed up on the second. I pulled the drive rather nastily, but it was long and, because the fairway was so wide, it still rested on the flat stuff. For the second shot I played a glorious seven-iron into the green. It was a lovely strike and made me feel more of a man from the moment of impact onwards. I thought it was on the green. Younis wasn't so sure. He was right. It was in a bunker again to the right of the dance floor. Only two to get out this time and two putts, so a six, but again that feeling that I could and should have been challenging for par.

At each hole I found ever deeper bunkers, and my mood worsened. It was getting really hot. Not in a heavy, damp Delhi or Calcutta way, but in a high summer in Provence sort of way. Also, before every shot Younis and I would have a spat about which club I should use. Younis would tell me how it's important to practise and hint that I was playing too much in my comfort zone. Both statements were true but sometimes you just want to hit a ball accurately to feel good. My round was also affected because I knew I was starting to get ill. India ill. Delhi-belly to the max ill. This would slay me for the next two days, my bottom becoming a tap for hissing, explosive liquid poo six times a day, my mind drifting off into dehydrated, underfed, trippy paranoia.

I played the eighth and ninth rather well, jettisoning my

malfunctioning driver in favour of a hybrid off the tee. I ended up with a five on the ninth in front of the old members, but by now the sun and my oncoming sickness were really getting to me. I secretly hoped Tom wanted to stop, which he did, and after changing we sat down on the balcony to rehydrate and to chat.

The old members were friendly and talkative, though melancholic. I told one – a retired brigadier in the Indian Army – that I occasionally worked for the BBC.

'Ah. BBC. Mark Tully.'

'Yes . . .'

'Mark Tully is a great man . . .'

'Yes,' I said, 'he has lived in India for 40 years now . . .'

'Mark Tully speaks excellent Hindi. He speaks Hindi with no trace of an accent.'

'Right,' I said, feeling that I was unfairly getting some rubbed-off credit for Sir Mark's linguistic skills.

'Why you guys playing here? You should go to Gulmarg – that's a proper golf course.'

They all seemed to have a nostalgic sadness about them – that no one comes to Kashmir anymore; that their golf course is empty; that from 1990 – when the violence escalated – Srinagar has become this war zone. Since that year it is estimated that 70,000 people have died in the conflict – twenty times as many as the numbers killed in Northern Ireland in thirty years of the Troubles. At the KGC you can still feel – just – the heartbeat of a different, more positive, thriving time. Not of a British time – though the sense of that is here still – but a prosperous time before the pain and divisions scarred this beautiful area and its proud people. It's the only occasion in India that I've felt this wistfulness and melancholia.

I saw an advert on TV when we were in Calcutta (1,000 miles away from Srinagar), subtly extolling the virtues of the Valley, and with the snappy slogan 'Help encourage tourism back to Kashmir.' But it was the only time I saw anything like this, and it is clearly not being listened to.

'The tourists have stopped coming because of the troubles here,' one old member said.

'Well,' I said brightly, 'we came . . .'

'Yes,' he replied, 'but the Western tourists are so small in number. It is the Indian tourists we need, and they do not come.'

Later, in the Hotel Broadway's five-star 'pub' we sat at the bar with Mohsin, a prosperous-looking businessman of my age, and Imtiaz, a white Anglo-Indian in his late forties. Imtiaz was proud to introduce himself to me as a Kashmiri, and spoke English in a thick local accent. They, too, had played the KGC on that day and wondered what I thought of the course. 'It's great,' I said, 'very pretty. But far too many bunkers.'

'Far too many bunkers? You have it dead right there! Those bloody bunkers are a pain up the backside,' Imtiaz said, and they both roared with laughter. 'Anyway, what are you doing playing there? You want to play at Gulmarg – that's a real golf course.'

***

Much later that night I am stupidly, sadly drunk again on Royal Stag whisky, and I can feel the sickness about to rise up through my body and pulverise my digestive system. I have bored Tom, always drunker, always less hungover than I, with my stories of personal woe that he has heard in every bar, every night, all over the Himalayas. And inevitably I tell him about my father, over and over again, as though somehow the telling will produce catharsis. It doesn't. I drink more and more, and within twenty-four hours my body has collapsed in diarrhoeic entropy and I am hallucinating. As I lay sweating in bed in Kashmir, the late monsoon rain now flooding the town, I start to think about what the hell we are doing here.

Lyrics from Stephen Sondheim's 'Somewhere' trip in and out of my mind as I surface and plummet in and out of clear thought . . .

2

Dreaming of Simla

Although Tiger Woods would never admit weakness publicly, few friends doubt that his father's death has fundamentally affected the golfer and cast a shadow over his innate sunny disposition. Above all, it almost certainly affected his relationships with women.

Daily Mail (1 December 2009)

I am standing at the priest's lectern in the pretty fifteenth-century church in Keyford-on-Sea looking out at the forty or so people gazing at me from their pews. I am about to address my father's funeral. My scepticism about religion and religious services is put aside for an hour, as I think to myself, *I am doing this for him.* I am very nervous and, as I struggle to think of the words to start my speech, my mind is focusing on two things: as his coffin was brought into the church by the anonymous, paid pall-bearers, Sondheim and Bernstein's beautiful song 'Somewhere' started to play over the PA. Just hearing the first verse nearly triggered the powerful tears I have been repressing all morning. My mother chose this song. They both loved musicals and *West Side Story* was the last musical they ever saw together. Three months later this song of great, against-the-odds, Romeo-and-Juliet love is transformed into his lament. I am overwhelmed by the perfection, the beauty of my mother's choice. But the speech that I'd meticulously planned, and felt confident about delivering, is now in jeopardy as I try to control my emotions. It's always the music at funerals that makes me cry. It mainlines.

And then there was this exchange with one of the undertakers which I can't shake.

It is 2.28 p.m. I am standing outside the church with my mother and the (very kind) vicar. We are saying hello to mourners as they arrive, accepting sympathies, deflecting the pain of others and the pain they are feeling for us. The service starts at 2.30. The organist is already booming out some dreadful, bass-heavy bombastic minor key dirge, and I'm dealing with my petulant Holden Caulfield anger that I'm participating in this phoney Christian ritual for a man who couldn't even name the four gospel writers.

I'm conscious that the undertaker has crabbed up to my side. He's already annoyed me by making us wait in the hearse at the church gates, while the car carrying my father arrives late.

Then he says out of the corner of his mouth, as though we are two spies exchanging passwords during a 'drop', 'Your mother tells me you work on *Big Brother*.'

'Er . . . that's right. Sometimes. I also . . .'

'Me and the wife: we're huge fans of *Big Brother*.'

My brain is in freefall. Suddenly I feel I'm in a *Monty Python* sketch. Surely this can't be happening? But it is. And I listen, stunned, as he gives me his opinion on the recent series, how it was all better when 'Nasty Nick' was around, his thoughts on Jade Goody, how 'the wife' tapes every episode. And I find myself forced into this chat, gossiping, *Heat*-style, about *Big Brother* housemates whilst my father's coffin is readied for its unexpectedly Broadway entrance.

Later on I reflect that it is all about the amazingly powerful tractor beam of celebrity. That somehow, however inappropriately, this man was compelled to talk to me, all because I had brushed against his TV heroes. He would tell his wife later about his encounter with me, and somehow they would both glow with the fourth-hand radiation of celebrity.

I wanted to hit him.

Grief can make you very selfish, very impatient, and quite nasty. And, for once, everyone forgives you. Grief is a charter to behave like a self-hating spoilt brat, and get away with it. For a while.

***

The last time I ever had a drink with my father, Tony, was in a pub round the corner from his local golf course in Lymington, Hampshire. I had just finished a month-long, intensive job, often working through the night. It had been four weeks of considerable stress, which at that point in my life I seemed to seek out like a ghetto kid desperately searching for glue or horse tranquilizers. The busier I was, the more stressed I became. The more stressed I became, the more alive I thought I felt. Pace, frenzy, lack of contemplation time – these seemed to blot out the underlying chaos that was simmering. Activity was my heroin. I was addicted to my poison.

I'd planned it out thoroughly: I'd hit some balls on the range, finish the job, grab a few hours sleep, then head down to my parents. As the only golfing non-motorist in the country, I have spent my life hauling a heavy and inconveniently designed golf bag around on trains and buses. I thought I'd hit the jackpot that month when I discovered in Tesco Borehamwood a budget golf shroud with wheels that you nestled your clubs in. That day I wheeled my clubs on and off several trains and buses, then dragged them for twenty minutes across semi-countryside and a town-fringe housing estate, through a rather boggy, waterlogged recreation ground, up across a bridge over the A1 and finally down into 'Nevada Bob's Driving Range'.

It had been quite a slog. My hands were cut because I'd been pulling the rough handles hard for so long. The bottom of the bag near the wheels was shredded, the seam had split and the bag was covered in mud. I cursed Tesco craftsmanship. Then I cursed my parsimonious self for buying a shoddy 'value' product. Then I realized that this was really not the intended use for this bag. It's designed for old men to wheel their clubs from their suburban double garage to the car boot, or from the airport baggage carousel to the awaiting trolley after the flight from Malaga. They're not made to be dragged across a commando assault course. As it turned out, this was good training as I was to spend months in India doing exactly the same, with a much heavier set of clubs, a suitcase and a rucksack full of computer gear. In 35°C with the monsoon tipping down.

***

Golf is so popular simply because it is the best game in the world at which to be bad.

A. A. Milne, 'The Charm of Golf' (1920)

He had wanted to play too, of course, but I wouldn't let him, knowing that his chronic sciatica would barely allow him to walk from the car to the clubhouse, let alone attempt eighteen holes. Anyway, that day I actually preferred to be on my own, to be in the open air, moving at pace up and down the fairways, enjoying the splendid views of the Isle of Wight and the Needles which loom across the water behind the club house. For years, I am ashamed to admit, I had found my father's golf slightly embarrassing to be around. But I loved our time together, and I know it held a fifty-fold meaning for him. I think our little half-day golf trips were some of the best moments in his life. It was certainly a few hours when he could have a good bitch about everything and chain-smoke his Craven A old-lady fags.

He was a terrible golfer. All his life. We played together for almost thirty years and he never for one second improved, even if we played every day for a week. He loved the game though. I knew that every April when I stayed up into the early hours watching the US Masters tournament from the beautiful Augusta course, he would be sitting in his armchair in the New Forest watching too. At every gripping last hole of Ryder Cup drama, I knew that wherever we were we would be both be shouting at the screen, screaming aggressively at the Americans.

For him, playing golf was a bit like digital technology. He just didn't get it. When I talked to him about computers, mobile phones or the internet I know he had no conceptual framework to begin to understand what I was saying. Whenever I did a project for BBC News Online, he would always ask me to tell him 'when it would be on so we can catch it', as though it was an episode of *Heartbeat* that had to be circled in the *Radio Times* so that it wouldn't be missed. The idea that it was 'on' *forever* was beyond his paradigm. Similarly golf. He had no concept whatsoever of what you had to do to play the game better. Many of us tried to tell him over the years. He'd listen politely, nod, thank us for the advice and then proceed as normal. He loved the phrase 'let it go in one ear and out the other', and I think this is what happened with golf tips.

And yet he had a fine mind. Even into his seventies he could take a car engine to bits, know exactly what wasn't working, and tell the young mechanics at the garage what to fix, how to fix it, and how much it should cost. And he was fantastic with analogue electronics. All my life he fixed my toys. Even when I was running professional recording studios I would take him all the broken cables, headphones, guitar pedals or speakers, and he would return them to me after a few months, mended. He saved me a fortune in replacement costs. He could do so many things I can't. The most obvious is driving cars. He was a car obsessive, adored Formula One and could tell you exactly what was happening in Michael Schumacher or Lewis Hamilton's car at any time during a race. He would have loved to watch recent seasons where the all-British pairing of Lewis Hamilton and Jenson Button is driving for the British-based McLaren team. We always felt they were *our* team, as their HQ is in Sheerwater in Surrey, very close to where I grew up.

He had one golf shot. I called it 'the push/shove/jab'. He really had no swing action whatsoever, and no timing or rhythm. No matter where he was on the fairway or in the rough, he would select a club (this club selection was basically irrelevant as the shot was always the same) and, with minimal backswing, jab hard into the ball, then stop on impact, with no follow through. Every shot the same. Almost every shot a disappointment to him. A normally mild and polite man, he would become filled with Tourette-like rage while playing golf. From various bushes and ditches on the course I'd frequently hear a distant 'SHIT' and 'OH FUCK IT'. It later struck me that the only other time I saw him show serious anger was when he was in Portsmouth hospital a month before he died, when he was angry with everyone – the nurses, the doctors (now paranoid, he thought they were 'experimenting' on him), and most of all, God, for calling his time too soon. As I sat on his bed, he grabbed my arm with his strong bony hand, looked me hard in the eye and, his body shaking, hissed 'You've got to get me out of this fucking place.'

But with golf he never seemed that bothered for long and when he fluked a good one he was ecstatic. We always diligently wrote down the scores and I always won. When I was a boy, he was happiest when we'd have a sit down between holes. He'd light up, I'd eat some crisps or a Mars bar, and he seemed the most relaxed and contented I'd ever seen him. He was no sportsman. Apart from golf, and kicking a football around with me as a kid, he never played anything; and he was totally disinterested in nature and the outdoors. He never understood my passion for rambling. 'Why not drive?' was his attitude. He was also to the right of Jeremy Clarkson on most environmental matters. But on the golf course with me he found some sort of peace I think, as did I.

As he got into his seventies his game worsened, but I started to care much less (perhaps shedding the embarrassed teenager skin), and other players on the course who we'd hold up minded less too. Old men hacking away on golf courses are treated with a lot of affection and a sort of respect by young players, the assumption being 'they were once really good, now bless 'em, they're still doing it, even though their game is clearly much reduced'. I think young players have a flicker of a moment of seeing themselves in thirty or forty years and hope that they too will still be hitting golf balls at that age.

Also, two new factors came into play. Firstly, he became rather erratic and forgetful during a game. He would play a shot, put the club on the ground whilst he lit a fag, then walk off without the iron. When he next needed that club, he'd suddenly realize what he'd done and I would have to go running back through the course, letting players galore through, to pick up the errant tool.

The other factor was that he started seriously to struggle to walk as sciatica set in for the pernicious long term. Gradually he found it difficult to even play more than two consecutive holes without being in a great deal of pain. He'd have a walking stick in one hand, an iron in the other, a fag hanging Jimmy Page-style out of the side of his mouth, and I would end up caddying the whole round for both of us, lugging a bag on each shoulder for nine holes, which really isn't that enjoyable, especially in the February rain. Our between-hole rests would lengthen as he tried to will the pain away from his lower back and arse. In fact, he was in so much pain I wondered if he was having any fun at all. But he kept wanting more. He loved the experience so much, and couldn't really accept that his body was telling him he couldn't do it anymore. And by now his putting was shot, too. He'd always been a decent putter – it suited his calm, measured, diligent temperament. But in the last few years he seemed unable to judge the weight of a putt at all. It was almost pot luck if the ball landed near the hole or twenty feet past it.

***

In 1947–8 my father worked for Lord Louis Mountbatten, cousin of the Queen, uncle to the Duke of Edinburgh, war hero, spin doctor extraordinaire, show off and general all-round Establishment good chap. In February of 1947 Mountbatten was appointed Viceroy of India, taking over from Viscount Wavell, but his hasty partition of India and withdrawal of the British led to some of the worst sectarian conflict the world has ever seen. This was a shadow that would hang over Mountbatten for the rest of his life.

My father joined the RAF in 1945, just in time to catch the end of the war. He was based in East Anglia for his whole period in the service, and it was here that he was recruited to join the flight crew of Mountbatten's personal aircraft (an Avro York), which would shuttle the last Viceroy between Britain and India as he negotiated with Gandhi, Nehru and Jinna. Many of these negotiations occurred in the Viceregal Lodge in Simla. I was once shown the table there where India was literally carved up.

He was the aircraft's wireless operator. It gives me pleasure whenever I work for BBC Radio to think that here is one trade that I have inherited from him, albeit tangentially. It was a forty-eight-hour flight to India. Nowadays it takes eight, direct. In 1947 they had to fly first to Alexandria in Egypt and would stop there for a few hours to refuel. Presumably Mountbatten was on the phone to Gandhi or sending express telegrams to Prime Minister Atlee as this was going on. Then the second leg of the flight took them to Karachi, in what is now Pakistan. After resting and refuelling the crew would then take the Viceroy to wherever he needed to be in India, although according to my father this seems to be mainly in and around Delhi.

The Karachi airbase, christened RAF Drigh Road, has had an interesting history. For several years before my father whiled away the hours there with his mates, it had been home to T. E. Lawrence, who had sought anonymity from his 'Lawrence of Arabia' fame by enlisting into the air force as a simple airman under an assumed name. Once it was discovered that he had been stationed in western India, rumours became rife that he was acting as a spy engaged on a secret mission against the Russians, in one of the final moves of the century-long Great Game. Conspiracy theories still abound on this bizarre stage of Lawrence's extremely odd life, though it seems likely that he was just after some peace and quiet. RAF Drigh Road didn't really agree with him. He wrote to Charlotte Shaw on 28 January 1927:

> The Depot is dreary, to a degree, and its background makes me shiver. It is a desert, very like Arabia: and all sorts of haunting likenesses (pack-donkeys, the colour and cut of men's clothes, an oleander bush in flower in the valley, camel-saddles, tamarisk) try to remind me of what I've been for eight years desperately fighting out of my mind. Even I began to doubt if the coming out here was wise.

In 1947 the base was handed over to the Pakistan Air Force and in 1977 Drigh Road Air Base was re-named 'Faisal Air Base' in honour of King Faisal II of Saudi Arabia.

As Mountbatten made history, the crew would be given a few days leave, and basically got up to no good. Tony disliked India. He always found my fascination with the country somewhat baffling. He hated the heat, he disliked the people, he despised the filth, but most of all he hated the food. In all my life I never saw him eat Indian food. He was in fact very distrustful of any food that had the affront to contain either herb or spice that wasn't salt or pepper.

My father loved telling yarns, often at great length. Some of them were gripping. And he certainly knew how to shape a narrative or rather, exaggerate and embellish a remembered occurrence. At his funeral I told the congregation some of his stories. My all-time favourite has the feel of an Ealing comedy caper.

To deal with the frustrations and need to kill time on their Indian trips the crew decided to have some fun and make a bit of money on the side. After I had been to Agra and seen the Taj Mahal for the first time, I asked my father if he'd been there. He told me that he had, but it seemed that he barely noticed the breathtaking beauty of the dawn light over the white marble tiles of the planet's most famous mausoleum, as he had other things on his mind.

The crew – with the full knowledge of the captain – worked quite a scam in Agra. They all would go to a carpet shop. Three of them would enter through the front door, engage the owner in conversation and make sure any other shop assistants were suitably distracted. Meanwhile, the other three boys would go round the back of the shop, find a way in and start loading beautiful, expensive Rajasthani carpets on to a waiting van. At a certain point they would drive off and rendezvous with the other three at the airfield. Whilst Mountbatten was high up in the mountains of Simla carving up the country with Gandhi, the hold of his plane was being filled with expensive looted carpets. When the Viceroy was ready, they'd head back to Britain.

As they flew low over the flatness of East Anglia on the final approach to land at RAF Honiton, two of the crew would open the doors of the hold. Once over a specific part of Thetford Forest, another of the crew would distract Mountbatten away from the sight of carpets being chucked out of his plane and landing amongst the trees.

The plane would land lighter, and Mountbatten would head off to London. In the meantime, a local farmer, in on the scam, would have driven a tractor with a trailer through the forest to the pre-arranged drop point and picked up the carpets. These he stored in a barn. Later on, an RAF truck would appear at the barn, the farmer would be given a fiver and the carpets would be whisked back to RAF Honiton. They would then be sold on the black market for considerable profit and the whole crew got a healthy cut.

It was perhaps one of the final acts of the four-centuries-long looting of India by the British. But never had it happened so literally under the Viceroy's nose.

I told this story at the funeral and was met by a wall of silence. I had expected some laughs. I hastily moved on.

I wondered if people disapproved as it cast the deceased as a petty criminal or at best a spiv (which he was a bit). Afterwards, my friend Mark told me that he could see that people had found the story touching and amusing – it's just that no one thought they should laugh at a funeral.

Tony adored Mountbatten all his life. My father, a deferential lower-middle-class man born in the 1920s, always looked up to the officer class and especially to aristocrats. Apart from meeting Dame Vera Lynn at a local amateur dramatic performance of the musical *Blitz* where she was guest of honour, Mountbatten was the closest he ever got to top brass. He remembered him very fondly. What a great man, so kind to the crew, etc. And he would always come to the cockpit and share his fine single malt whisky with the lads before the end of every journey back to London.

Mountbatten was blown up by the IRA in 1979. I remember my father being devastated. All the critical material that's been written about Mountbatten in recent years wouldn't matter to him. My father's relationship to him and admiration of him was almost Hindu – an unbreakable ancient feudal master–serf dynamic. Somehow the glory of the great man's celebrity rubbed off.

***

All along it was my father who gently fostered my love of golf. It was the one interest we really had in common and from when I was a small child I think he could sense this. But golf for him was also about class. After leaving the RAF, he was in awe of his boss for many years. This officer-class chap was called Ray Sanders, and owned a small chain of musical instrument shops in the western suburbs of London. Mr Sanders lived in a big house in Gerrards Cross, Buckinghamshire. And he was a member of the posh Denham Golf Club – perhaps the only golf club in

Britain that has a mainline train station named after it. The management of the firm used to go on industry conference weekends, and golf was a part of this. Dad had to play to fit in. It must have been slightly socially agonizing for him, not really being a golfer, so he cleverly worked it that he would organize the tournaments, but not necessarily play. I think he smelt the proximity of the bourgeois life he'd always yearned for, and golf was both a passport to it and somehow a block rejecting entry. For my father the bar of a local golf club felt like the Garrick Club. It was an officer's mess, to which he'd gained access by the back door. This is a feeling I have had (and continue to have) all my life too.

My mother and I would often join him during these conferences. Normally they were held in Bournemouth. When in 1977 I saw the crazy golf course in the Pleasure Gardens there, I was immediately hooked. I adored it. I loved the fantasy side of it – that you had to get this ball through a tunnel, over a stream, into the castle, out of the pirate's mouth and into the hole. The course is still there. I played it recently. It's still ace.

Seeing my delight, we started to play crazy golf, and then the more grown-up putting greens wherever we went. A few years ago I was in Bexhill-on-Sea to look round the recently refurbished art deco wonder, the De La Warr Pavilion. I was startled to find at its western tip the putting green, which we had played on twenty-five years previously, still open. From putting greens, I progressed to pitch-and-putt courses – the one in the middle of Sandown Park racecourse was a particular favourite, not least because in the café afterwards there was a Space Invaders machine which was almost as good, if not better, than the golf.

Then, when I was ten or eleven, we started to play nine full-length holes on easy courses, like the one in the grounds of the swanky Oatlands Park Hotel in Weybridge. We once got shouted at by some stuck-up toff who complained that we didn't have a golf bag each, and that we were sharing clubs. This was the start of a lifelong and continuing loathing of – and fascination with – the reactionary pomposity of many golf people and golf clubs the world over. The simple fact was that we couldn't really afford all the gear but loved playing, so we played it with charity shop clubs and found golf balls.

Neither of us really knew what we were doing. In fact, it was only when I had the first golf lessons of my life at the age of thirty-six that a pro told me I was gripping the clubs wrong – like I was holding a baseball bat. It's a bit like my guitar playing – technically woeful, but often effective.

***

Ca sera la plus magnifique de toutes ces ruines.

French Prime Minister Georges Clemenceau, on looking at the half-built city of New Delhi (1920)

The spark suddenly, beautifully ignited in October 2005 when I saw a simple wooden sign on which was engraved the words 'golf course'. I was near Simla and later would discover that the sign pointed to Naldehra, the golf course Lord Curzon (Viceroy of India 1899–1905) himself set up at his favourite beauty spot. My imagination was on fire: *the British had built golf courses at their hill stations.* In the middle of the Himalayas there must be courses with the best views on the planet. I had a sudden desperate need to find these courses and play them. When I returned to Delhi at the end of that trip I drove past the Delhi Golf Club in the centre of the city. That night I Googled it and saw the pictures that made my mind up. Here was a course constructed by the British in the 1920s amongst the ruins of a seventeenth-century Mogul palace, as they were building the Empire's biggest folly – the city of New Delhi. The poetry of the gesture was fantastic. At the very moment when the British Empire was about to implode, the Raj built a golf course on top of the previous colonial rulers of India – the Muslim dynasty who it had taken over from two centuries before.

I yearned to play this course, but had to go to weddings and head home soon after. However, the idea grew and grew, and the more research I did the more I discovered that there were British-built golf courses all over India, almost all connected to hill stations or to the bigger cities. I wanted to play at Gulmarg in Kashmir, which claimed to be the highest golf course in the world, and at the Shillong Golf Club – the wettest golf club on the planet; hit a few balls whilst revelling in the luxury of the Madras Cosmopolitan Club, and visit the course at Kodaikanal where tigers and leopards are rumoured to roam across the fairways. And I wanted to play at Delhi where, amongst the ruins of the Mogul palace, there are cobras in the rough.

An idea formed. I was intrigued to know how the British used these courses, what they had meant to them and the role they had played in the social life of the Raj. But, parallel to this, I was keen to know how today's Indians, propelled by the dynamo of the economic boom, are taking to golf; I wondered which courses are being used, which are derelict and which abandoned. In 2011 India had for the first time two players – Jeev Milkha Singh and Arjun Atwal – in the world's top fifty ranked players. This can't be a coincidence – there must be a link between the recent success and gradual westernization of India and an interest in that most class-sensitive of sports – golf. One reason why the British and the Indians mostly got on for so long was because both cultures were (and still are) obsessed with class. The highly complex Hindu caste system had almost met its mirror in the deeply nuanced class structure of Georgian and Victorian Britain. Both countries were a bunch of huge snobs. And I wondered if golf, both then and now, somehow expressed these class aspirations and assertions.

I was looking for the right moment to go – when my interest and need were at their zenith. My father dying made me want to run and run; whilst arranging his funeral I was catapulted into action, and I started to imagine a trip – my own Raj fantasy with a bit of golf on the side.

3

A Cobra in the Face

Every white man's life in the East was one long struggle not to be laughed at.

George Orwell, 'Shooting an Elephant' (1936)

Like my father, I too hated it at first. India and I had a very protracted courtship, a mutual antipathy that bloomed into passion only after many years. I was plunged into India at twenty by my friend Simon. He'd already been to Rajasthan, ridden on camels in the desert near Jaisalmer, seen the Taj, bathed in the Ganges at Varanasi and got the T-shirt. Simon had made good use of his gap year before Cambridge, while I was hungry for more and more book education, and went straight up to university. In my second year, Simon told me he was going back to India, but this time to the south, and taking his girlfriend, Audrey. It seemed an exciting adventure before the final university year began so I jumped at it. I obtained one of the freshly invented student loans to pay for the Pan Am air ticket, and somehow convinced my girlfriend Karen, a Kent girl who'd never been out of the country before, that she should come with me.

I'm not sure what I expected. I'd read a few books about the country, seen *A Passage to India, Heat and Dust* and *The Far Pavilions,* but I was acutely ill-prepared for the reality of the place and was stripped down to the rather naive, sheltered suburban schoolboy that I still was in essence.

The first night in India was one of the worst of my life. We arrived at Bombay airport late in the evening to find that Pan Am had forgotten to put my rucksack on board the plane at Frankfurt. After filling out reams of lost-property paperwork (Indians love paperwork – another thing the British and Indians share), we headed outside the terminal building to wait for a local bus. We felt we were too poor and 'authentic' to hail a taxi. As we waited, a beggar woman tapped me on the shoulder from behind and started asking for money. She was carrying a small cobra, and she thrust it in my face, indicating that I should make an offering to the serpent for luck. I completely freaked out. At that stage in my life I was phobic about snakes in the way only a still basically adolescent man with severe Freudian hang-ups can be. One of my anxieties about coming to India was that I would see snakes everywhere. People had told me not to be ridiculous, but here was proof positive that the entire country was writhing with vipers.

The bus came; we boarded it. Then as now many travellers' first experience of India is the drive into town from the airport through the infamous Azad Nagar slum. It is Asia's largest shanty town, it is *Slumdog Millionaire* territory, and it is vast and extremely startling. Some young backpackers have been known to turn their taxi round and head straight back to Gloucestershire on the first available flight after experiencing this. After an hour the bus stopped in a very dodgy looking back street. The driver refused to go any further unless we and the three female Indian passengers on board paid him a sizeable backhander. It was two in the morning. We were already terrified, jet-lagged and hungry, and with no particular plan. We paid up.

Eventually we were dumped outside Victoria Terminus train station. This is one of my favourite buildings in the world and a masterpiece of absolutely over-the-top Victorian neo-Gothic. It looks like a trippy, Gotham City version of London's Natural History Museum. And it is vast, easily dwarfing London's great stations. However, that night the architecture was unimpressive as I thought I was going to die. We assumed (incorrectly) that no hotels would be open, so we decided to wait on the station concourse until dawn. Ninety per cent of the floor space on Indian stations is taken up by sleeping bodies at all times of day, but especially at night. We found a space and tried to fit in. To handle our fear we played hangman all night.

We really thought we were about to be seriously harmed. In reality these places – and most of India – are incredibly safe. It's much more dangerous hanging around London's King's Cross at one in the morning than amongst the poor families in Bombay getting some kip before their morning train leaves. But the strangeness, the foreignness, of the situation completely threw me. I was totally disoriented, as though everything I'd been brought up to think about how life is lived was not true here. I didn't know how it all worked, and I didn't know how to act. I felt like a lost child.

At dawn we found a hotel near the station. To this day, budget hotels in the big cities in India are hell-holes. Our room had a huge pet rat – which in a wonderful echo of *Fawlty Towers* the hotel manager kept saying was a 'mouse' whenever I complained. There was also a swarm of huge, buzzing, flying cockroaches that flew directly at our heads. We hid under the mosquito net and read Dickens.

The rest of the trip proceeded in a similar manner. Simon

would pick an obscure town in the plains of Karnataka to visit, we'd get there by train (steerage class in those days – again, it was more 'authentic'), bus, rickshaw or ox cart, we'd check into some dump of a hotel and spend three days or so looking at the local ruins. I hated it. We all did. Even Simon, I think. But we all pretended it was fab, a *really great* experience. The heat and the wildlife drove me nuts. Our room would be so full of mosquitoes, ants, geckos and a million other assorted fauna at night that I took to stuffing scrunched-up pages of *The Times of India* into every possible crevice where beasties might get in. My biggest fear was, of course, that a king cobra would come slithering up my body late at night like in a James Bond film. It didn't. Audrey and I decided we actually had always quite liked each other and spent agonizingly English moments working out if we should actually do something about it. We didn't. Karen was plucky and game, but probably hated me for bringing her here. Simon kept going, bless him. I've always felt I let him down.

I found the squalor a real challenge to my cosseted worldview. I hated the constant staring, the hassle, the people trying to sell you things and not taking no for an answer, the limbless beggars, the child beggars following you around, the strange diet and the maladies it created, the horrible hotel rooms, the claustrophobic death-trap buses, the ubiquitous irritating wildlife and the lies that everyone seemed to be telling you all the time to get something from you; I also hated that our sex drive had slipped to below zero, our only consolation being reading Dickens and thinking of that distant trip back to the motherland.

I was probably feeling many of the things my father felt when he was in India forty-five years before.

We cut the trip short and headed back to London after five weeks. I told everyone what an amaaaaazing experience it had been. You know, really, like, spiritual. I insisted on eating largely vegetarian Indian food, and would walk in the road through Walton-on-Thames to show how much I'd gone native. I spread out a huge map of India on my parents' dining-room table and talked my father through (with meticulous detail) our route, our crazy encounters and our stomach disorders. I could see him straining to remember stuff from his time there, but I don't think he'd made it much further south than Karachi and Agra.

Karen and I split up. So did Simon and Audrey. India at least had achieved something. We all moved on and I forgot about India for several years.

***

> *That the capital of the Indian empire should thus be hanging on by its eyelids to the side of a hill is too absurd.*
>
> Lord Dufferin, Viceroy of India (1885)

I had dreamt of Simla for many years – ever since I watched *Simla,* a Channel 4 programme about the town, in 1997. The idea of Simla bewitched me, and seemed to speak to something ancient and English in me. I felt a strong urge to go there and connect with something mysterious and fundamental in myself.

I discovered Salman Rushdie around the same time, who reignited my interest in the sub-continent. I thought (and still do) *Midnight's Children* to be an absolute masterpiece. I was delighted when I eventually made it to Srinagar in Kashmir where the book's opening sequences are set. This year, by chance, I also stayed in the cottage in Kalimpong in West Bengal where Kiran Desai lived with her mother Anita, and where she wrote her Booker-winning novel *The Inheritance of Loss.*

I also loved Vikram Seth's monumental 1,500-page epic, *A Suitable Boy.* I adored the simplicity of the storytelling, the beautifully drawn characters and the warmth of the book. I realized I understood this world and felt a connection with it. I also greatly admired Seth in interview. He seemed wise, seer-like, an Indian intellectual Dylan. Rushdie and Seth had opened my mind to a different India to the one that had shaken me ontologically. And I was fascinated by it.

That Channel 4 programme about Simla fascinated me. I had never heard of Simla before. I had certainly never read Rudyard Kipling, who so famously celebrated it. I was schooled in literature first by disciples of F. R. Leavis at college, and later by free-thinking hippy intellectuals at university, and Kipling had no place in either canon of dogma. In the net draped between Eliot, Milton and Yeats on one side and Pynchon, Ginsberg and Vonnegut on the other, Kipling fell through the holes.

From then on I became more and more interested in the British in India, and particularly how they relaxed. I felt the clash of cultures acutely, and somehow identified with it. Perhaps I too was looking for an England that was gone, like John Major and his vision of cricket on village greens, spinsters riding bicycles and fine cask ale – a sort of forever Ambridge. The more I discovered about India, the more I saw myself connected, through shared history, to this country, but most of all, of course, to the small number of British who made their homes – and often their fortunes – there.

***

After my slow, meditative, stress-busting solo round, I was waiting for the white Ford Escort to turn into the car park of the golf club. Waiting for this car to pick me up as I had since I was a teenager. At the wheel, chain-smoking, my father, who had spent the last forty years chauffeuring me around – the six-hour each way trip to university six times a year, picking me up in the early hours drunk from teenage suburban parties, or being my roadie when I crammed the car full of guitar amps and drum gear when I was gigging around Surrey in my early twenties. The first glimpse of that small white car was always a calm rush of reassurance to me.

He pulled up and we loaded the golf clubs and trolley into the boot; I scraped and knocked the mud from my spikes, and changed into my trainers. Dad took this opportunity to drain another Craven A into his lungs. My mother hated him smoking in or around the house so he grabbed his fix whenever he could.

I felt a little guilty about not letting him play with me, so I suggested we go to the Waggon and Horses for a drink. He loved this idea, and I too liked our intimate man-to-man relaxed time together. Sometimes I think he was happiest when he was driving, with me in the passenger seat. Those long trips up the A1 to Durham with my student gear never seemed to bother him in the least. Indeed, it was when I saw him at his most calm. He was, above all, a driver, an automobile man, and I think he felt the same sort of peace that I do when I step into a recording studio; you feel like you're home.

We were the only customers in the pub. They had Wadworth 6X ale on tap and I persuaded my father to try it. Not in any way a drinker (I never in my whole life saw him inebriated), he had grown to like the taste of bitter and I enjoyed introducing him to beers that I thought were quality. We sat in a corner table with our pint and a half and chatted. I can't remember a word we said to each other – we probably talked a lot about *Big Brother*, as he made a point to watch the TV shows I was working on. But I remember feeling how good this was, this proximity, this back-and-forth flow of love and respect. It was possibly the most perfect relationship I will ever have.

During the drink he complained about a persistent dryness at the back of his throat that wouldn't go away. He couldn't quite quench his thirst, and it was starting to annoy him. I told him to drink some water, rather than the tea with which he almost totally hydrated himself. It seemed such a minor complaint from a mostly strong, healthy old man. In four months he would be dead from kidney failure and cancer that was diagnosed too late. By the time the US Masters was on in April, he was in such pain that he didn't even bother to watch it.

***

After he died I stripped down my life. I had been juggling so many things it was all getting too chaotic, and now I had all this grief to handle. I packed in my recording studio business and decided that now was the time to find the British Raj's golf courses. Golf was the one thing my father and I had really shared. Every shot I played would make me feel closer to him. It would shake me up, I thought, but also connect me to my past, to the history that makes us British, to my father. I needed a project to take my mind off everything; something outside of myself to reshape my brain and deflect it from the intense, dark introspection that had become its default mode. I wanted to run and run. I wanted to be anonymous. I wanted every sense to be challenged every hour of every day. I wanted my eyes to start looking out again, rather than inwards. I knew I had to be in India, on the move, with a quest. I needed golf, calm and beauty more than I ever had. Perhaps I needed to be as free as a child again, living each day for sensual pleasure, without responsibility. I needed simply to focus on contorting my body in such a way as to produce the perfect air parabola of a sweetly hit pitching wedge. Golf is a martial art with a ball; a channelling of *chi*; a linking of all the body and mind's energies; an anti-chaos.

Some Westerners flee to an ashram in Rishikesh to

reconnect the shattered shards of their personalities; some find a sort of peace in the easy drugs and beach-bum life of Goa's Anjuna beach; some trek far into the Himalayas by the Nepalese border, finding solace in altitude and ascension; others dive head-first into the Mumbai party scene or teach in a Rajasthani orphanage. I guess I wanted to do the same thing, but with a bag of golf clubs on my back and Kipling tucked under my arm. India is generous to the mad. Wherever you are in India, there is always someone very near doing something far madder than you. Hinduism is a faith that welcomes the eccentric.

I stayed up night after night into the early hours planning and researching the trip. I would spend my days in the British Library digging up anything I could find on golf in India and Raj history. The characters and backgrounds of the petit bourgeois pen-pushers, soldiers and pioneers of the East India Company and later Anglo–Indian society resonated with me. These people *seemed like me.* The utter academic hush of the Asian and African Studies Room itself helped to soothe my mind. I planned a trip that lasted two months; I ended up staying far longer.

My great friend Tom Aldwinckle agreed to join me in Calcutta, play some golf and take the pictures. It took a while to persuade him that he wanted to go up a mountain in Kashmir in full golf gear to look for a golf course that might not actually even exist, but Tom had had a horrible year, splitting up painfully with his partner, and wanted something fresh, fun and quirky too. He sent me a text confirming his involvement in the project: 'Mate. I must admit I don't give much of a toss about India. But as long as you can guarantee me ten tonnes of Kiwi backpacker minge then I'll go wherever you want me to.'

We both had golf, sex, alcohol and adventure fantasies for the trip. It seemed we were heading to the hills for similar reasons to the British of the Raj.

I let him down. We were seriously off the tourist trail in the monsoon season. In most towns we were the only Westerners around.

4

The Punkah Wallahs of the Tollygunge

I have done the one unforgivable thing by not bringing a dinner jacket and am obliged to have dinner in my room as a result. The whole of India is one enormous conspiracy to make one imagine one is in Balham or Eastbourne.

Robert Byron, letter to his mother, 1929

The cold glass of Coke tasted like nectar from the gods. I don't know if I've ever been more thirsty. Or wet. Or hot. Or embarrassed about my driving. The Coke sugar-charged me and I zoned back into the chat of Mrs Sharma's old Calcutta gossip gang. These three ladies had kindly let me go round with them, as Tom, still lamely pleading jet lag, decided he wasn't golfing today, preferring to sit on a sun lounger and work on his tan.

It had been tricky getting a game. First, the Starter told

me it was fine to start right away, but when I came back with my clubs five minutes later he seemed disappointed that I was on my own, and insisted that I wait to join a two- or three-ball, even though no one had teed off on the first for about half an hour at that point because of the heat. Then he noticed my shirt and demanded that I change it. All right, it wasn't strictly a polo shirt, but it was damn smart and pricey, and I felt a bit annoyed. Shirt changed, I sat and waited for a game feeling a little like a tart on the sidewalk waiting for a trick. After ten more minutes a middle-aged, sporty looking lady in purple and pink golf gear came over, a few sentences of Bengali were exchanged between her and the Starter, and she turned to me: 'Well, if you don't mind coming round with three old ladies, you'd be most welcome to join us.' In my finest English tones I told her what an honour it would be, if they could put up with me. She sort of smiled, then walked off to the ladies' tee, fifty yards away. No names exchanged.

So I wasn't that relaxed as I walked out on the first tee, which is basically part of the 'Wills Shamiana', the wonderful alfresco café-bar on a veranda of the Tollygunge Club, Calcutta that walls the first tee and eighteenth green. It is one of the most pleasant spots that I know to pass the time, snack and watch golf. Everyone pretends to be chatting, but really all are slyly eyeing the golf, enjoying the grandstand nerves of the players.

But this time it was me being watched. I reassured myself that all would be fine. After all, when I played this hole the previous day I shot the most sweet hybrid off the tee to the centre of the fairway with great carry and an exquisite ping-pop sound. My four-step hybrid mantra was once again in my head: ball by heel, slow backswing, long follow through and, above all, head down. All I have to do is the same as yesterday, where I fancied I could hear the delighted oohs of the spectators behind me.

But I was tense, hot and rather hurried. I should have taken longer, gone through the routine better, but I just went for it and hit a terrible, shocking yanked top that dribbled along the ground barely past the ladies' tee. I was so angry that I marched up to the ball, still clutching the hybrid, and clattered it 120 yards up the fairway. Also mostly along the ground. It wasn't pretty but at least it was away from the Starter, the café, the sniggering caddies and my own shame. I then watched as the ladies each took out genteel lady-woods and played very short, very elegant, extremely textbook shots into the centre of the fairway.

I was slightly confused as to what the etiquette would be. Would the ladies ignore me, annoyed to have a useless foreign hacker foisted upon them? I imagined this was the one chance in their week to gossip away from men, and here was I, a big, clumsy, sweaty man who needed their attention. I need not have worried. I was conscious one of the ladies was heading towards me. Short, squat, in her sixties, she bounced up to me and boomed: 'HELLO THERE. I AM MRS SHARMA AND THESE LADIES ARE MY GOOD FRIENDS. WE ARE SO GLAD YOU COULD JOIN US. PLEASE RELAX, DON'T FEEL ANY PRESSURE AND ENJOY THE GAME.'

She had a cheekiness about her. She was clearly the boss and I instantly liked her. And it did set me at my ease. My third shot was almost a beauty. In fact, my mood was so monsoon knife-edged that morning that I think had that shot turned out differently the whole round would have changed. Such is the fickle effect a golf shot can have on one's long-term karma. I hit a great five-iron, squeezing it on a straight line past the trees, and I watched it parabola beautifully towards the green. I was already doing the maths: if this lands near the hole, I can putt for par – quite a result after the agony of the first two shots. The ball finally landed on the left bank that fringed the green. It could have rolled nicely towards the hole, but instead took a nasty bounce and ever so slowly slipped back into a bunker.

Oh God.

I hate bunkers. Why now? Why here? Three posh, serious Calcuttan lady golfers and four caddies who could beat me in their sleep would all observe me in a bunker. I watched as the ladies very neatly kept punting their balls a hundred yards at a time, taking three or four to get on the green, then neatly putting for four or five. I took two out of the bunker then two-putted for seven. 'WELL HOLED,' Mrs Patel thundered cheerily.

This would be the pattern for the rest of the round. On the fourth, as another sliced drive went high and long over the perimeter fence and into the nether reaches of the city, Mrs Sharma turned to me and said: 'YOU KNOW, WE PLAY "BORING GOLF". IT'S WHAT YOU DO WHEN YOU GET OLDER. IT'S NOT MUCH FUN TO WATCH BUT IT KEEPS THE SCORE DOWN!'

She had a point. Every hole the ladies played with the same concentrated efficiency. They rarely strayed from the centre of the fairways; they rarely hit longer than a hundred yards, but their card read far better than mine. They were marking each other, and I only once heard a 'seven' being guiltily communicated at the end of a hole.

The round progressed at first in a heavy silence, which disarmed me a bit. Was my presence causing this silence? If I weren't here would they be nattering and hooting and having a great time? But gradually I realized that firstly, the heat really made all but the most essential chat a needless waste of energy – sometimes you had to will the strength to get the words 'good shot' out of your mouth – and secondly, that for these ladies, their round of golf is a quiet, focussed, almost solemn affair. They are serious about their golf, clearly work hard on it, and treat every shot with a craftswoman's care. I thought of the matey in-between-shots banter that men do, and realized that actually most of the time I too would prefer the silence, the time to reflect, to enjoy the beauty of the course (and the Tolly, as it's called, is gorgeous), to shape and plan my life, to express through golf the exuberance and the neuroses of my current consciousness. To 'play boring' . . . I've thought about this a lot since. I think it's hard for most men to deliberately play boring. Their machismo wills them to attempt the extravagant, showbiz shot: the ambitious drive over the water rather than the six-iron layup. But for most of us high handicappers that means 50 per cent of the time we end up in trees, brooks, other fairways or slicing on to someone's veranda. I think men start to play boring when their bodies start creaking. They then have to play boring. They glamorise it as 'percentage play' but it is 'playing boring' by the back door. And I think I like it.

The heat was unbearable. By the second hole my yellow shirt was drenched in very visible sweat, and I crossed my arms whenever I talked to one of the ladies to try to hide the sweat marks ridging my diaphragm. I was dripping constantly. When I bent over to putt, big drops would fall from my face; I seemed to be sweating from every pore in my backside too, which made walking uncomfortable, as it felt like I was wearing a huge, sodden nappy. I was embarrassed. Not only was I playing extremely erratic golf – a wonderful 180-yard five-iron to the green and a lovely putt would be followed by the horrendous slash of a drive on the next hole – I was also not in control of my body. The ladies were all clearly mothers and grandmothers – Mrs Khan, the best golfer of the three, told me that she used to play four times a week, but that the kids have reduced that to once a week – and I began to feel like an awkward, gangly teenager trying to hide his wet dreams from his parents. By the fifth I considered heading back. This is silly, I thought. It's meant to be fun.

And then: an oasis. 'WE WILL REST HERE FOR A FEW MINUTES, AND HAVE A DRINK,' commanded Mrs Sharma. 'Here' was a small drinks pagoda before the sixth tee, where not only can you top-up on Sprite, Pepsi or (if you are insane) tea, but there is a bucket containing small white towels soaking in ice. All four of us – I slightly more feverishly and inelegantly – covered our faces, heads and arms with these towels, which felt amazing. The bar-wallah brought us cold(ish) water to drink. I gulped down three cups in a row. And I realized that the ladies – with the possible exception of the indomitable Mrs Sharma – were struggling with the climate almost as much as me. Mrs Khan, in particular, seemed in a grumpy mood about it – even though she was playing excellent, controlled golf. 'Why are we playing at this time, Bibi? It is too hot, no one else is playing . . . we must be bloody stupid.' The kind lady agreed, but I noticed that even in this heat she was wearing a long-sleeve shirt and golf gloves on both hands. She must be roasting. Quite a price for modesty.

Mrs Sharma told me about her life in golf: she had been playing at the Tolly for forty-five years off and on, had not played too often for twenty years of that when she was raising the kids, but was now back with a vengeance, and played four times a week. Once she was Ladies Captain here, and her daughter was a professional golfer. Her son was scratch. She never mentioned Mr Sharma senior. Perhaps he had passed away. Or worse, perhaps he was rubbish at golf, and so ostracized by the rest of the family. She complained to me that the British made it difficult for women to play golf, but that in all her years here, women golfers were always treated well.

These girls were seriously posh, and I rather liked them. At first, I thought they never looked at, let alone talked to, their caddies, but I started to notice that very discreet, corner-of-the-mouth, non-eye-contact conversations were happening between player and servant, and that this 'boring golf' was something of a team effort. If I listened carefully I could hear a caddy murmuring 'Slightly to the right, madam' into Mrs Patel's ear as she chipped in on a downward-sloping green. And for every putt, they would point – either with the flag or a club – the line of the putt. I noticed, too, that the caddies often placed the balls in better lies for the ladies, or positioned a fairway ball on a slightly raised piece of grass, creating a natural mini-tee. The previous day I thought they were doing this for Tom and I to make us feel good, but it seems that this is *de rigueur.* Most shots therefore become tee shots, which is a nice if rather unethical perk.

The Smart Indian Golfer–Caddy relationship mirrors the Brahmin–Dalit caste dynamic of Hindu India as a whole, with the starters and office managers lodged in the middle. Golf is class obsessed, and I discovered that even within the British Raj 'Club' communities, there were incredibly subtle class-based distinctions about where one played sport, which a Hindu with the caste system in their DNA would easily comprehend and to which, perhaps, they would warm.

Sir Ridgeby Foster arrived in India in 1933 to work for ICI and eventually became chairman of the company. An Indiaphile, he remained in the country after Independence and made these comments about the club hierarchy in Calcutta in Charles Allen's collection of oral history, *Plain Tales of the Raj*:

> People who worked in shops were known as 'counter-jumpers', and even the general manager of one of the biggest stores in Calcutta could not get into the more select clubs. If he was in commerce and therefore acceptable, the first club the young man joined was The Saturday Club, which was a social club for dancing and squash and swimming . . .

> Next there was The Tollygunge Club . . . a very select club with a six-year waiting list, which had a golf course, a racecourse and a swimming pool . . . Then when a young man got more senior there was the Bengal Club, which was famous for its cuisine and was quite a landmark.

Of course, for most of the Raj, Indians were banned from membership of these institutions. It was not until the 1920s when the doors were reluctantly opened to a few Indian members. Many have seen this club-level segregation as a major factor in the spread of dissent amongst the intellectual and business classes of India: if only the smart, clever Indians had been allowed to play golf at the Tolly with the sahibs, then they could all have had a good chat, and sorted out any civil unrest peacefully. Beneath the racism seemed to be the old terror – fuelled by the 1857 'Mutiny' – of Indian men consorting with Englishwomen. The mutineers' behaviour towards the British women in the cantonments of Delhi, Lucknow, Cawnpore and elsewhere had so shocked the homeland that it created a lasting psychic trauma for the British. Women were violated during the Mutiny, but many of the reports were grossly exaggerated by the press both in India and at home; also, the equally horrific retribution handed out by the British – which often included the violation of native women – was played down. So the sexual relations between Indian men and British women changed for good at the point when the Raj was officially established. It is no coincidence that the two most famous novels about the Raj – E. M. Forster's *A Passage to India* and Paul Scott's *The Jewel in the Crown* – both have the (alleged) sexual assault of a white woman by an educated Indian at the heart of their narrative. Forster wrote his book in 1923 – precisely when Indians were being allowed into clubs like the Tollygunge for the first time.

Sir Ridgeby goes on to describe the evening life at a typical club:

> On almost any evening you would see the club verandah, usually a long deep area which was cool and in the shade and fitted out with cane chairs and tables, occupied by literally hundreds of people . . . They would be busy chatting among themselves, drinks would be flowing freely and you would repeatedly hear the exclamation 'Koi-Hai' which was a call for one of the servants to come and attend.

Helen Mary Chitty, wife of a High Court Judge in Calcutta, described a similar set-up in Rangoon (then part of British India) after a round: 'A sociable circle of wicker chairs and a choice of cool drinks await one at the end of the round, and on some evenings a native band plays as we sit and rest, and the stars shine out and the air grows fresh, and there are (few) less pleasant places in the world.'

This description of the so called 'basket chair circles' is the Tolly to this day. The basket chairs, the veranda, the chat and the drinking still exist around the first tee. Unlike the peacocks I would see in Delhi or the monkeys of Naldehra, the only dominant animal on this course these days seemed to be strange mutant-looking wild dogs that dashed across fairways, looking like they hoped you wouldn't see them.

At dinner later, we met Christina, a middle-aged Anglo–American academic, specializing in the history and development of non-governmental organizations. She hates golf, but once a year she comes here alone, for two weeks, to write. She writes in the deluxe air-conditioning of her room, then comes down for meals, whiskies and to pass the time of day. 'The Tolly is my favourite place in the world,' she said.

The iced towels must have refreshed me as I hammered my six-iron off the tee on the par-three sixth straight and purposefully, and it landed four inches off the green. Then an awkward thirty-yard, nine-iron chip to within three feet of the hole ('GOOD CHIP,' foghorned Mrs Sharma who throughout the round was wonderfully complimentary towards any of her playing partners who produced a bit of class), and a putt for par.

By the eighth I was on reserve power; staggering up the ninth I was fantasizing about great Indian air-conditioning situations I've experienced – the booking hall of Victoria Terminus station in Mumbai, a second-class carriage on the West Coast Konkan Railway, the Oberoi Hotel in Delhi, that first reviving blast of cool as you ascend towards Simla . . . they all felt delicious.

'YOUR SHOT MISTER!'

My reverie was shattered and I dutifully drove into the lake. After putting out, the ladies invited me to join them for a drink at the small refreshments tent before the tenth. It was the best glass of Coca-Cola ever poured. We chewed over the round. I apologized for my extremely erratic golf. 'OH DON'T WORRY, WE DID NOT NOTICE,' Mrs Sharma decreed very graciously. One of the ladies was unimpressed that I was going to Assam next, and advised me to fly rather than take the train. I asked her if this was because the trains were very crowded or hot. 'Oh no,' she said, 'it is because it will be full of people from Assam.' She rolled up her nose as though she'd just smelt something bad.

After spending several hours rehydrating and re-establishing my normal bodyweight I walked around the club and like most who come here – and, of course, like the British for over a hundred years – fell for it. The bog of Tollygunge was made into an indigo plantation by a British family, the Johnsons, in 1781, and was later acquired by the exiled family of Tipu Sultan to form part of a princely estate. Tipu had trumpeted a militant Islam in the face of colonial oppression before being defeated by the future Duke of Wellington in 1799. Allowing the defeated prince's family such a generous exile is perhaps a mark of the pre-Raj British at their best. In 1895 the property was bought from Tipu's descendants by the Tollygunge Club Ltd, led by the Scottish banker Sir William Cruickshank, who converted the Johnson home into the clubhouse. Traces of the course's heritage remain: the first hole is called 'Tipu Sultan' and the posh restaurant in the clubhouse is 'The Mysore Room', from which I got kicked out for wearing 'the wrong sort of sandals'. They were in fact flip-flops bought from Tesco, Borehamwood.

This clubhouse is magnificent, and one of the finest preserved Raj buildings in India. The grand hall – or Wills Lounge as it is known – is a wonderful room, barely changed in a hundred years, beautifully cool; and I was surprised how empty it always was. A few kids used it to pass the time, but otherwise Tollygungians preferred to sweat it out on the veranda rather than bask in the air-conditioned glory of this Raj gem. The library off the main room is a very pleasant sit, and I donated to it the John le Carré book I had just finished. I'm sure if le Carré had been born a century earlier he would have been working for MI6 on the north-west frontier, running secret missions against the Russians during the Great Game, rather than against their Soviet grandsons in East Berlin. When I find a room like this I like to sit and fantasize; people it; make it bustle with an historical re-creation of how it was used. When the space is so well preserved – like the Windamere Hotel in Darjeeling, or the Mehrangarh of Jodhpur – this is easy, and the past, the Raj, seems touchable. In this room, on the golf course, indeed anywhere in the grounds of the Tolly, it is possible to forget where you are; to forget that next to the high wall guarding the long, lush fifth fairway, there is a row of slum houses on the other side, shit in the street and the chaotic honk-honk crazy bustle of Calcutta traffic. At the Tolly, you can forget where you are. Which to the chronically homesick Britisher, I guess, was always the point.

I went to the range to sort out my driver. The staff there seemed surprised to see me. It was 2 p.m., desert hot. I'd just showered, shaved and changed. I felt good and fresh, although even the three-minute walk to the range carrying my golf bag had started the sweats again. I hired fifty balls and started hitting. At Sidcup World of Golf in Kent – my normal practice place – I hit off fifty balls in about ten to fifteen minutes. Here it took an hour. Every drive required so much energy. The heat was making my limbs heavy, my concentration short and my clothes rapidly pure liquid. I got my driver working, but every shot felt like drilling the heaviest pickaxe into the hardest rock. In the bay next to me one of the staff arrived with a bag of balls. We said our hellos and smiled. I thought he was going to hit a few off. But then two upper-class kids arrived with a bag of junior clubs. Both aged about eleven and kitted out in trendy sports gear, they started belting balls off the tee with swings resembling Sachin Tendulkar's when he hits a straight drive over long on. Short, sharp, fast, with a vicious flick of the wrist on ball impact. They were noisy little gits, competitively challenging each other, passing on tips and often talking loudly on their cell phones to their parents. These little maharajahs owned this place and they knew it. Two things occurred to me: one, these short little kids were really good at hitting a golf ball, and two, I realized that the role of the staff guy I had greeted was to stand by the tee and place a new ball on it each time one of the brats had made a shot. *So that they didn't have to do it themselves.* Throughout the whole session, the boys never said a word to him or even acknowledged him.

This reminded me of a thought I'd had in the Wills

Lounge: that in the years before electricity and air conditioning, the British sipping their drinks and chatting in that beautiful room would have been cooled by vast ceiling fans, operated by punkah wallahs – men who pulled a rope up and down, all day, to operate the fan. They didn't exist to the Raj, they were a mechanical cog in a system constructed to comfort them. At the Tolly, the Raj punkah wallah has morphed into the golf assistant to the Calcuttan upper class.

***

A poor man, with hardly more
Than a garden plot, he did not want
To send me to Flavius' school,
Where the sons of the local yokels went,
Schoolbags hanging from their arms
Carrying their two-bit tuition every Ides

His son, he dared to take to Rome for schooling
In the ways which any knight or senator
Would have his son taught
My clothes, the trains of servants,
(it's how the city people go about)
If anyone had seen me he would have believed
They were furnished to me
From the family fortune

Horace, *Satires* 1.6

I am fifteen years old and sitting next to my buddy Big Daz at the back of Mr Tingay's O-level Latin class. On the mouldy pre-war wooden desk on which I rest my elbows lies volume four of *The Cambridge Latin Course.* I have been learning Latin, without for one moment thinking how gloriously irrelevant it will be to my future life, since the age of eight. (I still find the '*Romanes eunt domus*' sketch in *The Life of Brian* hilarious because that is my memory of Latin lessons and Latin masters at school, always shouting at you for getting the word order wrong or that genus takes the locative case when its motion towards . . . or something or other . . .)

In the last few weeks, however, I have started to take more notice than usual in Latin class. For the first time, we have been introduced to Roman poetry. No longer is the lesson a unison sing-song chant of *amo amas amat amamus amatis amant*; now we have poetry to translate, dissect, analyse and discuss. I'm hooked. We start with Catullus and Juvenal, and I'm struck by how modern it all seems, how piss-taking, undeferential, sly, sarcastic and satirical. In short, good for schoolboys on the cusp of a mild teenage rebellion enwalled in a public school. Then, with Horace, amongst all the social comment I discover tenderness.

I remember clearly when the class translated and discussed the lines above: the agonizingly slow crawl through each line to fillet out its meaning; the snail's pace hack through conjugation, mood, declension and word-ending agreements. Word by word the meaning started to come through, and I realized that in Horace I had found a kindred spirit; this man, 2,000 years ago, had lived through the same experience as me. I realized that these lines are about Tony and me.

My father may not have been a freed slave who piled his small emancipated earnings into his son's education, like Horace's, but something of the dynamic is the same. He was a man from a modest lower-middle-class background who left the education system at seventeen and joined the RAF, then after the war bummed around the film industry (these days we call it 'freelancing') for most of the 1950s before landing a job selling the new hi-fi record-playing systems in the HMV shop in Oxford Street. He then became assistant manager of a chain of music shops in West London in 1965, and it was this period that was his most successful. He lost this job in 1981 after the Currys group bought out this small private firm and laid off the senior staff. For a while he was desolate. He was from the 'You've never had it so good' generation, hoodwinked by the illusion of perpetual career and wealth ascension, anchored around regular and greater moves in the property market. I lived in six houses in my first thirteen years. It wasn't that my parents were restless, or moved for their work, rather that they had been led to believe that buying and selling houses was how you rose up the social ladder. Once, when he was skint, my father said to me 'We've got out of being working class; we became middle class; we're not going to slip back.' Being a child during the Depression of the 1930s inured and hardened my father, and gave him a lifelong fear and suspicion of unemployment, the dole queue, charity, the homeless, socialists *et al.*

He became a travelling piano salesman for a couple of years before moving to another chain of music stores in Bracknell, which ended rapidly and badly a few months later when the bosses were all found to have their fingers in the till.

When I read Horace for the first time, the economic glory years for my father were gone and never would return. He was working in Bentalls department store in Kingston. He was back selling hi-fis and fridges. I was sitting in one of the best, most expensive public schools in the country studying Latin, my gold star education sustained by immense penny-pinching at home, a couple of dodgy high-interest loans, a very kind godfather and a headmaster who went out of his way to structure the payment of the school fees so that my father could somehow meet them. All this so I could read 2,000-year-old poetry written by a man whose experience directly mirrored my own:

Although if my nature is decent enough,
A few frailties but otherwise fine
(just as one notes a few moles on a handsome body)
And if no one can fairly complain that
I am a liar, a lowlife, a playboy,
If, honest and innocent, I can
Brag about myself a bit,
If my friends love me –
I have my father to thank for this.

My parents never pushed me much academically, for which I am grateful as I think it made me discover what it actually was I wanted to learn about. I became a tutored autodidact, and it suited me. They also had low expectations about what this expensive education could achieve. They came home stunned late one night after a parents' evening when they looked at me in a very funny way and said, 'Your teachers were all very complimentary to you; they think it's worth you trying for university' – a comment which made me wonder what they were sending me to this school for if not that. The next morning Mr Thompson, the young trendy History master, said to me, 'Your folks are amazing; they are the nicest parents I've ever met. Normally in a place like this you get these awful demanding parents yelling at you as to why their little darling isn't going to Oxford; your parents were stunned to be told that you'd go to university, and immensely grateful to me that I was being this kind about you.'

Like Horace, I was socially out of place at school. I am sure that I came from the poorest family, but I really didn't care and wasn't in any way ashamed. Like Horace, I was proud of my father and the sacrifices he made for me. Half the boys were sons of well-off senior professionals – surgeons, judges, accountants. Then there would be a smattering of bankers' sons, diplomatic offspring, high-ranking civil servants' children, mixed with a few sons of really famous and powerful people. One of the Rolling Stones sent his boy there and a senior minister in Mrs Thatcher's cabinet followed suit. This man was a political star, and exceedingly handsome and charismatic. One evening the headmaster summoned the parents of prefects (I felt I was the token arty, prole prefect and that suited me fine) to sherry and canapés in the Great Hall. Underneath the sombre portraits of dour-looking headmasters dating back two centuries, my parents mixed with the *haut monde.*

They returned to our little suburban terrace buzzing with tales of chatting to this proto-Portillo. I was proud of them. In Thatcher's Britain, it seemed the class barriers really were coming down, and my father was a Norman Tebbit shaking the austere, landed hands of a Macmillan or a Douglas-Home. The only other boy from a similar background to me was my friend Rob whose father was a scrap-metal dealer who had shrewdly made a fortune. Rob and I wore our shoulder chips with pride, almost like badges of coolness.

At one point I knew secrets at school that could seriously disrupt the political life of the country. A son of another leading politician was involved in a marijuana-smoking ring on the Common. The gang was busted, suspended and the whole affair was hushed up. As prefects we were encouraged to be discreet with the information. With the Tory Moral Crusade – anti-drugs, family values, etc. – in full swing this could have caused considerable embarrassment. Similarly several of the senior prefects were suspended or kicked out once when it was discovered that they had formed a homosexual orgy group, who in free periods and lunch breaks would meet at a secluded spot on the Common and get down to it. These scandals were never big news, always hushed up in a terribly English – and media-savvy – way.

Like Horace, without my parents' investment, love and

encouragement I wouldn't be who I am or have experienced the wonders I have. I think their greatest triumph was their modesty and that I was barely aware of any difference between me and the other boys in the school. It was never an issue. I was accepted, befriended. The struggle, the sacrifice, was done behind the scenes, away from my lived experience. I was able to flow. Horace made me see the difference but also filled me with pride for my own father:

> He didn't care if later someone would object
> That I had become an auctioneer or an agent,
> As he was, chasing paltry profits.
> Nor would I have complained. But seeing where
> I've come, I owe him even greater praise.

5

The Rain People of Shillong

The young Anglo–Indian arrives in the country, as a rule, burdened with prejudices and misconceptions regarding native character. One person has told him that the natives of India are 'great liars'; another that they are 'dreadful thieves'; and altogether, he has unconsciously drawn for himself a picture of the 'mild Hindoo', in which the worst horrors of the Mutiny, human sacrifice, suttee, infanticide, thuggism – to say nothing of sensualism and mendacity – are the prevailing colours.

E. C. P. Hull and R. S. Mair,
The European in India (1878)

In August 2009, His Excellency The High Commissioner for India in Brunei wrote to the estimable *Golf Digest India* magazine – India's leading golf publication – to criticize Shillong Golf Club:

> 'The Gleneagles of the East' (Shillong Golf Club) is suffering from near extinction and needs urgent attention . . . the sanctity of the course has been non-existent for a long time – encroachment on to course land; a thoroughfare for pedestrians; picnicking on the fairways and greens; playing soccer, cricket, archery, etc.; parts of the course are filled with litter. People would even urinate and defecate in the 'hole', so much so that the greens had to be barbed wired. The condition of the course is pathetic. The greens cannot be called greens at all.

He goes on to say that 'there is a lack of clarity about the lease of the land taken since the time of the British'. No one is sure who exactly owns what, it seems.

We had planned to go to Shillong expecting a soaking. We weren't expecting it to be a dump, and it was proving such an arduous mission just getting there that His Excellency's words, read on the train north from Calcutta, made me think that I might have made a mistake dragging us to the wettest golf course on Earth.

In fact, we found that everything the High Commissioner had written was true, but that Shillong is still one of the most beautiful, playable, interesting and, actually, really well-kept courses in India.

Oh, and we got soaked. Really monsoon drenched. Twice.

***

After the intense, claustrophobic, body-drenching heat of Calcutta, we were grateful to board a train at the magnificent, frenetic Howrah Station to take us on a seventeen-hour overnight journey to Guwahati in Assam, where we were sure we would somehow travel on to Shillong. The train journey was eventful, as Tom had the first and only homosexual experience of his life. A young Guwahati 'doctor' took a shine to his muscular form and offered him a free reflexology session, during which the physician told Tom that it was clear from examining his palm that his testicles were swollen. There followed an invitation to his private, curtained-off bunk, which Tom, ever the polite Englishman, accepted. The curtains were drawn, and deep massage commenced, with the doctor's hands starting at Tom's feet and slowly working their way up to his inner thighs where Tom called a sudden, nervous halt to proceedings. The doctor then suggested that he stay and they could 'talk' all night until the train arrived at Guwahati (ten hours away). Just talking. Tom ran.

We arrived exhausted at Guwahati, a seemingly prosperous crossroads town and now capital of the north-eastern state of Assam, provider of 60 per cent of all India's tea exports. It was elevated to regional capital after it was suddenly declared in 1970 that the remote hill station of Shillong, the capital of British Assam, was no longer in Assam, but in fact in a new, tiny state called Meghalaya (literally, the 'abode of clouds' in Sanskrit). The Assam area and southern China are the only places on the planet were tea is found indigenously. Since 1838 it has been exported from here (usually through the auction houses of Guwahati) to Britain. The British have long had a taste for this brew. In fact, most of what we drink every morning – PG Tips, Typhoo, etc. – and what is called internationally 'English Breakfast Tea' is actually Assamese. Assam tea rapidly became a craze in London, and soon British entrepreneurial tea planters were hacking down huge areas of jungle to establish plantations to cash in on this boom. It is the descendants of these men, I think, who also had a taste for golf.

We found a jeep that was willing to go up into the hills,

and after the clubs were strapped to the roof-rack, we set off. Neither of us was in the best of shape, having suffered for many days now with various typically Indian gastric disorders. It was a four-hour journey, extremely bumpy and very twisty, so that we had to hang on all the time and clench our stomach muscles, as a sharp, forty-five degree bend would appear every hundred yards or so. Tom threw up. I nearly passed out.

What improved was the climate. That horrible heat of Calcutta and Guwahati was slowly transforming as we rose to a very pleasant Chilterns-in-June feel. The bush around the roads was as near to jungle as I've seen in India, and yet the climate felt mild. In fact, after three hours of driving it had gone through mild and into chilly. And rainy. And suddenly the district's long-standing nickname of 'The Scotland of the East' started to ring true.

A few miles outside of Shillong, we rounded the enormous Umiam Lake (a very scenic reservoir), which, in the drizzle and chill, did indeed resemble a Highland loch. I recalled the disproportionate amount of Scots in the Raj – about 35 per cent of all British people in India at any one time from 1858 to 1947 were from north of the border. These people must have got to the Shillongese hills and thought they'd found home.

I wonder if they knew when they started building just how wet the place is? Perhaps they thought these were just a few inclement, passing showers.

Perhaps they liked it.

***

We were almost certainly the only Western people in the town. We were without doubt the tallest men in Shillong by several inches, as the local Khasi people who make up most of the population here are on the short side. The townsfolk are very friendly, but it all felt like a wet resort town out of season – Worthing in December perhaps. The hotel was empty and the incredibly nice smiley staff became slightly irritating with their over-eagerness to help us. They seemed so bored – they just wanted something, anything, to do. And Shillong isn't really a looker, like Simla or Darjeeling, partly because it's bigger, partly because it doesn't have a panoramic location and is covered in seemingly ubiquitous mist, and partly because it's hard to see much trace of history here.

Except at the Shillong Golf Club, founded in 1898 by a group of British civil servants who built a nine-hole course, which was then upgraded in 1924 to its present eighteen.

It wasn't raining so we headed straight to the club to play. It was deserted. No phalanx of aggressive caddies wanting your bag, no sniffy old members sizing up your attire and no jobsworth starters or junior admin guys determined to put obstacles in your way – just a beautiful yellow and green British clubhouse and the first and eighteenth fairways. It all looked lovely. If damp.

We reverentially entered the clubhouse and were eventually discovered, as we pored over the old winners' boards and Raj-era golf cartoons hanging on the wall, by the Course Manager, who was happy to let us play.

On the first tee we noticed two striking things: firstly, there were no hole flags anywhere, indicating where to aim; secondly, there were no golfers. None. But the holes looked handsome, the fairways wide and well maintained, so we set off, guessing at each tee where the hole actually was and some of the time getting it right.

We saw what His Excellency meant straightaway though.

People were crossing the first fairway – using it as a cut-through, not bothering to look out for golf balls. Once we'd played around them, we realized that two young ladies in bright saris were sitting on the bank next to the green, right where you'd want to pitch in to attempt par. Too polite to shout at them to move, we played ever-so-careful low chip-and-runs on to the green, and the ladies watched us putt.

Walking up to the second tee we passed two young, thin security guards who smiled, slapped their truncheons into their palms a few times, and gave us a look that said, 'Are you sure you want to be playing now?' And then when we mounted the raised second tee we saw fully His Excellency's problem. It's a 430-yard par four. Seventy-five yards to the front is a small grouping of ancient Stonehenge-like monoliths that are a protected heritage monument. Another seventy-five yards on there is a rather busy road completely intersecting the fairway. On this road buzzed rickshaws, trucks, taxis, cyclists, carts and pedestrians. To the left as we looked down the fairway a very competitive game of cricket was being played on the muddy, wet red clay surface of a school playground. Watching the game were about fifty teenage students of both sexes, many of whom spilled on to the golf course or were crossing it to get to the snack stalls by the seventeenth green. It was wonderfully anarchic. And there we were at the top, wanting to hit five-irons amongst this melee without injuring anyone.

In Britain, after you play your shot, you shout 'fore' if it is going to land near someone. In Naldehra, the practice is to shout 'ball' in the general direction of where you want it to land, and then hit it anyway, even if there are people likely to be underneath. In Shillong on the second tee, we shouted 'ball' and 'fore', and eventually 'hey!' and 'oi!', but no one seemed to care. We, it seemed, were in everyone's way not vice versa. It reminded me of one of my favourite jokes ever, which Robin Williams tells. Here's the difference between cops from New York, LA and London: in New York cops say 'Stop or I'll shoot' and then shoot anyway; in LA cops shoot anyway then say 'Stop or I'll shoot'; in London, policeman say 'Stop . . . stop . . . please stop . . . it's my job'.

So I thought, better just go for it, and if I hit a small child or smash the window of a rickshaw, at least I had yelled first. It was the time to be accurate, certainly, and I hit a very nice-looking straight shot, which landed in the ditch by the road. Tom's ball nicked the edge of the Stonehenge structure, whizzed high into the air and ended up just in front of the ditch. Human casualties: none.

The ditch was vile – full of the sorts of mounds of accumulated garbage and excrement you find in many open spaces in India; my ball had landed right in the middle of a pile. I had to jump in to get it out, which felt a bit like a scene in *Slumdog Millionaire* where a child ducks into a tank of faeces in order to find a coin.

The following day when I played the second hole, more random fun happened. I had taken a three-iron off the tee this time, intending to clear the monolith, the ditch, the kids and the road in one go. Which I did. I was delighted with my 190-yard straight shot. Then with horror I saw a couple of small children bend down and pick up my ball. I screamed at them – 'hehehehoioioi' – and waved like I worked on a runway at Heathrow, until they finally noticed, got the point that it was mine, put it down and walked off. But then a male teenager picked the ball up a few seconds later. Again the screams and the waves. He looked at me, holding my ball, about fifty yards away. 'It's my ball, put it down where you found it, I want to hit it,' was what I was trying to communicate through limb semaphore, and repeatedly patting the ground. He seemed to understand me, put his thumbs up and then slung the ball at me in the fast, fizzy way a fielder zings the ball in low to run out a batsman attempting a risky single. The ball torpedoed straight into the ditch of hell. In I went again.

However, as we progressed, disturbances considerably reduced, and we started to really enjoy this handsome course. We lost a lot of balls, as seemingly decent shots landing in the middle of the fairway would disappear into monsoon-bogged land. But we were accompanied by two kids who seemed to want to help us and were good at digging balls out of weird places. On the fourth there were goats grazing on the boggy fairway. By the seventh, the rain came. Suddenly, and tremendously, it rained and rained as though God was in grief. We donned our waterproofs, put up the umbrellas and played on, with the thunder rumbling and Tom giving me instructions what to do if lightning started right over us: put the golf clubs down, don't head for the trees and save the children first.

Shillong is about thirty miles from Cherrapunji, nestling into the Bangladesh border. This spot is, according to the records, consistently the wettest place on the planet and Shillong isn't far behind. I obsessively logged on to Indian meteorological websites for weeks before we came out, tracking the progress of the monsoon and checking rainfall. In one day just before we left for India, Shillong had 150 mm of rain. I wanted it to be wet. But I hadn't counted on the thunder. It took me two days to realize what the weird atmosphere was in this seemingly pleasant town with pleasant people. At first I put it down to a sort of remote border-town mentality, but I realized after time that it was the thunder . . . an ominous, black, electric presence, always there, really messing with your head, like constant PMT, I imagine.

And as we spent a few days in the town, we realized why no one plays golf in the afternoon. Because it always rains in the afternoon. Heavily, every afternoon. So the Shillong Golf Club members finish up by lunch and the greens keepers put the flags away, not imagining that anyone would want to play in the heavy rain.

The eighth – a long straight, wide par-four – isn't really a golf hole at all, but the local Lover's Lane. Along both sides of the fairway, barely hidden by the bushes, are dozens of teenagers in pairs huddled under big umbrellas, making out with each other. I've never seen more young puppy naughtiness anywhere in India – not on The Maidan in Calcutta or Delhi's Lodi Gardens, or even indeed Mumbai's Chowpatty Beach. We felt guilty that we were disturbing them by whacking balls through their idyll. The rain was tearing down but the couples didn't seem to mind. These are Rain People, I guess. More than Mancunians or Scots, these are people with rain in their DNA, as used to coping with the rains as a camel trader deals with the sun in Rajasthan. When we caught their gaze we said a very English 'Good afternoon', and were met with blushes and giggles.

I played a fine six-iron approach to the green, but as I had played it uphill I couldn't see where it had landed. As I had used a luminous ball and had hit it straight, I wasn't that bothered. However, as I crested the hill and looked down to the green, I was slightly surprised that that part of the eighth and the attached ninth fairways were being used as a football pitch by a group of young teenage boys. My ball would have landed right in the middle of their pitch, and it was nowhere to be seen. The football match continued. None of the boys would look me in the eye. Hmm. Anglo-Indian golfer Helen Mary Chitty, writing in 1901, had a similar experience when playing a course in British Rangoon: 'Occasionally one finds the direct line from tee to green interrupted for some hundred yards by a native football or hockey team most picturesquely turned out in turbans and hobnailed boots, and a brilliant jersey surmounting the flowing shirt tails.'

We played the tenth, and then decided to head slowly back to the clubhouse as we were now soaked to the core and not really enjoying it anymore. On the way we played the sixteenth, seventeenth (back over the school-kids, the rickshaws and the road) and finally up the majestic eighteenth fairway in front of the clubhouse, where I was two inches away from chipping in for par.

The course claims to be the second oldest in India after the Royal Calcutta. Although so does Gulmarg and so does Pune. Sporty Indians like their superlatives – most centuries, best bowling figures, the oldest, the highest, the wettest, the thunderiest . . . and this can get quite competitive. I was nearly kicked out of the Shillong clubhouse when I suggested that this claim may not be as clear-cut as all that.

Around the clubhouse walls are pictures of men from the Assam Rifles regiment who have had a long-standing association with the club. In fact, the regiment, along with the Meghalaya State Government, has been funding the development of the course. This is a great golf course, one of the most enjoyable I played on in India, the local hazards adding a lot of fun to my rounds and certainly creating a warm, friendly informal atmosphere. It was as though everyone was taking their exercise (or trying to get a snog), but in different ways. However, I can see how, to those brought up on the sacred slopes of Delhi Golf Club or the Tolly, this sort of thing is deeply annoying. If it was my club and I wanted to play three or four times a week these things would probably stop being charming and become irritating. But as in most areas in Indian life – as in Britain – this is also about class. People who play golf here tend to be upper-middle class or flash, aspirant entrepreneurs. Golf is status. Having the riff-raff on the golf course is not how it should be, I suspect many think. And they'd think it, too, in Tunbridge Wells or Cheltenham.

As with Naldehra's crazy design and traffic congestion, so the Shillong Golf Course issue seems to represent some profoundly Indian dilemmas.

The shit in the holes does have to go, though.

6

The Lost Courses of Senchal

Three cars.

The first is driven by Stirling Moss. It is 24 April 1962 and English motor racing daredevil Moss is screeching round St Mary's Corner on the Goodwood race track in Sussex. He is pushing his pale green Lotus 18 Climax to the limit, trying to make up lost time as he lingers disappointingly in seventeenth place. He is one of the greatest racing car drivers ever, known for his panache, daring and fearlessness, and he has the air of a Spitfire pilot. He is a 1940s era *Boy's Own* British hero, on the cusp of the 1960s social revolution, six months before Lennon & McCartney have their first hit.

My father is in the crowd, thrilled by Moss, his hero, capturing it all on Super 8 mm film. Apart from the scream of the cars and the whoops of the patriotic fans, my father hears the rat-a-tat flicker of the film moving round the cogs and motors of the camera. Through the lens he sees Moss take the corner at 110 mph, lose control of his car, hurtle 150 yards off the track, across lawns and into an eight-foot high embankment. There is a huge crash, a little exhalation of smoke then a few seconds silence. My father keeps filming, but nobody and nothing is moving: the Lotus is a mangled, distorted wreck; somewhere inside it is Moss, who is cut out of the wreck after half an hour, lies in a coma for a month, half paralysed, and will never race at this level again.

The second is a white Ford Capri with a funky red stripe down its side heading out of London's West End, along the Embankment. It is 10.30 p.m. I am seven years old and about to lie down on the back seat to have a nap on the long journey back home to the suburbs. My father is driving and my Uncle Norman is in the passenger seat. I hear their banter, but can't follow its arcane, blokey dingdong meaning. I am so tired, but also exhilarated, as I have just had the best day of my life.

Star Wars exploded into Britain at Christmas, 1977. Within a week it was smashing box office records and touts were marking up £2 tickets to £30 – this in the middle of a time of economic hardship, industrial unrest and recession. Kids from my school started to come back from London trips, relating what they had seen, and it all seemed like the most exciting, wondrous thing in the universe. Then they'd start appearing at class with *Star Wars* sticker books, comic book adaptations and – best of all – plastic dolls of Luke, Han, Leia and Vader. Not only did it sound incredibly exciting, but the peer pressure was immense and, increasingly, those in class who had not seen the film became ostracized.

With no internet or other genuine mass-market communication networks, publicity about anything was all about word-of-mouth back then. I'm not sure my parents had even heard of *Star Wars* until I started begging them to take me to see it, and they were slightly baffled by my desire to go. They just didn't understand how amazing the sound of a light sabre was, or a laser blaster, or Chewbacca's yodel, or Vader's asthmatic diction. Eventually – and possibly because my father had discovered the film starred Sir Alec Guinness, another of his heroes due to his Ealing Comedy films – they relented, and our party travelled up to London to see it.

Before we reached the Leicester Square cinema, however, there was an extra treat. We parked off Covent Garden (still a fruit and veg market in those days) and walked down to the Strand. It was then I saw for the first time in my life the beautiful sight of the glowing golden arches on a ketchup-red background. For the other big new craze amongst schoolboys was McDonald's food. Their simple beefburgers had become a schoolboy obsession for us, and friends would come back from London trips telling of the wonders of a Big Mac or a triple-thick banana shake. Even now when I go into that same McDonald's on the corner of Villiers Street and the Strand, I feel a sense of childish excitement. I remember sitting with my father and uncle, looking out into the drizzly black London evening, eating a cheeseburger and feeling in sensual paradise.

Then we walked up to Leicester Square, and after securing popcorn, Coke and a *Star Wars* photo book, found our seats in the auditorium. The houselights were dimmed, the screen's curtains parted and from the pitch black came the mighty 20th Century Fox logo and the studio's bombastic fanfare theme music, cutting quickly to the swoosh of John Williams's magnificent title theme. Then there was a black galaxy with an infinite amount of twinkling stars, and *that* text in yellow, crawling away and up the screen. An engine rumbled and an amazing, vast spaceship passed over my head, and I felt my mind popping and fizzing with wonder.

It is still the best day of my life. Nothing has ever matched that.

The third car: a few months after Stirling Moss's crash, the British Motoring Corporation launched a small car, called the Austin 1100, aimed at the mass market. The Mini Clubman may be the iconic era-defining car of the Swinging Sixties, but it was the Austin 1100 which was the speedy, reliable compact car of choice for less groovy folk across the country. It is April 1983 and I am in a yellow Austin 1100 with my father on the M4 heading west into thrashing rain. The twenty-year-old wipers creak and groan and intermittently attempt to fight off the incoming storm, like the Spartans at Thermopylae, or Luke and Han faced with legions of stormtroopers when trying to blast their way out of the Death Star.

We are in this small leaky car because I am a man in love. My little obsessive twelve-year-old brain is fixated with an Australian actress called Janet Fielding, or more precisely, with Tegan Jovanka, the sexy air hostess she plays in *Doctor Who*. Always in the TARDIS dressed in her lilac flight attendant gear, with a cute matching fez that she rests on the side of her head, French beret style, she has triggered a pre-pubescent lust in me that I struggle to contain. The Tom Baker and Peter Davison Doctor Whos were my obsession, my escape, my every second thought, and Tegan was my pin-up girl.

I have heard that Janet Fielding will be at a Doctor Who convention in Longleat, near Bath . . . answering questions! Signing autographs! Looking gorgeous! I ask my father if we can go and, of course, he says yes. However, as the weeks go by I overhear snatched conversations between my parents about this excursion. My father has no job; we have no money; and he has sold both our cars just to have some cash to live on. We are in a bungalow in Weybridge that we all hate, and our belongings remain unpacked in boxes in the dining room. For the first time in his adult life he has no car, the object that defines and expresses him most. I feel the tension of these times, but immerse myself in science fiction, fantasy and comic book worlds. I go for long solitary rides on my Raleigh Chopper and create a makeshift putting green of the front garden, with a trowel, using flower pots as holes. My father makes me flags out of bits of old rusting pieces of tin on wooden sticks.

Late at night I hear them strategizing in the kitchen about the Longleat trip; there is strain in their voices; now and then a voice is raised, then shushed. We can't go to Longleat without a car, it's a simple as that, and I begin to lose hope that I will ever meet Tegan.

Then one morning on the driveway there is a yellow Austin 1100, with its bonnet up and my father's head and shoulders buried deep inside the engine, trying to breathe fire into it. I can hear him curse as the machine will not start. There are greasy, oily rags littering the driveway, along with cans of various mechanical lubricants and potions intended to inspire the internal combustion engine to ignite. Spark plugs are checked, changed; the exhaust pipe removed, examined, cleaned, replaced. At one point, with the car up on a jack, he disappears underneath the chassis on a small homemade tray with wheels, a wrench in his hand. As uninterested in cars as ever, I return to my fantasy world and leave my father to attempt his motor-mechanic alchemy on this rusting bone-shaker. After a while there is a BANG, a whizzing sound and a yelp of glee. I can hear an engine gently purring. I look out my window and see my father, with crazed Einstein hair, topless, covered in grease, smoking a small cigar, gazing at the car, a slight smile of triumph on his lips. It is the first time I've seen him smile in a long time.

I stand the other side of the trestle table to the seated Tegan Jovanka. I am unable to speak, dumbstruck by the Australian vision in front of me. She smiles that Tegan smile and hands me a photo of herself that she has just signed personally for me . . . to Grant . . . love from Janet Fielding, with three kisses and an exclamation mark. I stare deep into her lovely hazel eyes and I feel a warmth and terror that is utterly new to me. Tegan smiles professionally back, and tells me cheerily to 'keep watching'. I hear my father thanking her for making my day then he gently nudges me to move on as there is a queue of hundreds of other boys (and a few much older men who should know better) queuing for some Tegan-love.

Within weeks of this trip my father had turned his life around, found a new job and money, and we had moved to a house that we loved. I changed schools, and soon my father could afford a new car. He traded in his now souped-up Austin 1100 for a second-hand white Ford Escort.

Thank you, Tegan, thank you, Janet. My infatuation with you pushed my father, gave him the momentum he needed to create a new life for us all. Making that car start was his own Doctor Who-like regeneration from one man into another. He regained his self respect, and I got to meet the space-travelling woman of my dreams.

***

This is a funny quiet sleepy little place, the air is certainly better than Simla – softer and less extreme. Through the rent in the fleecy veil (the traveller can see from Darjeeling) clear and clean against the intense blue sky the snowy summit of Kinchinjunga, the culminating peak of lesser heights converging upward to it and all ethereal as spirit, white and pure in the sunshine . . . we are uplifted.

British Indian explorer, adventurer and spy,
Sir Francis Younghusband, in
The Heart of Nature (1921)

The omens were not good.

I'd added a few days in the hill station of Darjeeling ('the Queen of the Hills') to our itinerary because I'd heard about two courses nearby. The Army course in Kalimpong, forty-five miles east of Darjeeling and run as a very gentle form of top brass R&R, has a counter claim to Gulmarg as 'the highest course in the world'. It is perched precariously amongst the mountains next to a Buddhist monastery. Senchal, the other course, seemed even more exciting. For it was here, I assumed, that the Calcuttan government pen-pushers holidaying in Darjeeling played their golf. The location sounded amazing: nestling by a pine-fringed lake on the famous Tiger Hill, where on a clear morning you can see Everest in the distance and, much closer, the mighty Khangchendzonga – the third highest peak in the world. The British had found paradise in the hills here in the 1830s, I thought, and had built a golf course with the best views on Earth.

'There is no golf course at Senchal Lake,' said Dushen, the young graduate IT guy to whom we gave a lift in our jeep as we painstakingly, gruellingly and very bumpily climbed up the winding road from Siliguri to Darjeeling at two in the morning. Dushen worked in Bangalore, 1,000 miles away, and was returning home to the hills to see his family for the first time in three years. He had grown up in the area and was adamant there was no golf there. 'You need to go to Kalimpong – there they have good golf,' he said.

'But on the internet there are many references to the course by the lake at Senchal,' I countered. And indeed there are. Lake Senchal is advertised as an attractive beauty spot for family picnickers. There is a nine-hole course there, they say, with a clubhouse and tourist lodge. Sounded great. If it was real.

Vikram, our Nepalese hotel manager, had a similar opinion. 'No, there is no golf in Darjeeling. I will arrange for a day trip to Kalimpong. You can play good golf there.' But I insisted that I had read a lot about Senchal golf course online. He looked puzzled. An Indian hotel manager would have given me a 'You're an insane and unpredictable tourist' look and wanted me to disappear. The Nepalese seem a more patient race, and Vikram promised to make more enquiries as I was so adamant.

I went online in the hotel while Vikram rang his mates. Sure enough, there was page after page of references on India tourist websites to a Senchal course. Whether this course was the British course I didn't know, but I assumed that someone could tell me at the clubhouse.

Vikram came back to me: 'OK, I have spoken to many friends who grew up here. There is no golf course. But there may be the remains of a British one. Kalimpong is where you play golf. My brother will drive you, yes?'

No!

This was a great lead and, to Vikram's bewilderment, I booked his brother to drive us the next morning halfway up a mountain, armed with full golf clobber to play on a golf course that no one in town believed existed.

11 a.m. the next day

A huddle of men: two very large Westerners with 'Tollygunge Club' polo shirts, golf bags, soft-studded shoes and Nike baseball caps with sun visors: four very short Nepalese – Vikram, his brother Shubash and two other jeep drivers. The six of us are in conference as to where the hell we're going. The more I insist there is a golf course the more the guys get into the game. Just to please us? I start to wonder . . . maybe they're thinking – OK if you two want to think there's a golf course, we'll say there is one. Then suddenly there's a breakthrough. I describe my fantasy of where I think it is: the pine trees, the lake, the nice families from

Bihar and Bengal picnicking, the view . . . and the boys go, 'Oh right – we know where you mean!' Rapid exchanges of directions in Nepalese, and it seems we're on to something. Tom and I set off with Shubash.

So us pioneering Hilaries start the long slog up the hill with our own sceptical jeep-driving Tenzing.

Of course, we didn't really factor in the mist. Or the rain. Or the cold. As we ascend – Darjeeling town is at an altitude of 7,000 feet, and we're going high above it – the weather, which was bad enough for us to put off a dawn trip to see the sunrise over Everest as visibility was so low, worsens. It starts to feel like the Hebrides in January. Visibility is reduced to about thirty-five yards. The car slows, headlights are on full and the precipice that the road nervously peers over becomes more canyonesque. It's all getting spooky. And I'm aware that even if we find this golf course, even if I'm right and everyone else is wrong, even if by some miracle there's nine lovingly tended greens with numbered red flags poking out of them, then the 'Thriller'-like fog and the now torrential drizzle will mean that play will be rather limited.

'Right,' I say to Tom, 'we're going to have to play the course as a succession of fifty-yard chips. I only have three balls left. None of them luminous. I don't want to lose any.'

'Right,' says Tom wishing, I suspect, that he was in a nice hotel somewhere near Alicante, with an attractive German blonde at his side by the pool.

After a while Tom furrows his brow and says, 'Why is this place called *Tiger* Hill? Do you think there are any tigers here?'

'Don't be ridiculous,' I say. But then I start thinking about the time, which I will describe later, when I was walking in the Nilgiris hills near Ooty and came, by chance, face-to-face with a tiger. I remembered how primevally terrifying that had been. Same kind of place, same climate, tea area. Hmm. Then I think about hitting golf balls into mist on an open space where you can't see much beyond a few yards. You'd never know what is out there waiting for you. Stalking you. Hungry. And I actually start panicking inside that I am leading all three of us on a foolish jolly that will see us all end up as tiger nibbles.

'Look, the chances of seeing a tiger twice in a lifetime, randomly, in the countryside are so slim, that statistically I'm the safest person to be with at the moment,' I offer, trying to make this a question of mathematics.

Tom doesn't look convinced. If he's not worrying about cobras in the rough or snarling she-monkeys chasing us across fairways, he's going to worry about tigers. But to be honest I really am worried, too. Stupidly, irrationally worried. It is, after all, called *Tiger* Hill.

A long uncomfortable silence. Tom cracks first.

'Er – Shubash . . .' he asks, his tone forced jokey-casual. 'You know this place is called Tiger Hill? Er . . . are there any tigers here?'

'No sir. Once there were many tigers, but no more, because . . .' and then he smiles cheekily, 'the British killed them all. No tigers here for eighty years.' He looks at me and I feel vaguely to blame.

'Sorry,' I say.

Further up . . .

We round a bend and pull in, the heavy drizzle cascading down through the fog.

Shubash says with a flourish, in the manner of a conjuror who is slightly unsure that the prestige for an under-rehearsed trick will come off, 'There: golf course.'

He points us to a sludgy footpath that goes up hill a bit before levelling out.

'Where?'

'We walk from here – I will help you carry your clubs.'

'How long's the walk?'

'Thirty minutes.'

'We can't carry our clubs for thirty minutes. And smart guys from Calcutta who play golf – they wouldn't pull up in their deluxe air-conditioned cars and be prepared to walk half an hour in the rain to the first tee.'

'Mmm.'

We walk a little down the footpath, the rain tunnelling down our already foul monsoon-smelling golf waterproofs. We find what we think is a large open grass space – though it is hard to tell its dimensions because of the fog. It certainly feels like golf course shape and terrain, but it is now like a muddy disused farmer's field. Is this really where the highest echelons of the Calcuttan Raj passed their time?

Shubash can see we're disappointed.

'There is a guy I know, further up the mountain, who is big expert on this place – the history – you want to go see him?'

So we get back in the jeep, starting to enjoy this search with seemingly two mysteries: first, where is the British course and, second, to what do all the online citations refer? A new course that was never finished, perhaps, or was itself discontinued soon after its completion?

Up, up, up twirling into thickening fog. Shubash seems to be muttering a prayer.

Finally, we pass a deserted temple and a barrier appears across the road. We have reached the ticket booth for the summit of Tiger Hill, where the following day we would witness one of the natural wonders of the world. Shubash goes first, and emerges seconds later to beckon me in. There is Mr Upreti, late fifties, and apparently the man who knows more than anyone about this hill. He speaks to Shubash, who translates – yes, there was a course here but long ago – during the British time. But soon after Independence the course was flattened, and they planted trees on it. The old clubhouse and the gate to the club are all that is left. Even Shubash seems excited by this. We find out where these are, and head back down the hill. After ten minutes we pull up. 'This is the place the man was talking about,' Shubash confirms.

We are standing at a ten-foot-high iron gate, padlocked, and supported by two grey slate pillars. Attached to the pillars is some very rusted barbed wire that stretches in either direction around the meadow behind. On top of the barbed wire is the skull of a long dead rodent. And behind the gate, twenty yards away, we can just make out a ghostly building in the mist.

At first the building seems to have the outline of a temple, but in the further glimpses we get when the wind blows the mist away for a few seconds we see a solid stone, tarnished yellow building, about the size of a drive-thru McDonald's restaurant, with its windows bricked in and steps leading up to a large front door.

Shubash points at the building. 'Mr Upreti says that is the, er . . .' He struggles to find the right word, 'Er . . . offices of the golf.'

'Do you mean clubhouse?' I say.

'Clubhouse! Yes. That is the word.' He smiles.

We duck under the barbed wire and walk around the desolate old building; there is no way in. I imagine rooms of billiard tables criss-crossed with duvets of cobwebs; old tournament winners' boards; a ghost bar with a few bottles of scotch on its shelves; a library with copies of *The Times of India* from the 1920s; and the starter's office where decaying scorecards and handicap lists from a century ago still rest on the shelves, but are now probably snacks for rats. Tom has been snapping away.

'Hang on – let me play some shots,' I say.

So I run back to the jeep, pulled out my pitching wedge,

my glove and a ball, and start chipping in front of the building. If this is the site of the old British course, then I am almost certainly the first British person in sixty-odd years to hit a ball on it.

'OK. Tomorrow we go to Kalimpong, yes? There is good golf there,' says Shubash.

***

The next day we woke at 3.45 a.m. to get to the top of Tiger Hill for the sunrise. Unlike the previous morning the sky was totally clear, and we were excited to see this famous view. We all stood facing the ridge of mountains 100 miles away, dominated by the awesome Khangchendzonga. Further back, 250 miles away, we could make out Everest, its wonderfully iconic steep triangular face and sharp tip resonating with the charisma of an A-lister forced to dwell among minor celebs. When the sun started to rise, a cheer went up, and the hundred or so people that were with us surged to the eastern end of the viewing promenade, like excited girls greeting the arrival of The Beatles.

After an hour's watching we turned to go. Then I saw it. I grabbed Tom. Amongst the immense vista below us I pointed to an area about a mile or so away. 'What does that land look like it's been used for?' I asked.

'Golf course' replied Tom.

Maybe my need to find the Lost Courses of Senchal had become obsessive, maybe I was seeing golf courses like Don Quixote saw windmills. But to me it looked like a patch of links-like land that would be perfect for golf. At the far end of this small plateau was a building. I asked Shubash what that was.

'Tourist lodge,' he said.

***

That evening I trawled the internet for images of either a golf course or even the piece of land I'd seen. I found none of the British course and I started to notice that there were very few images of the newer one (if it existed). In fact, there was only one image that kept appearing in all my searches: a green, a flag and a backdrop of pines. No golfers. If you typed any other golf course I'd played on in India into the same search engine you discovered a lot of holiday snaps of golfers hacking away. Furthermore, I could find no formal or bloggy reviews of this course. Surely, I thought, someone would have written something about this place? And yet all these tourist sites listed Senchal as having a nine-hole course. I can only assume that there were plans drawn up for a tourist course that were not carried through. Or maybe it was half laid out and abandoned.

Tom was sick for a few days so we agreed he'd stay in Darjeeling while I headed to Kalimpong to see if anyone there knew anything. Apparently the golf is good there.

7

Coffee with the Colonels at Kalimpong

The talk in mess is very bad at times . . . nothing but scandal about people in the station . . . the bad seem to have the upper hand.

The young Francis Younghusband on his first military posting (1921)

Kalimpong lies 4,000 feet above sea level, and forty-odd miles east of Darjeeling. Both places were British hill stations, both have the same architectural relics of Raj, but the climates couldn't be more different. Where Darjeeling is cold, wet, damp and foggy – kind of like a November England – Kalimpong feels gently tropical. It's pleasantly hot – London in July if you like – but with enjoyably breathable fresh air. At night the insects hiss and trill cacophonously, as if we were in the middle of the Bengal jungle a few hundred miles south. Hungry mosquitoes buzz en masse at dusk; the odd scorpion is seen outside the hotel rooms; little lizards dart about the golf course; and the bush is green lush and exotic.

At the Durpin Hill's summit is the Army golf course, the vast Army base, the Durpin Buddhist monastery and a large colonial lodge ('Dr Morgan's House') that is now a state-run hotel. Oh, and the views are astounding. On a clear day you can see the snow-topped Khangchendzonga. As you tee off above the clouds, high on the second to the green 215 yards far below, you feel like you are hitting into the great black rocky peak itself. The scale of the mountains as backdrop is immense. Sometimes I was so involved in golf self-hatred I forgot where I was. Then I would look up from my introspective rage and be astounded once again.

I kept wondering why golf had come to this area only relatively recently. The Army course dates from 1972. Before, this land was a swampy bog called Dhan Dhania Park. Yet it's exactly the sort of spot the British chose for their hill station links: up a mountain, panoramic views, cool temperature, awkward hillside, breeze. So why no golf?

I think it's to do with who exactly the British were that came to Kalimpong. Some hill stations were dominated by military people, some by government and civil service employees and their families, others by the established and entrepreneurial business classes, and some by tea planters. Each gave a slightly different texture to the hill-station society. Kalimpong was the domain of the Scottish (and Swiss) missionary. I suspect they were far too busy evangelizing and working for the good of the local community and the Lord above to be bothered about playing something as frivolous as golf. Maybe it was even thought of as slightly immoral. They made great efforts to win over the local Buddhists throughout the nineteenth century and their legacy can be seen all over town today – from the many white churches to the famous Dr Graham Orphanage, set up in 1900, and now a school of up to 1,300 pupils. Though Norden, a local businessman and ex-pupil of this school, told me interestingly that 'even though we had Christianity rammed down our throats every day, none of us really converted, as to us, compared to Buddhism, Christianity seemed such a simplistic religion; we asked for more from our faith than their God was offering.'

The British grabbed the town in 1864 after the Anglo–Bhutan war with the Gurkhas (otherwise spelt Gorkhas). It was a strategically significant gain. Kalimpong was on one of the old Silk Routes, as the nearby Nathula and Jelepa passes provided good access between India and Tibet. It was still being used in the nineteenth century as a through-point for trade, especially furs and food. The British moved in and tried to pitch it as a slightly warmer, quieter alternative to Darjeeling. Of course, from its inception the staff of the East India Company had never really given two hoots about religion. From the early seventeenth century onwards their progress was about hard cash, and whatever it took to keep and increase the flow of money back to their shareholders in London. This is why, despite Clive of India and Wellesley's brutal wars of conquest, there was considerable harmony between the cultures in the first 200 years of the Anglo-Indian trade cooperation. Indians loved trade as much as the British. It suited both. Many of the problems seem to have commenced with the missionaries. From the early 1800s on, they came in large numbers with one aim: to convert the heathen. Some say that it was the uncompromising nature of the missionaries and educationalists that in turn led to the spark of the 'Mutiny' in 1857. This, after all, was triggered by the strike of Hindu and Muslim soldiers in Meerut, protesting as they thought that they had to bite into pig- and cow-fat sealed gun cartridges in order to load their weapons. Whether this is true no one seems sure anymore, but it was taken as the final insult from over-zealous Christians disrespecting local faiths, and proved the powder-keg for the massacres that followed.

As I wandered across the veranda of the clubhouse I caught site of a thin Sikh in a '113th Regiment Engineers' blue tracksuit. He seemed very edgy and nervous. There were two middle-aged men on the first tee and a third, older one barking orders into a phone nearby. The Sikh signified that this was the Boss and that all dealings should be referred to him. The Boss stared hard and stonily at me, and looked me up and down (I was pleased I had shaved). Then I noticed his eyes fix on the Tollygunge Club logo on my polo shirt. He thrust out a hand for me to shake and met my eyes solidly, saying, 'You are most welcome – which country? England? Very good,' before carrying on his phone conversation.

I started changing on the veranda and was sorting out green fees with the caretaker when I noticed an ominous silence aimed in my direction. The caretaker was nearly shaking. The Boss, driver in hand, was belligerently glaring at me. I realized my nattering was interrupting his warm-up routine. I apologized. He grunted acceptance, then pulled the ball rather horribly into the left-side rough.

The Army has such a strong presence here because of the campaign for an independent Gurkha state – 'Gorkhaland' – which by the 1980s had turned very violent. The Gorkha National Liberation Front made a strong, aggressive push for statehood during this time, calling a forty-day general strike, which in turn led to riots in Darjeeling and Kalimpong: 1,200 people were killed. I spoke to one local who pointed around where we stood and said that there were heads rammed on to stakes all the way down this road. It was this period that Kiran Desai wrote about in her Booker Prize-winning novel *The Inheritance of Loss*. By coincidence I was staying in a small 1930s wooden cottage called 'Magnolia' in which she and her mother, the equally eminent writer Anita Desai, had lived. Each night as I swatted meaty cockroaches with my flip flops, I imagined the Desais sitting as I was in the front parlour, writing and looking out on the same porch and bush.

It's a lovely course: tight, slim, criss-crossy and hilly, and you have to hit straight. Very straight. All the time. A wayward shot can end up cascading down a mini ravine and could start an avalanche. High on an eyrie, facing the mountain, a thick belt of meringue cloud below me and a liquid clear, stratospheric blue sky above, I hit a good five-iron off the second tee, and whilst it was in flight I dreamed of par. It bounced nastily and clattered down a steep bank, meaning two chips and two putts for five. But when the view's that good, who really cares?

The fifth is the most vertical golf hole I've ever played. Ninety-three yards long and about the same up. If your pitching wedge tee-shot misses the green you could roll back all the way down to the tee. I missed the green by a foot, but thankfully the ball embedded itself in a ridge. Standing at a horrible angle, I overhit my chip in, and it ended up on a road behind the green, next to a large white stone sign depicting a cartoon golfer and the slogan 'You are in paradise – enjoy it'. Sometimes here you can even hit a beautiful shot, dead straight, full distance on to what you think is the plushest piece of fairway, only to find that your ball is nowhere to be found. It has dribbled down into the valley hundreds of yards below.

As I sweated up and down the hills, I kept bumping into the Boss and his mates. I enthused about the course, and they seemed pleased. After the seventh I walked up to the Golf Greens Café by the side of the road.

'Do you have any Coke?' I asked.

'No sir.'

'Water?'

'No sir.'

'Er . . . chai?'

'No sir. No drinks sir.'

Silly me, why would I think they'd sell cold drinks at a café on a hot day? I returned to the eighth tee and played the last two holes well. The ninth green lay next to the clubhouse and stood atop a steep motte and bailey mound with bunkers ridged down the front. I could see the Boss's gang watching from the veranda. I took out a seven-iron and hit a beauty, landing on the green.

Nearly.

In fact the ball had lodged next to the wall of a muddy semi-bunker thing next to the green. With the Boss watching I had a sort of etiquette panic. There's no way I could play a stroke, as the ball was basically next to a solid mud wall. I couldn't get any backlift. A caddy wandered on to the green and held the flag for me, perhaps expecting me to become all Phil Mickelson and chip in. I suspect I could have shifted the ball a bit – this seems to be what Indian club golfers do every shot – but I didn't want to be seen as a rule-breaker in front of the Boss, who I assumed was a military man. He had that sort of moustache. I grabbed my pitching wedge, carefully placed the head behind the ball, then with no backswing whatsoever, scoop/flicked the ball out on to the green. Not very far, leaving a huge putt for par. Which I missed. Still the approach shot seemed to have impressed them, and the Boss asked me to join them for coffee on the veranda.

The Boss and his friends, it turns out, were all colonels. The Boss is the Secretary of the club. When I criticized the state of Shillong's turf and admired his, he beamed with delight. We talked about the course. Colonel Varghese (slightly bigger moustache than the Boss) managed to get in that he got a hole in one on the vertical fifth three months ago. His name is on the honours board for this, and he got a mention in *Golf Digest Magazine*. I asked them if there had ever been a British course in Kalimpong. They were certain there hadn't been. They mentioned the old British course at Senchal, and I asked them about the more modern course there – had it ever existed? 'Yes,' said Colonel Sarkar, 'but it was no good, and now it does not exist.' Colonel Varghese then told me about a British course I hadn't heard about. Apparently British tea planters built a nine-hole course at Dalgaon in Assam, on the way back to Shillong. It still exists, though it would seem that it is 'under repair'. However, one state government website suggested that it should be improved and updated as it would be a good facility to offer for holidaymakers from the nearby Chalsa resort town. This website describes the golf course here as a 'potential sector with promising investment prospects'.

The colonels also suggested that a third golf course, aside from Kalimpong and Gulmarg, has a claim to being the highest course in the world: the Haa Dzong course, near Hasimara in neighbouring Bhutan. The colonels had played there as the Indian Army has a large presence in that area of 'the mountain kingdom'. Golf is advertised on the Indian Army's advice website for this station as a good way to relax. The greens are all mountain browns.

The Boss barked orders at his staff to make me feel as comfortable as possible, get me anything I needed and ensure that I was safely placed in a taxi when I wanted to leave. It's the closest I've ever got to top brass. Tony would have been proud of me.

***

O, fie! Hold, hold, my heart;
And you, my sinews, grow not instant old,
But bear me stiffly up. Remember thee!
Ay, thou poor ghost, while memory holds a seat
In this distracted globe. Remember thee!

Yea, from the table of my memory
I'll wipe away all trivial fond records,
All saws of books, all forms, all pressures past,
That youth and observation copied there;
And thy commandment all alone shall live
Within the book and volume of my brain,
Unmix'd with baser matter

William Shakespeare,
Hamlet, Act 1, Scene 5 (1601)

The vicar mumbled something holy sounding from the little black death book he cradled in his open outstretched palms; the coffin was lowered with faux solemnity by the pall bearers wanting their lunch and beer. We shuffled a bit. It was overcast and chilly, even for June. There were a few sniffs.

The irritating undertaker stepped forward and, with a theatrical cough, said, 'And now, ladies and gentleman, we invite you to throw earth on to the coffin.'

Oh God. I had a middle-aged Holden Caulfield voice constantly babbling in my head: how phoney; ridiculous ritual; suburban am-dram for the falsely melodramatic.

As we were about to step forward, he continued, 'Please don't be shy of the earth. It isn't real earth, it is a synthetic earth substitute, so your hands will not get dirty.' He gave a little chuckle; the weaker-willed, easily led of the gathered mourners echoed this chuckle.

I wanted to push him violently into the grave and cover his weaselly chops with his bloody astroturf. Death is messy, the body decays, falls to bits, people go mad, all previous order is broken up. How dare he pathetically try to sanitize it for us with his throw-and-go soil? Death is chaotic and painful. A Jewish friend told me how, in her faith, the dead body is laid out and the relatives come and wail, openly, insanely, letting the full force of the grief pour out in communal ululations. This seems a more honest way to deal with the dead. Grief is the messiest set of emotions a human can feel. At that point I despised the Christian Church and the parasites that earn their living in the sub-industries supporting it for packaging up this ancient human entropic suffering. The Hindus, who burn the body in the open air on a wooden funeral pyre or float the corpse down the Ganges from a funeral ghat, seem to understand more what mourners need from the death ritual: theatre, immersion, a sense of the epic, apocalyptic and transcendent, of worlds being crossed. Anglican Protestant ritual seems to be about the brushing of grief under the carpet. It's too embarrassing, too impolite and might upset the neighbours. A death is an end of the world, a star collapsed, sucking into its black hole all those that relied on it. It deserves a highly operatic marking, not a mumbled, drizzly, astroloam burial.

After the funeral we all went to the local Harvester, had microwaved chilli con carne and garlic bread, and made small talk about what had been on TV the night before. About *Big Brother*. Somebody said how inconvenient it must be that my father died at the busiest time of my year. I wanted to wail.

8

Banana Leaf Brollies in Bangladesh

Everywhere we go/The people want to know/Who we are/ Where we come from/We are the Army/The Barmy Barmy Army/We are the England/The mighty mighty England

Barmy Army chant at Mirpur Stadium, Dhaka (March 2010)

It was when Gary, dressed in full black burqa, hijab and niqab, ran through the Dhaka hotel lobby with a can of Heineken in each hand, fag stuffed in his mouth, and barged his way into the nearest ladies toilet to throw up, that I thought it time to leave my lunch with the Barmy Army and head back to the cricket match.

The Army's generals had arrived in the Bangladeshi capital a few days before the match started, and were alarmed to discover that it was almost impossible to find any lager in the whole city; it wasn't actually illegal, it's just no one here really drinks lager, or anything alcoholic much really. There are no bars, except in the five-star business hotels, there are no off-licences, and in the average budget fleapit that Gary and his mates would stay in, there was not a drop of the amber fluid deemed essential for any Barmy trip.

So, they worked out where the ground was (in the suburb of Mirpur), then scanned the nearby area for appropriate venues; a short cycle rickshaw ride away was the Hotel Delana with whose manager they did a deal: if twenty of them guaranteed to stay in the hotel could he get them some lager? The manager said that this could be arranged. Yes but we need somewhere to drink it . . . together. So the manager handed over one of his empty function rooms to the Army for the duration of their stay. The well-drilled platoons of the Army went into immediate action, like a crack unit of marines, converting a bland empty space into the ideal Barmy environment; first, massive widescreen TVs were procured, a satellite feed was set up to the ESPN Sports, Star World and Neo Cricket channels, and these were all positioned at suitable places around the room to ensure maximum audience enjoyment. Then the room was decorated; bunting was the main theme, with streamers, wall hangings, mobiles – like a Christmas office party the morning after. Thick black curtains were draped over every window to ensure total focus. Finally, the Heineken was solemnly brought in. It felt like a working men's club in Nuneaton.

The problem was that the manager had managed to secure them one Heineken crate of thirty cans. And was charging the Army 350 taka (over £3) per 300 ml can – three times the price it would be in Nuneaton, and I guess ten times the cost price in Dhaka. Bear in mind it only costs 50 taka to get a day's entry into the test match. That's equivalent to buying a beer at a Lord's test for £350.

But the price wasn't the problem. It was the quantity. Big Dave, the Army's Drinks Tsar – everyone has a rank in the Barmy Army, and a job, which they take *very* seriously – looked the manager hard in the eye: 'It's not enough mate. You don't seem to understand. I would drink that in a few hours. We each need a crate like that every day.' Once the penny dropped, an endless stream of Heineken was found, and resulted in the bizarre sight of smartly suited Bengali waiters standing behind a small table in a *Phoenix Nights* meets darts from Frimley Green atmosphere, handing out cans of Heineken (each costing more than their daily wage) to overweight, topless men from Grimsby and Hartlepool. When it would seem that the Heineken was running low, orders would be barked, and another waiter would appear with a fresh crate; twenty-four hours a day, lager on tap, in one of the most populous Islamic countries in the world. The curtains were always drawn, the overhead neon strip lights always on; the cricket trundled away on the massive screens which the Army followed with half an eye while getting steadily wasted as the day progressed. The Sky commentary voices of David Gower, Nasser Hussain and the Army's patron saint, Sir Ian Botham, murmured ubiquitously away in the background like the chants of high priests at a Hindu festival.

I worked out the Army's routine. The hardcore few fought off the hangovers and lack of sleep and made it to the stadium in time for the teams coming on to the field at 9.25 a.m. (Play starts considerably earlier here than in England as it gets so darn hot later in the day.) When the England team, led by the stand-in public school and Cambridge officer-class captain Alastair Cook, jog on to the pitch around then, the twenty-five or so Barmies stand up as one and sing at full pelt, in terrace-chant style, the great British hymn 'Jerusalem'. William Blake's words, set to music in 1916 by Sir Hubert Parry at the instigation of that great man of India, Francis Younghusband, as part of his First World War morale-boosting 'Fight for Right' campaign, roused me each morning. The England players, a hundred yards away in the centre of the pitch, seemed to like it too. They would always turn towards the singing Army and, whilst they stretched a few muscles, with gestures and waves would make the Army feel that their singing was welcome, that somehow it was pumping them up, filling them with Englishness, making them think about their sweethearts and making them proud.

At the end of the song ('in England's green and pleasant land'), the England team would clap the Army, as indeed would we, all unified by a sense of community in an alien place. It felt like an Anglican mission in the middle of the Bengali jungle belting out hymns to keep the tigers and native heathen at bay, like Katharine Hepburn's African congregation murdering English hymns in the middle of the jungle to a bemused Humphrey Bogart in *The African Queen.*

Matt Prior, the burly Essex wicket keeper loves the Army and they love him. Every day he would run up to the Army and stand waving and clapping his big gloves at them. In return there would be hearty shouts of 'Morning Mattie' and 'Have a good one today, Mattie son.' It was all somehow touching. The other England player who interacted most with the Army was the usually haughty and aloof Kevin Pietersen. In this post-imperial 'England' team made up of South Africans, Irishmen, Welshmen, second generation Indians and Pakistanis, and a back-up wicket-keeper born in Papua New Guinea and raised in (of all places!) Australia, it was the seemingly-only-in-it-for-the-money-and-glory KP who connected with them the most. This was partly because Alastair Cook always made him field in the most boring places of the outfield, far away from the action in the middle; placed at long leg or third man, KP would come over and chat. My companions Zoe and Daphne (who had something of Miss Quested and Mrs Moore from *A Passage to India* about them) liked this as apparently he is quite a stud; when he turned back round to face the play they both noticeably quivered as his perfectly shaped bum swivelled into their view.

Ironically it was the Australians who coined the name 'Barmy Army'. The 1994–5 Ashes tour of Australia was so disastrous for the England team that the local press concluded that England's fans must be insane to keep following a team so unable to win; so they dubbed them 'barmy', and I guess that rhymes with 'army'.

Most of the Army are big boys. Those that aren't are lean, muscly men from the north who would sit on their own in the stands, topless and in skimpy shorts with a massive flag of St George draped in front of them and their lower league football team (the likes of Grimsby Town, Scunthorpe United or Port Vale) black-painted around the cross. There are a few girls, but not many; those that are there tend to be big, too. Everybody has a nickname. I made friends with 'Edgy Eddie', a man of considerable charm, but debilitated by a terrible stutter, and 'Serious' Steve, who again seemed very calm and pleasant on the surface, but had apparently been part of Millwall FC's notorious 'Bushwacker' hooligan squad, and served several sentences in the 1980s and 1990s for grievous bodily harm and affray.

Griggsy was in charge of the songbook. His pre-tour task was to collect and create the Army's favourite chants. When one of the Army fancies a sing-song during the match, he can sing out, 'Heeeeeey Griggsy, Griggsy, Griggsy . . . sing us a song, Griggsy.' At which point Griggsy would select from his files something appropriate to the situation. Each player has their own song. My favourite was about England's young, very tall fast bowler Stuart Broad, whose father also played for England. It went: 'He's big, he's bad, he's better than his dad, Stuuuuart Broad, Stuuuuart Broad.' The other one that made me laugh was (to the tune of 'The Lion Sleeps Tonight' and in reference to the lack of booze in the country): 'In the jungle, the Bengal jungle, it's orange juice tonight.' Maybe you had to be there, but the more I sat with them, the more I liked them and the more I realized how much they loved the cricket. I mean really loved it, and were as knowledgeable about form, averages and selection policies as any wised-up cricket-crazy teenager in a Mumbai backstreet.

So play would commence at 9.30 a.m. Between then and 11 dribs and drabs of just-got-up, ill-looking Barmies would dribble into the ground and join in the fun. Lunch was at 11.30. At 11.15, all the Army in the ground (about seventy) would exodus en masse. We had christened one of the main entries into this ground the 'Goat Gate' in that to get into this large international stadium, you had to jump across an open sewer and scrabble across a parched dry piece of red land where some goats were tethered. Outside the gate at 11.15 would be waiting an armada of cycle rickshaws who had soon cottoned on to the Army's routine. Bengalis are not big men, and you could see them hoping they wouldn't get the seriously fat Barmies, or worse still get one of their seriously fat wives, too. The flotilla would then set off, groaning and clanking its way the half mile to the Hotel Delana. The Army would head to their bar and get the beers going, then spend most of the rest of the afternoon in the room getting very drunk and watching the match on their widescreens – a match which was happening *for real* half-a-mile away and which they had paid to go and see. Zoe and I spent one lunchtime there and had fun, though these boys drink so quickly I found I had sunk four cans without even thinking, and it was barely noon.

It was all a giggle, but Gary's burqa pushed it too far for me. The waiters and the hotel staff looked deeply shocked but powerless to object. Harmless Brits-abroad fun had crossed an old imperial line and I headed out, feeling a little self-righteously like Mr Fielding in *A Passage to India* who always escaped British cantonment parties when the racism got too much.

***

Whilst Tom trekked in the hills, I watched all five days of the cricket with friends from a Surrey cricket club, out on holiday. The evenings were spent in the company of our hosts – friends from the British High Commission in Dhaka.

David, a High Commission big cheese, fixed everything for us and couldn't have been a more welcoming host. Within an hour of getting off the plane I was in a minibus of similarly jet-lagged chums on a sightseeing tour of Dhaka. The truth is Dhaka hasn't got many sights and is not a looker, but I was so trippily jet-lagged that you could have shown me the Milton Keynes one-way system and I would have been impressed.

David knew about my golf obsession and had fixed me up to play a round the following day with Sakhawat Hossain Sohel, one of Bangladesh's top golfers. I was thrilled and nervous in equal measure. This felt like playing with Ian Poulter or Lee Westwood. What would I find to say to him as yet another ball disappeared into the trees/deep rough/water/neighbouring field? I always tell people I'm not that good, it's just no one seems to believe me; they think it's modesty or something.

I had to pick up David's clubs. I was quite excited by these golf sticks, partly because I was fully expecting them to be several thousand pounds worth of quality metalwork, which would be nice to play on for once rather than my thirty-year-old ultra-light graphite shafts that were outmoded long before Culture Club split up. I always feel my golf game is the equivalent of playing tennis with a wooden racket and somehow just managing to compete. But I was also excited because of who had used these clubs before me. The previous week David, an expert string-puller and networker, had himself played a round of golf with former England cricket captains Mark Butcher and Paul Collingwood, and Ashes-winning spinner Ashley Giles. Apparently Colly was fantastic and nearly hit a hole in one. Butch had used David's spare set of clubs and had left them for me at the reception of the second most deluxe hotel in Dhaka. I was delighted that the last set of hands that had touched these shafts were those of Butch. I was a Junior Member of Surrey County Cricket Club (his team) as a kid, and made weekly pilgrimages to the Oval to watch them play. I thought his ingrained palm sweat on the rubber would connect me to this on some molecular level.

David's wife Sheila is also a golfer and had a weekly lesson, so I hitched a ride in her enormous 4 x 4 to the Kurmitola Golf Club, which was built on its current site in the mid-1960s after being forced to move when the government claimed its original land to build the new international airport. Sheila described Kurmitola to me as 'the best place in Dhaka'. Wow. I was expecting Augusta.

We pulled into the car park and were predictably circled by caddies. We picked two at random who helped us out with our gear, set up our trolleys and busied themselves with becoming familiar with the ins and outs of our bags. I received a quizzical glance when they discovered the emergency toilet roll I had tucked into a pouch. Next to us another big diplomatic car drew up. A harassed-looking middle-aged Englishwoman emerged from the car and was approached by some other caddies. I thought nothing of it until I heard her shriek petulantly, 'I told you to not touch my clubs; did you not hear me? My driver will take my clubs from the car.' I looked round to see a chastised over-eager caddy apologize to the woman as the smartly suited chauffeur brushed him aside and took his mistress's pink lady-bag out. Her tone was sharp, imperial. And somewhere in it was the weary racism of someone who needs to go home, but is stuck here.

It was 9 a.m. but it was mighty hot. I was meeting Sohel at 10. I had a brand new bag of clubs to get used to so I went to the range. By 9.15 I was soaked. The clubs were good, but I was now drained of all energy and I had to play a round with the country's number one golfer. Oh God, I wish I'd had breakfast. Sheila smiled at me from a nearby bay. At least I'd shown her that I could hit a golf ball and wasn't a complete dilettante idiot. And she could tell David I wasn't going to break his clubs.

The club is owned by Koreans, and most of the players there that morning were Korean women, and a few mostly older men; the managers in the club seemed to be Korean, the menial workers were Bangladeshi. It's odd. Even Sohel – the Lee Westwood of Bangladesh – was deferential to the Korean man who ran the pro shop, which we had entered to buy me a shirt as by the end of our round mine was a sodden, smelly mess.

I liked Sohel – twenty-four, bright, energetic. And bloody marvellous at golf. I didn't disgrace myself, but it's hard to play good golf with a top player whilst still trying to think like a journalist and grill him for information and juicy ephemera as you walk between shots. I hit a decent enough straight, if not very exciting, 220-yard driver on the first that cleared the water. 'Good shot,' he said, while his caddy grinned. Sohel took his driver and blasted it 300 or so yards into the middle of the fairway, with a perfect line in to pitch at the pin. 'Good shot, Sohel!' I said. I kept saying this after every single shot he did, as they were all of a standard I have rarely seen. By the fourth I was bored of telling him how good his golf was. He knew anyway. I stopped being a gentleman and saved my breath. Every hole I hacked away for one, two or more over, while he parred and birdied as though it was the easiest thing in the world. Often I felt he was barely concentrating on the game and was on pure autopilot. On the green fringes when I was chipping or pitching he would point to the exact blade of grass where he thought I should aim to land the ball. I believed him and he was always spot on.

On the par-four fifth I holed a long put to claim five. Sohel missed a four-footer and similarly bogeyed. 'Hey – you got a five Sohel, yes?' He looked at me, gave me a curt nod and an attempted smile, and looked faintly irritated for the first time that morning. 'I did too . . . so that means . . . we halved the hole!' I was thrilled, and probably said all this with too much elation in my voice. 'Well played,' he mumbled and headed off to the next tee.

Sohel told me that he had recently played as part of the Bangladeshi team in the 2010 South Asian Games, where they had won a team gold. I was impressed, and even more so when I discovered afterwards on the internet that he had played, and triumphed, despite having heard that his father had passed away the very morning of the tournament. Sohel is quoted as saying: 'It was tough for me to give full concentration. But I knew it well that if I played badly we would lose the gold. I just tried to forget everything and focus on my own game and help the team win the gold.'

It made me remember how, in the immediate impact of grief, you do keep going and how it is essential to work. If you stop, you disintegrate. It also made me think what a remarkable young man is Sohel. He is vying to enter the Asian Tour pro circuit and I hope he does, then he won't have to waste his time with hackers like me.

He texted as we played and as the round wore on started to take incoming calls, which I didn't mind. I know he was doing this as a favour to David – whom he coaches – and for the (very small) sum of cash David had told me to give him at the end of the round.

After the round, Sohel got me a Coke and sat down with me. He waited for me to sit first before he did. His caddy hovered five yards away on the other side of the drinks veranda's low wall. I could tell Sohel wanted to go, but felt, I think, that I had to dismiss him. He couldn't just *go.* I was starting to feel embarrassed that I was keeping him, so I drew our meeting to a close, and as I shook his hand slipped into it the 1,000 taka note that David had told me to give him for his time. That's £10. For three hours of one of the best golfer in the country's time. Imagine doing that to Lee Westwood.

The course itself I found slightly dull. It's modern, expensive-looking, well designed and irrigated, and there are obstacles and challenges wherever a very high handicapper like me wants to put the ball; there are holes surrounded by water and bunkers, which I inevitably found, and there is a solitary tree placed in exactly the spot that blocks your view of the green if you slice your tee shot. If I lived in Dhaka, I know I would get to love it, and maybe I would think it was the best place in town. There weren't too many alternatives.

***

Each night we ended up in the Bagha Club. This was set up by British High Commission and Development people in 1979 to provide a few home comforts from the challenges of Dhaka life. Often in the day we would lie in our trunks around the small pool and have Heineken served to us; diplomats' children would splash about while we read, sunbathed and savoured this semi-tranquillity – even though Gulshan Avenue, one of Dhaka's crazy main thoroughfares, was just a hundred yards away. For lunch we would sit in the café, read a three-day-old copy of the *Telegraph* or *Times*, and eat beans on toast, fish fingers and chips or a Caesar salad. The beans almost tasted like Heinz. At night we would go to the upstairs bar and drink lager after lager with the other expats. After too many we would end up in the TV room and watch live football from England, whilst playing drunken darts.

The club grandees – smelling a profit – even opened the Bagha's doors to the Barmy Army, who for a £5 admission charge (a huge sum in Dhaka) could drink their (sizeable) guts full at the bar. The Army were quaintly deferential in this environment. Men amongst officers, it felt. I had been forbidden to go to an old British hill station area near the Burmese border by my High Commission friends – too dangerous, they said, high risk of kidnapping. It turned out most of the Barmy Army had been up to these hills the previous week, happily drinking, smoking and singing their way across the jungle.

The bar area was mostly for men whilst the downstairs was dominated by women and children. The whole building was the size of a large five-bedroom detached house in Barnet, and it felt like a piece of home – like a British social or gymkhana club from a hundred years ago, in fact.

One afternoon we went to the British High Commission shop. Inside, the homesick Brit can purchase every familiar British brand name – Heinz, Kellogg's, Branston, Kit Kat, Ready Brek, Marmite, Tetley's tea – at above UK prices. I worked out that I had paid Sohel ten cans of Heinz beans at this rate for his time. It's a consumer hymn to British tastebuds and, I'm sure, most welcome.

I stayed in a palatial High Commission flat that resembled a swanky apartment on New York's Upper West Side. Carrie Bradshaw's Mr Big would be happy with this place. It had three-and-a-half inhabitants. Myself in the comfortable guest room with en suite by the front door; Malcolm, the official resident, a kind but tough Glaswegian who had been a development officer for thirty years, in the enormous master bedroom; and Jim, his mate, a retired and rather portly old Dhaka hand, in the other gargantuan bedroom. There was a pleasant open living-room area in front of windows and a balcony which we never used. Similarly there was effectively another wing of the place consisting of a huge smart lounge for entertaining; cosy it wasn't, impressive, certainly; we never went in there. Nor did I ever sit at the table in the enormous dining room. No, the three of us would squeeze every night into Malcolm's tiny 'snug' room and watch English or Scottish football, or the Indian Premier League cricket beamed into Dhaka live from across the border. We listened to 1970s rock like Rod Stewart, Deep Purple and Free, surfed the net and talked about Bangladesh – which both of them were passionate about. Unlike some of the expats I met in Dhaka these two had really gone native, and were good men genuinely striving to improve the country's lot. Only after a few too many whiskies did their humour become slightly sharp. I saw them as benevolent Graham Greene characters – men with pasts, rather more comfortable in the tropics than at home, and true old-fashioned humanitarian liberals devoted to aid work. I admired them both, and when I rather apologetically thanked Malcolm for the room, and offered to find a hotel in the morning if I was outstaying my welcome, he looked hurt and horrified. 'Mate', he said, 'you are so welcome here – this is the Queen's apartment – we all own it – it's your apartment – it's your taxes that have paid for it, stay as long as you like.'

Malc took me to a restaurant called Spaghetti Jazz one night. The humidity had been building up all day and a thunderstorm was clearly about to explode. It was hard to walk even a hundred yards; it felt like you had to carve your way through the thick, treacly air. Your clothes would be drenched with sweat after a short walk.

When the burst of late monsoon came, the rain was sudden and immense, and broke the horrible moods that we all seemed to be in. The restaurant itself is a wonderfully messed-up example of the confused cross-cultural influences that congeal on the subcontinent: a restaurant in Bangladesh with Bangladeshi waitresses serving Italian food to a group of Brits whilst black American jazz plays, and within walls covered with pictures of John Coltrane, Miles Davis and, rather incongruously, Wham.

The next morning, constipated with pasta (and with Tom still away trekking up mountains), I took the train to Chittagong.

***

Bengalis are not the tallest people, and the further south you head towards Burma, the smaller they get. Chittagong made me feel clumsy, too large and awkward. I became a Peter Crouch, I felt like a freak, a gangly giraffe of a man amongst sturdy Lilliputians. I also had one hell of a migraine. Chittagong was on pre-rains PMT. The whole town was ready to blow. I was on edge all the time. Grumpy, surly, grizzled, uncharitable, tetchy and irritable.

Chittagong is the industrial capital of Bangladesh, and as I wandered the city streets I did get a sense of bustling manufacturing and light industry. When I drove out I was more aware of the shipyards and the associated trades. Chittagong is the tenth most rapidly developing city in the world. That doesn't mean it's very nice to be in – it isn't. But that stat does mean that it must have been really, really bad before.

It wasn't that the hotel staff were unfriendly, more that I just baffled them. There are only three reasons why

Westerners come to Chittagong – to watch cricket, to head off to trek in the jungle of the Chittagong Hill Tracts or to see the infamous ship-breaking yards, and take photos of once mighty liners and tankers being slowly ripped apart *by hand* in the harbour. These dismantled ghost ships are a striking sight, but the shipyard authorities have become very nervous recently as they have been accused of dodgy environmental practices (for example, some of the ships can release asbestos into the atmosphere when they are dismantled this way) and worker exploitation. Now you can only see the yards by the back door, with a guide, and with a series of bribes being paid.

So when I told the hotel staff I was here to play golf, they weren't sure what to think; when the next day I emerged in top-to-toe golf costume and hailed a rickshaw to take me to the Bhatiary Golf and Country Club, they must have thought I'd really lost it. Perhaps being English gave me a certain leeway for eccentricity, but even so.

After twenty minutes driving west out of town, the rickshaw stopped and my driver announced 'We are here!' I looked round, but we clearly weren't anywhere near the here that I needed to be at. He pointed to the other side of the road at a white, cheap concrete building vaguely in a Bauhaus style with the GlaxoSmithKline logo on it. I realized this is where he thought I wanted to go. GSK HQ. I still don't understand why he thought this. I persuaded him to continue into the hills. We stopped every five minutes to ask directions from passersby to whom I showed a golf ball. Sometimes these directions were good, sometimes hopelessly wrong. Finally, and now well out of the city, rickshawing through green hills, farmland and empty roads like a small chuff-chuffing steam train well out of its depth on modern intercity rails, we arrived at the club and looped down its long drive to the clubhouse.

The journey had put me in a stroppy mood, the heat

and muggy atmosphere was oppressing me, and I wasn't really up for this round. Still, having come this far, I had to proceed, and the course looked pleasant enough without being that interesting. It was 11 a.m. No one else was playing. As the odd spot of rain dappled my brow, I kind of knew why.

The clubhouse was large, modern and spick and span. The club was built in 1984 on Army-owned land, after the Chittagong area had been without a course for nearly twenty years since the British Nutanpara course had shut down. I picked up on 'What on earth is he doing here?' looks everywhere. I kept my head up, my gaze level, back straight, Quentin-Crisp-style, and acted as though my being here was the most normal thing in the world. I asked to borrow some clubs for the round, and was given the most horrible-looking and horrible-feeling set I have ever encountered.

These clubs panicked me and I asked if there was a driving range where I could try them out. 'Of course,' said the bookings guy, 'your caddy will take you there.' The 'driving range' turned out to be the fairway of the seventeenth hole, which clearly no one was expected to be on for the next few days. We were joined by a twelve-year-old boy with a bucket of thirty balls. Out of nowhere a man appeared, claiming to be a golf pro and trying to interest me in taking lessons with him. He didn't look like a golf pro. Then his mate joined us. Silent type. So I started hitting balls watched by four people all standing right next to me. The caddy started to place a new ball down on a tee after I had hit a previous one, as I had observed in Calcutta. The more I told him not to do this, the more he did it. I couldn't win.

As I hacked and hacked with these horrible clubs, all four decided to chip in with bits of advice – head down, sir, topped it, sir, tee too high, sir, etc. Utter humiliation. I was hitting the ball very badly. Every time one of the knacker's yard clubs connected with the ball, a massive 'Clang!' reverberated through the hills. By the time I'd hit sixty balls I was soaking wet, had a temple-bursting throb in my skull and didn't want to be there. Also, all the boys agreed that it was about to rain, Heavily. Like it does every day at this time, idiot.

I kept going. I can't remember much about the round as I was so appalling, and the monsoon came crashing down when I was on the fifth. Within thirty seconds all my clothes were sodden. We ran for a sparse group of trees, but they afforded little protection. My caddy ran off and reappeared with a big banana leaf which he held over my head in a touching but pointless attempt to mimic an umbrella. The rain was just too heavy. Now and then it would stop, we'd play another hole, then it would start again. After I hit one three-iron fairway shot, the club flew out of my hands and landed twenty yards away, such was the slipperiness of things. Somehow we staggered on with me scoring two, three or four over on most holes. I hit one beautiful full nine-iron approach shot from the rough, over a tall tree and on to the ninth green. It was the only strike all round that would indicate to anyone that I knew what I was doing.

After putting in on the ninth, and with the rain cascading down, I decided enough was enough and, declaring the game over, stomped off into the clubhouse. I bought a new shirt and headed to the empty upstairs bar, the size of a modern airport departure lounge. The rain fell and fell. As I sat in my wet pants and trousers, with my shoes and socks off, I felt miserable. I ordered a Coke and a club sandwich, held my head in my hands and felt like crying. What the fuck was I doing here? The desolation and loneliness of the last few months, which normally golf can keep at bay, flooded back into me. I was alone in the hills near Burma, going mad, trapped in a looped British eccentricity, like the

Dombey & Son-reading English madmen in the Amazonian jungle at the end of Waugh's *A Handful of Dust.* I felt so far away from love, from friends, from the life I was meant to have. I felt shattered. The booze and partying in Dhaka had distracted me for a while, and now I was on my own again.

9

Mrs Chitty and Mr Blair in Rangoon

'How was that one?'

Karen dipped her head slightly towards the microphone as she said this. She looked at me with wide, vulnerable, imploring eyes through the thick soundproof glass between us.

I summoned up some professionalism. 'Really good. Best one yet. Really liked that new thing you did with the melody on the chorus – definitely keep that. Do you want to try one more, or do you want me to do a comp of all the takes you've done so far?'

'Can we do one more?'

'Of course, no problem. Let me just set up a new track on the computer . . .'

Bloody hell.

In the live recording room Karen stepped back from the mic and started doing odd hissy exhalation vocal warm-up noises that sounded like the war dance of a Papua New Guinean tribesman. She was short, wide, crew-cutted, Canadian and gay, singing songs of break-up and heartache with a country-rock feel. She wasn't awful, but she wasn't very good. We'd been recording since 9 a.m. It was now 5.55 p.m. and I'd had enough. The meter was still running but I was shot. And her voice and winsome lyrics were getting to me.

She did another vocal take that sounded pretty much like the last one.

I pressed the intercom button on the mixing desk, and said into her headphones: 'Excellent take, well done . . . do you want to keep going or shall we knock it on the head for the night?'

An eternity passed while she considered, then: 'Would you mind if we started fresh tomorrow? I think I'm straining my voice a little now.'

'No problem,' I said, rapier quick. 'You've done really well today – go get some rest and we'll continue the good work tomorrow.' At what point in my life did I learn to talk this bilge?

She smiled edgily, nervously, nodded, took off her headphones and headed for the door.

After she left I sat down, at last alone in my studio, and stared out of the window. The day before I had received a call from my mother who sounded very shaken, very unlike her. I had asked her how my father was, and for the first time she hadn't spun me a positive line like a slick recording engineer to his rich clients, but had simply said in a weak, tired, cracking voice, 'Not good.'

It was the first time I took my father's illness seriously or considered it as something that might not go away like a bad cold. It was the first time that the word 'terminal' came into my mind. I didn't know what to do. You've seen those moments so often in films or in books, but it takes so long to realize that it is real and happening to *you*, and if you don't act then the moment will pass by. It was my mother's birthday. I needed pushing, positioning. I was stuck on a marooned ice-breaker in the North-west Passage with no charts.

I sought the advice of someone very close to me, who just said, 'Go. Go now. It'll cheer your mother up. Forget the session tomorrow. Just get on a train now.' If she hadn't pushed me I would never have seen my father alive again.

I left the Hampstead studio and slowly made my way to the New Forest, half reading Orwell's *Burmese Days* on the train down, and walked the forty-minute journey from the station to my parents' house through pitch-black lanes, freshly ploughed fields and footpath avenues roofed with oak canopies. I love the country round here, and I reached my parents house at 10 p.m. in a good, calm, relaxed mood. I had forgotten my set of keys so I rang the bell and forced my face into a 'Happy Birthday, Mother' look.

I heard their confused voices from within. 'Who's that at the door so late? It must be Grant . . .' Both their voices sounded high-pitched, strained, desperate.

'Happy birthday, Ma! Thought I'd surprise you . . .'

'Thank God you're here,' said my mother opening the door to me, looking ashen. 'It's your father, he's had a fall, I can't get him up; we've already had the ambulance round once tonight.'

As I entered the lounge I saw my father lying face down on the floor in his pyjamas. He looked appalling, so thin and old and sick.

'Hello, mate,' he squeezed out.

His legs had seized up for the second time that night, and when he had tried to get out of the armchair they had given way. I put my arms underneath his armpits and with some strain hauled him on to the sofa. Though shrunken and bony, he was still quite a weight.

We all paused a moment. My mother put the kettle on. My father's speech was very slurred, his lips were dry and cracked, and there were blotches all over his face. I had never seen him so thin.

We decided the best thing would be to put him to bed. Good idea, except that meant getting him upstairs. It took me twenty minutes to drag, pull, push and manoeuvre my father up the stairs. At one point his pyjama trousers slipped down, revealing his bony arse. It was the first time I had ever seen it. I was shocked. I felt his humiliation. There was no meat left anymore, just weak old bone ready to snap.

Both lying on the landing at the top of the stairs, we paused for a bit, panting, sweating; I could feel the pull on my arms, legs and shoulder muscles. With one final effort I dragged him on to the bed, and slowly swivelled him round ninety degrees so that his head would be on the pillow.

I lay down next to him as he groaned intermittently. I never imagined I would have to do that. He had helped me up so many times in my life, and suddenly the roles were reversed.

I knew now this was serious. Really serious. I cancelled Karen's recording session. She seemed even more relieved than I was.

The next day he had made no improvement. The doctor came round and we almost forced him to find my father a hospital bed. While we waited for an ambulance to take him to hospital I once again lay next to him on his bed; he would doze in and out, mutter something, or wake up in a panic and grip my arm tightly. I tried to chat to him, but it was a struggle for him to articulate anything by now, so in the end we just lay there in silence.

I now knew he was going to die. I still could not believe

it. Sometimes I wanted to laugh. My mind couldn't quite catch up with the reality of the situation.

The ambulance came, and he lay down inside it. Just as the paramedics were going to shut the doors he looked up and said, 'Where's my cane?' I handed it to him, but his confused eyes barely registered either it or me. I waved at him, the doors were shut and the ambulance drove off.

And that was that.

***

> *In Burma many human rights abuses are directly connected to the regime's drive to develop the country for tourists. More than one million people have been forced out of their homes in order to 'beautify' cities, suppress dissent, and to make way for tourism developments, such as hotels, airports and golf courses.*
>
> Press release from Burma Campaign UK, endorsed by Aung San Suu Kyi (2004)

The Burmese pro-democracy leader, and legitimate ruler of the country, Aung San Suu Kyi, was released from twenty-one years of house arrest on 13 November 2010. She has been a heroine of mine for many years, after I saw an incredible interview with her in the 1990s, when she was still permitted the sort of guests to her residence/prison at 545 University Avenue, Rangoon, that could enter with cameras, tape recorders and notepads, ready to broadcast her brave words to the world. And it was because of her that I decided not to go to Rangoon after Chittagong and search for the course of the old Rangoon Golf Club, next to the architectural marvel that is the Golden Pagoda.

I was close to Burma in Chittagong. At the Bhatiary Golf and Country Club I knew that Myanmar, as Burma's military dictatorship rechristened the place, was barely fifty miles away. However, even though what we now think of as Burma was part of British India until 1947, I had already decided not to go.

One day, sitting in the Asian and African Studies eyrie of the British Library, flicking through its online archive catalogue, I found an entry that caught my interest. It referred to a file of one Helen Mary Chitty, and included a golf reference. Intrigued, I called up the file, and a few hours later was presented with a blue A4 folder in which were two notebooks.

In the front of both was inscribed:

> Helen Mary Chitty
> 1900
> notebook
> 'Malabar Hill, Bombay'
> 'Western Lodge, Romford, Essex'

I loved the juxtaposition of Malabar Hill – now the Beverly Hills part of Mumbai and the most expensive real estate area in the world (more expensive than the smartest bit of Manhattan) – with dear old Romford, grazing ground to the Essex Man, the White Van Man, M25 Man, Thatcher's aspirational lower middle classes, snooker player Steve Davis and home of the legendary Hollywoods night club. I discovered that Mrs Chitty (1859–1932) was the wife of Sir Charles William Chitty, who after a stint as a magistrate in Bombay, became a High Court Judge in Calcutta between 1907 and 1919.

Both notebooks were six inches by three inches and contained about a hundred pages. The one with a magenta cover consisted of the author's short stories. I read these with considerable pleasure, especially as I assumed I was probably the first person to look at these notebooks since they were bequeathed after the author's death.

There were ten stories in all, five of which – 'An Indian Elopement' 'A Holy Fakir', 'The Delinquencies of a Daughter', 'The Bite of a Cobra' and 'A P and O episode' – were published in *Pioneer* magazine, according to notes made presumably by the author on the contents page. The stories were written in black ink in a flowing, easy to read hand, and feel like B-list Kipling tales; a softened-up, unsatirical, more titillating version of *Plain Tales from the Hills*. They all have gentle plot twists and generally happy endings (unlike Kipling).

In 'The Bite of a Cobra' a young girl in the hills is desolate when her beau Harry runs off with her cousin Violet. However, she saves Violet from a rampant cobra's bite by pouncing on it and cutting off its head. In this glorious Freudian story, though, the cobra has already sunk its fangs into Violet; all fear she will die, but it turns out the snake's fangs were not venomous as it was a snake charmer's beast and had been drained of poison. It ends, 'If I recollect rightly we paid four rupees to the disconsolate owner to make up for the loss of his toothless favourite'.

But it was 'An Indian Elopement' which I found most interesting:

> then so often with the advent of the cherub comes, I must admit it, the slight neglect of their papa; he is rather encouraged to amuse himself, and then when the day comes that the poor mother lands again in India without the children, and finds the long hours too lonely for words, she is no longer essential to her husband who had thoroughly learnt how to fill his leisure time without her.

This husband has an affair, as does his wife on board a P&O boat back to London. Both affairs continue in the open, and all four end up sharing a bungalow together in the hills in a bohemian *ménage à quatre* to enjoy the snipe and duck shooting.

These people couldn't behave like this at home. The stiffest imperial footsoldiers and pen-pushers became proto-sexual bohemians in the vanguard of a new modernist morality – these arrangements having more in common with the Bloomsbury Group than the stern moralizing late Victorian world back home.

The other notebook looked identical, except it had a royal blue cover. Inside was a similar set of handwritten stories, though with more non-fiction pieces included this time. The author had noted on the contents page that many of them were 'not published'. One, however, was published in *The Times of India* and another one in *Pioneer*, and, most intriguingly, there was a chapter called 'Golf in Rangoon', listed as being published in *Golf Illustrated.*

My heart started to race. I felt like I'd discovered something here. Not only was this woman an interesting chronicler of mid-Raj era life, but she was into golf. My head was buzzing and my heart thumping, and I had to look up and around the extraordinarily sedate Asian and African Studies Room to see if my inner excitement was bothering the whole room. As no one seemed to mind, I turned to the first page of 'Golf in Rangoon'. Inserted into this page was a small mauve piece of thick tissue paper, and on it there was a small pencil sketch of a pretty young woman with short-cropped hair, viewed from the side and wearing a smart dress while playing a violin. Quite why it was placed here at the start of a chapter about golf I could not imagine; still more, I wondered who this beguiling woman was. Mrs Chitty's daughter? Mrs Chitty herself?

I started to read the chapter and my golf nodes bulged. Mrs Chitty was clearly a keen golfer and immensely knowledgeable about the game. She describes, hole by hole, a round of golf at a Rangoon club. It is fascinating reading.

She says that the club has 250 members and that lady players are 'almost unknown, and the three or four wives who wish to play, are admitted as belonging to their husbands on an unwritten condition of not obstructing the links'. Remarkable then that she was such a keen golfer, though as she says in another piece ('An Interior'): 'I am an Anglo–Indian, and, as such (I gather from Rudyard Kipling and others), not so straight laced as my British sisters.'

Feeling like a Treadstone operative in *The Bourne Supremacy*, I tried to work out where the golf course that she was describing actually was, and better still – to see if it is still there. The best clue Mrs Chitty gave me was that she says, 'from the club house you look due east, straight across the maidan . . . and at a distance of about half a mile rises a slight hill . . . crowned by one of the wonders of the world, the Golden Pagoda'. The pagoda 'blazes away in the setting sun till you shade your eyes and look away if you do not want to be dazzled into missing your first shot'.

This is the astounding fifth-century Shwedagon Pagoda, more commonly known as the Golden Pagoda. It is still the most sacred Buddhist pagoda in Burma and, several years before Mrs Chitty, Kipling had come across it: 'Then, a golden mystery upheaved itself on the horizon, a beautiful winking wonder that blazed in the sun, of a shape that was neither Muslim dome nor Hindu temple-spire. It stood upon a green knoll, and below it were lines of warehouses, sheds, and mills. Under what new god, thought I, are we irrepressible English sitting now?' (*From Sea to Sea and Other Sketches*, 1899.)

Zooming in on Google maps, I searched modern Rangoon for this ancient wonder. Sure enough, to the west of the temple was a large green plot of land, seemingly covered with trees, shrubs, red-brown earth and outbuildings. But Google was telling me this was the 'People's Park', not a golf club. Suspicious of this very totalitarian-sounding moniker, I zoomed in further to the limits of pixilation, and found what I was looking for. Underneath the new pathways, and between the statues and fountains dedicated to heroes of the military junta, there was the clear ghost of a golf course in the layout and structure of the land. Many of the fairways that Mrs Chitty had played on over a hundred years ago were still just visible underneath the grim regimentation of the state-sponsored perambulation facility. I wanted to jump up and down, and only the presence of the silent old sages in the room held me back. I'd found a lost golf course of the Raj! Of course, I wanted to find out more and, obviously, play it.

After a bit of digging I discovered that it was a nine-hole course, connected with the nearby Pegu Club, which had been set up mostly for British officers. The British occupied Burma from 1885 and the men from the flourishing Rangoon business world wanted to play golf. The present Yangon Golf Club at Danyingon was established in 1909 boasting two golf courses, one of which was the nine-hole course on 2nd Mile Pyay (Prome) Road, which is now the People's Park. There is still a red timber, clubhouse-looking building on the western side of the park, which has the appearance of a Raj building. According to documents I discovered, a small, timber clubhouse was built on the course in 1904, and Mrs Chitty wrote that the clubhouse was 'of brown teak, raised for two or three feet on solid wooden legs to avoid being swamped in the rains and roofed with wooden shingles coloured a bright dark red, and trimmed round the edges with carved white boards'. I felt sure this was the building I was looking at a century later.

On her round, Mrs Chitty came across many quirks with which I was to become familiar. For instance, she found the run of an Indian course to be crazily dependent on the extreme weather conditions: 'The balls run amazingly on the hard dry earth, but in the rains half the plain is under water, and the grass grows knee deep, and the score increases proportionately.'

She describes how the greens are maintained against the odds: 'The greens show up like emerald islands on the dusty yellow maidan, and are most beautifully kept by our able Hon. Sec., Colonel Crawley . . . after sunset you see active bare legged figures watering the precious grass from Chinese buckets, dangling from yokes of bamboo, balanced across their shoulders.'

A round was 15 shillings (75p), caddies could be hired for 2p per nine holes. She had mixed feelings about these bag carriers:

> The little brown-legged caddies, with their brilliant coloured plush caps, ragged shirt or little jacket and linen waist cloth are all natives of India, as the Burman is too lazy, even as a small boy to do an unnecessary stroke of work. With a few exceptions, they know little of the game . . . but they trot cheerfully along, carrying a handful of wet sand tied up in a piece of dirty rag to build up the Tee . . . their warning of 'fore', addressed impartially to a regiment on parade or a wandering bullock, is enough to wake the dead.

Other hazards on the course included 'A large bank of earth, some twenty feet high, with a ditch beyond it, relics of the days when earth works were thrown up in attacking the great Pagoda, runs almost due east and west across the maidan, and makes a formidable hazard to drive over towards the second green, 295 yards to the north Bogey 4.'

And like I would later find at Wellington Gymkhana Club, there was the sense that she was playing in the middle of an Army base: 'the only hazards here are close to the tee in the shape of a small garden and well, enclosed in a low fence, and a shed which shelters a little cannon. The garden is out of bounds; if you run into the gun shed there is no penalty.'

She also passed on some good tips: on the sixth, there is a 'most unpleasant military erection of mounds and ditches . . . But it ought to be well left behind by a brassy or cleek, and a cautious approach, bearing in mind a deep drain close behind the green, should enable you to tie with Bogey in five.'

I wanted to play this course and thought it would make an obvious extra excursion once I had reached Chittagong. But the more I researched the more I realized that to go to Burma and play golf would be supporting the generals; that Aung San Suu Kyi explicitly asked tourists not to visit; and that all the Free Burma campaigns in the world endorsed this opinion. As I dug deeper I found more reasons not to go. Golf courses there, it seemed, often designed and built by Western golf companies, were the playgrounds for the top echelons of the military junta.

I also found a 2003 US Congressional Report on Burma, which noted that 'drug dealers are often seen playing golf with high ranking generals and hold high positions in major banks'.

So, for the only time in my life, I resisted a game of golf for political reasons.

A few months later, Aung San Suu Kyi was freed but the political future of the country is as uncertain as ever.

There is another excellent piece in this late Victorian storyteller's collection. 'A Trip to Rangoon' is a fantastic description of a journey through a cyclone from Calcutta to the Burmese capital, and I felt a kindred spirit in someone determined to battle all the natural obstacles the subcontinent can throw at them for the sake of a good game of golf. Mrs Chitty was much better at non-fiction. Her writing really comes alive with a sharp observational eye. She also inadvertently reveals subtle prejudice and racism towards the locals that were very much ingrained in her class at that time.

Elsewhere, in 'Bar Club', she describes a dull evening at the club: 'I seized on an ancient "Quarterly Review", and tried to stimulate a fictitious appetite for our fiscal policy. Interest in the outside world is apt to wane on these hill tops after an afternoon's golf.'

Quite right, madam.

***

George Orwell, that most brilliant of essay writers and keen golfer, wrote some of his best material (including his novel *Burmese Days*) about his time as a rural policeman in Burma in 1923–7. Burma (and Assam) were places to which no soldier or civilian wanted to be assigned. It was hard, lonely, wet frontier country, and often the only other British people around were rough, heavy-drinking, moody tea-planters. Orwell clearly grew to hate both the job and being a cog in the colonial wheel. As revealed in 'Shooting an Elephant', it gave him a very sharp, forceful, self-hating view of the dying empire at its seediest: 'With one part of my mind I thought of the British Raj as an unbreakable tyranny . . . with another part I thought that the greatest joy in the world would be to drive a bayonet into a Buddhist priest's guts. Feelings like these are the normal by-products of imperialism; ask any Anglo–Indian official, if you catch him off duty.'

Eric Blair (as Orwell was christened) was a keen golfer as a young man, and perhaps he saw a lot of the values he came to despise at Henley-on-Thames Golf Club where his father Richard was Honorary Secretary and where he used to play alongside the preposterously named Prosper Buddicom. The official history of the club notes of the Blairs that 'Father and son were keen golfers and frequent users of the course. The father played a lot with an 11 handicap; the son played as a junior.'

Orwell, left-wing creator of *1984* and scourge of the idle bourgeoisie, kept that one quiet, eh?

10

The Tigers of Ooty

Two nations . . . locked in an imperial embrace of such long standing and subtlety it was no longer possible for them to know whether they hated or loved one another, or what it was that held them together and seemed to have confused the image of their separate destinies.

Paul Scott, *The Jewel in the Crown* (1966)

Three months after the funeral, two days before the trip . . .

I am in Walton, my home town, where I am most centred, where I feel closest to what made me 'me'; closest to what I have lost, closest to my father. Here I can bathe in delicious, delicately sad nostalgia. In the last few weeks I have travelled a long way from myself, have stretched and expanded myself, have become the person I always sensed I could be, and then unexpectedly almost collapsed into the man I feared I might become.

I look out on to the street outside my friend's flat where I am staying and I see the road that my mother and I used to walk down thirty-five years ago to visit friends who lived by the allotments that are still there. There is a verdant alleyway that follows a stream opposite that I love. For the two minutes it takes to walk down, I feel like I am deep in the countryside. It still makes me calm, radiant, connected.

I look out on these streets of my childhood and realize that Walton is the only place I've ever felt at home. And this wanderlust, this running that has become the rhythm of my life for ten years, has been a search for a new Walton of the soul – in Brighton, in London, from country to country, person to person . . . I run and I run but I always come back to Walton, to home. Now I run to India, like a love-hurt East Indiaman or a French foreign legionnaire. I run to forget. I run to remember.

It has rained overnight. I open the front door, and the damp green smell is so rich to me; it is the smell of my childhood here. I sit in my friend's garden, in the same street that I lived in as a child, and the sounds are the same as they were all those years ago . . . the birds, the shuffling of the trees, the odd car, the odd distant train, the bees, the rustle of rhododendrons; above all, the suburban peace of the place. Chennai will fry my brain, upheave my emotions and kill my sleep urge. Walton is the anti-Madras.

I walk through the most familiar streets I will ever know; I amble past houses I used to live in and my first school where, every Wednesday lunchtime, my father would be waiting for me in his white Ford Capri. Wednesday was his day off throughout his life – a legacy of when almost the whole of Britain had half-day closing on that day. He'd be leaning on the bonnet of his car, smoking, looking out for me as I emerged excitedly from the school compound. He'd hand me a lunch box with cheese sandwiches from my mother, which I'd eat as we drove to Hankards Toy Shop in New Zealand Avenue, where the owners would be expecting us. I'd select a Matchbox or Dinky model car to add to my collection, peruse the more expensive toys that I knew were out of our league, then head back to school. My father and I had two connections throughout our life: up to the age of eight or so it was cars, and then golf bound us together. He tried hard throughout his life to pass on to me his passion for the internal combustion engine, and for those first few years I went along with it. I was fascinated by James Bond's cars or the minis from *The Italian Job.* I especially liked cars when they did things they weren't meant to do – fly, jump, crash or drive through sewers or down staircases. One of my favourite games with my father was called 'Traffic Jams', which we would often play when he came home from work at six every night. This game involved lining all my model cars up in a long serpent-like coil around the lounge, and then ramming them into each other as though it was the nadir of motorway pile-ups.

I think we discovered golf to fill in the gap left when I abandoned 'Traffic Jams' and any interest in automobiles for the rest of my life.

Mr and Mrs Hankard eventually retired and an Indian couple, Mr and Mrs Patel, took over the toyshop. I think they were probably the first Indian people with whom I ever had a relationship. Twenty years later they sold out to developers rebuilding Walton town centre and, I would guess, made a fortune.

I walk past the local football ground where my father and Uncle Norman took me to see my first matches, the library, the youth club, WHSmith, the war memorial, and feel connection with that child, that teenager that was formed here. I walked then, I walk still. The overriding memory of my early childhood is walking round this town with my mother. She didn't drive, so we trudged. We made a daily pilgrimage to a row of shops called 'The Halfway' to source the food for that night's meal. There were no convenience stores then, no corner shops run by Bengalis or Punjabis, no Tesco Metros, no fast-food outlets. Walton housewives would process from one end of the strip to the other, dropping into the baker's, the butcher's, the greengrocer's, the newsagent's, the chemist's and the needlework shop, as their mothers and their grandmothers had done. We kids had to come, too, as there was no 'childcare' then. If you had an au pair, a nanny or a child minder you were proper posh, and probably lived in Weybridge. Almost all these shops are gone now. But the baker's is still there. In fact, I will go there soon to buy my lunchtime sandwich. The facades are the same, though. The old Barclays Bank is a DVD and games store; Mrs Trimby's wool shop is an Indian takeaway called Guru Express. I will walk down this street in a short while and 50 per cent of me will be in 1976.

When British civil servants returned from India after twenty or thirty years out there, they often retired to the places of their childhood. There is an exhaustion after India, of course. It's just too fast, too busy, too crowded, too hot, too noisy, too depressing, too stimulating; but there's also the sense that you see and feel things in India that no one back home will understand. You don't fit in to the cities or the social to-ing and fro-ing of genteel society; so you retreat to the quiet and familiarity of your childhood; you simplify your life and reconnect with the child you were.

I have come home. But I'm not even meant to be here.

What's more, my stomach has packed up. This is meant to happen in India, not before you leave. The stress of the last few months is expressing itself through my bowels and intestines, because during the immediate aftermath of death, there is not the time to deal with it fully, emotionally.

That comes slowly, again and again, as time moves on. I am shitting out the nostalgia of the forever lost.

Tiger Woods has now lost the world number one status he held for 281 consecutive weeks to our very own Lee Westwood, the chirpy, self-doubting perennial nearly man from Worksop. I am reminded about something the great French footballer Michel Platini said when asked to compare the genius of his compatriot Zinedine Zidane to Diego Maradona. Platini thought for a while then said: 'Zidane is great, don't get me wrong; but you have to remember what Zizou can do with a football, Maradona could do with an orange.' Tiger's fall is a tragedy of sorts and has definitely set the democratization of golf back a few years. If only brand Tiger hadn't been so clean-cut, so perfect, we wouldn't feel the sting of his hubris so keenly.

Just before his almost brilliant comeback at the US Masters in 2011, Nike, one of Tiger's sponsors who stayed loyal to him, transmitted an incredible advert in an attempt to repackage the penitent Woods in almost Hamletian guise: Woods stared directly into the camera – at us – for thirty-three seconds, whilst the voice of his dead father Earl intoned on the soundtrack 'Tiger I want to find out what your thinking was. I want to find out what your feelings are and did you learn anything.' Never has a sporting redemption been so public. Earl Woods thought a lot of his son. Perhaps in a way all fathers would echo this silently to themselves about their boys. In 1996 he told *Sports Illustrated*: 'He is the Chosen One. He'll have the power to impact Nations. Not people. Nations. The world is just getting a taste of his power. He will do more than any other man in history to change the course of humanity.'

It should scare me how much fathers love their sons, but it doesn't.

***

Only those who strongly believe in Rebirth should risk going near.

Warning placard, complete with tiger head and crossbones, outside tiger pen in Ranthambore nature reserve (2010)

Replied the page: 'that little buzzing noise . . .
Comes from a play-thing of the Emperor's choice,
From a Man-Tiger-Organ, prettiest of his toys

John Keats, from *The Cap and Bells; Or, The Jealousies: A Fairy Tale* (1819)

I am in the Nehru Gallery of London's Victoria and Albert Museum looking in horror and amusement at 'Tipu's Tiger' – a near life-size clockwork model of a tiger devouring a soldier in the garb of the East India Company. Until I saw it up close, I did not realize quite how savage an automaton it is. Two massive incisors on each side of the tiger's jaw are buried deep in the soldier's neck, plunging into his jugular. The expression on the man's face is beyond pain; it's almost a blankness, a surrender, a release, an acceptance. The tiger is not the largest, but it is incredibly bulky, impressing us with its power and strength, in comparison to the small, brittle, snappable, *chewable* Englishman. The tiger's paws are holding the man down with some force at the shoulders and knees. This man ain't going anywhere. In a rather bland room of Indian textiles, jewellery, watercolours and porcelain, the clockwork tiger is a notable highlight, and is justifiably one of the museum's most viewed artefacts. A gaggle of ten-year-old British Asian schoolchildren brush past me in matching luminous pink anoraks. They swarm and bustle around the tiger cabinet with glee, shrieking how cool it is, how 'sick', how 'bad', how 'wicked', and how disgusting at the same time. This is the stuff of ancient childhood tribal terror: to be eaten alive by a savage wild animal – one of our earliest fears passed on in our coding, in the muscles of our adrenal glands for 100,000 years. Those children are confronting a primal, ancient human fear. So do I, every day, especially after the fate of the unfortunate soldier nearly befell me. I know what that fear is. I have looked it in the eye.

Tipu himself, seemingly consumed by anti-British hatred (well, we did kill his father) and his own tiger iconography, commissioned this toy himself, and apparently delighted in watching the spectacle. There are organ pipes inside the tiger's body that make it emit a terrible growling noise while the hapless soldier wails in pain. One of his arms also rises and falls in helplessness and distress. It is thought that Tipu was intrigued by a news item widely reported in India and Britain in 1793, only months after he had been compelled to sign the Treaty of Seringapatam (which formalized his surrender). A young Englishman out hunting near Calcutta had been carried off by 'an immense royal tiger . . . four and a half feet high and nine long', sustaining fatal injuries. The poor victim was the son of Tipu's British conqueror, General Sir Hector Munro. After Tipu was finally defeated, and his possessions seized by the East India Company, the tiger ended up in London as a prize exhibit in the Company's Leadenhall Street HQ.

The British took a decent revenge in this tit-for-tat iconoclasm. I walked down the aisle of the British church of St Stephen's, high on a hill overlooking the hill station town of Ootacamund (the Simla of the South, or 'Snooty Ooty' as it was nicknamed). I looked up at the roof and saw the fine wooden beams that form the backbone of the structure. These strong red teak beams were taken from Tipu's palace at Seringapatam, after the Company dismantled it. These beams, which held up the citadel of the last southern outpost of staunch Muslim resistance against the British, had now become the skeleton of this remote outpost of Christian triumph. As the Ooty congregation raised their eyes to their Lord, they would be reminded of their culture's triumph over Tipu and over Islam. The insult could not be plainer.

Tigers are on the up in the state of Tamil Nadu. According to an October 2010 report in the *Times of India*, a hundred tigers have been clocked in the state's three tiger reserves, while in the rest of India, tiger numbers are dwindling. A hundred tigers. Only a hundred in an area the size of Wales. There is a lot of Tamil tiger blood on British hands. The reason for their growing numbers is the healthy prey base – an abundance of bison and deer helping the race for survival. Also the Tamil authorities have a hardline attitude to controlling poaching. However, globally the news is more bleak: the World Wildlife Foundation says there are only 3,200 tigers in the wild now, compared to 100,000 a century ago. Some tiger experts predict that if their habitats are not protected they will be extinct by 2022 – the next Chinese year of the tiger. Their habitat is being destroyed by deforestation and construction and they are still a valuable trophy for poachers.

So it is all the more incredible that I saw one in the wild a few years ago.

***

A long time ago . . .

Ravi, our guide, picked us up at dawn, to catch a public bus a long way out of town, and then start walking into the hills proper. It felt like walking through a warmer version of a Scottish glen. In fact, many of these small valleys are still called 'glens' locally – named by Scottish tea men 150 years ago. The historian Lord Macaulay located the vibe more south of the border. To him Ooty's landscape seemed like 'the vegetation of Windsor Forest or Blenheim spread over the mountains of Cumberland'.

Ravi had a small spliff and handed it round. I didn't want to come across a cobra while stoned, so declined. My friend Sophie and Chris, a young teacher from Milton Keynes who had joined us that morning, lapped it up. This was clearly a sales pitch that Ravi did to all his tour groups to see how they responded to the weed. As my companions responded very favourably indeed he told us we were going to visit a man of the local Toda hill tribe who had some more. A walk across the valley led us to a straw and mud hut, where we had some tea and scored a bit of dope from the farmer. Sophie, Chris and Ravi set to work rolling spliffs and chomping away as we continued our bracing walk through tea fields, across brooks, into light pine woods and across meadows. I wanted to be clean. I was half relaxing into this and half on cobra-alert. Also, my stomach was weeping pus from the boils I had obtained after sunbathing stupidly in Goa for several days without using sunscreen. The thin watery pus was leaking through my T-shirt, whose material was rubbing against the open boils. I was sore, embarrassed and not looking good. Being stoned just wasn't an option.

The scenery of the Nilgiris Hills was gorgeous – it was not the gargantuan landscapes of the Himalayas, but big, quiet, beautiful, very green, and punctuated by the grey and granite of high rocky tops. Ravi declared we should stop for lunch, and we all sat on a large rock overlooking a handsome deep valley. There was no noise except for the rustle of the breeze through the patch of reeds that spread away in front of us and the chirp of birds. We unwrapped our lunches and started to eat in silence, contemplating the view. Sophie and Chris had a spliff on the go, which they toked on in between samosas.

I had sensed it coming for about ten minutes without fully being consciously aware. Some prehistoric part of my

DNA kicked in, an unmodified bit of coding from when we were hunters and hunted; it was the moment in my life when I felt most Darwinian. My forefathers' senses had got them through the evolutionary rough and tumble, had saved them from danger, had lead to the randomness of me being me; these inherited senses from the Stone Age, was triggered when I most needed them and may have saved all our lives.

It was as though there was something flicking in and out of my blind spots – a suggestion of a presence, the brushing of a patch of reeds and then nothing. The sensation was so slight that I would shake myself away from it each time I felt it. But somehow, I had the feeling I was being watched; I had the feeling I was being advanced on whilst I grazed; for the only time in my life I was on edge, because I realized on an atavistic level, that I was *prey*.

We kept eating and contemplating the scene. I kept seeing these ghost images and sounds, like floaters in your eyes that you can't stare at directly. Whenever I looked there was nothing there. The other three had finished their lunch now and were reclining on the slab, passing the spliff around. I couldn't relax. I sat alert, straining my senses, listening to the subliminal, sensory input chitter chatter, like I remember Daredevil (The Man Without Fear) doing in the Marvel comics I loved as a kid. I wasn't scared, as I had barely acknowledged to myself that there was a problem; I just felt *watched*.

I decided to relax. I envied the other three their carefree stoned state, and cursed myself for being so anal, anxious and unchilled. I glanced at my samosa, and moved my head downwards to take a bite.

Then I saw it.

Just a flash of orange in the reeds that my brain mainlined into the extreme front of my consciousness.

That orange shouldn't be there.

I looked at the orange patch in the reeds, then allowed my head to move slightly to the right. My brain couldn't process the data quickly enough. I felt like I was thinking in mud; then I saw a black stripe, the another orange patch, then a white bit.

Oh . . . my . . . God.

I continued to run my eyes slowly across this image, barely twenty yards away; the orange-black-white pattern seemed to repeat over and over again across a vast canvas, and then I saw its enormous grotesque catty head, and its eyes locked on mine, and we stared deep into each other's souls.

I am about to die.

And I realized why man and beast sometimes do not run when they are being hunted; how they can get frozen in the fear of the moment; how the charisma of the hunter renders the prey helpless and all you can do is wait for the kill. Surrender.

A more prosaic bit of me decided to take action.

I suddenly forced myself to stand up and with all the power of my lungs I screamed out over the valley 'THERE'S A FUCKING TIGER! THERE'S A FUCKING TIGER!'

They probably heard this in Mysore. I started jumping up and down on the spot and furiously pointing at the huge beast barely a tennis court's length away from us. If we're going to die, I thought, best to go down shouting. My yells had penetrated the potheads' trippy brains, and Sophie was first to react. Scrambling up and standing behind me she shouted: 'Where? Where's the fucking tiger?'

'Over there, for fuck's sake!' I yelled back.

'Oh my God, you're right. It's a fucking tiger. It's fucking enormous.' She said, and started giggling. Fucking marijuana. We were all about to be eaten, and she found this funny. The other two reacted slower and, still digesting the information, were looking round in the wrong places for what we were freaking out about. They too were shouting now, and we all must have looked and sounded like the platoon from *Dad's Army*.

Then the tiger looked at me again. And I swear, it shrugged contemptuously. As though communicating to me, 'You lot aren't worth the effort.' And it slinked off, beautifully, majestically, with a gorgeous side to side swivel motion, like an A-list catwalk model. It slowly disappeared back into the reeds.

Ravi and Chris hadn't seen it. Indeed Ravi was sceptical that I had until I convinced him that there was no doubt in any way ever that what I saw was anything but a huge, slavering tiger beast. He looked sad. He said he'd been in these hills for twenty-eight years and never seen one properly. I realized that I'd been here three hours, and outdone him.

I was shaking, adrenaline pumping through like I've never known before or since. Sophie was now rolling on the ground, holding her sides, giggling helplessly and muttering, 'A tiger wooohooo!' I felt like I was the sane, Martin Sheen one in an *Apocalypse Now* world of madness.

I wanted to get the hell out of there, as quickly as possible, but Ravi insisted we head to the nearby tribal village to warn the local farmers to bring their cattle in so they wouldn't be attacked. So the four of us walked across an open plain for about half a mile. I was terrified. There was nowhere to hide; we were sitting ducks if the tiger was still around and peckish.

But we made it to the villagers, who seemed surprised and concerned about my news, though in a relaxed, these things often happen round here sort of way. We had tea, then kept trekking, though for the rest of the day I was in a heightened state of alert – over-hearing, over-seeing, over-adrenalized, seeing tigers everywhere, in every bush.

The day continued to be surreal. We ended up lying on the top of sacks of tea on a lorry, looking up at the beautiful, starry night sky; then we all waded through a snake-infested swamp to meet the local drug baron so that my friends could score a tiny bit more weed. I felt, rather bizarrely, that I was there as 'muscle'. I was pissed off with all of them. I'd never felt so many extreme things in one day.

But I felt elated: I looked a tiger in the eye, and it had a backed off. If I'd had a shotgun, it would have made a great rug.

Raj tiger hunter Jim Corbett came to mind. In *The Muktesar Man-Eater*, he wrote:

> For a long minute there was no movement or sound, and then I caught sight of her. With the forlorn hope that my bullet would miss the saplings and find the tigress I threw up my rifle and took a hurried shot. At my shot the tigress whipped round, came down the bank, across the hollow and up the path on my side, as hard as she could go . . . what I took to be a wounded and a very angry tigress was coming straight at me; so, waiting until she was two yards away, I leant forward, and with great good luck managed to put the remaining bullet in the rifle into the hollow where her neck joined her shoulder. The impact of the heavy .500 bullet deflected her just sufficiently for her to miss my left shoulder, and her impetus carried her over the fifty-foot drop into the stream below, where she landed with a great splash . . . I . . . saw the tigress lying submerged in a pool with her feet in the air, while the water in the pool reddened with blood.

***

Eight years later Tom and I were staying in some luxury for a change. After our separate northern adventures we had rendezvoused in the southern hills, where we had been told there was great golf to be found. I remembered from last time how wet and cold at night Ooty can be, and thought we deserved something special. Wherever I could, I found us Raj-era British buildings converted into hotels so I could sniff out the British ghosts. So I booked us a large room in the Maharajah of Mysore's Summer Palace on Fern Hill, overlooking the town and its magnificent British-created lake. This place appealed partly for its opulence, but mostly because I'd read on several websites that it had its own golf course attached. We arrived in the dark early evening after a long, uncomfortable, boring six-hour drive. The higher we climbed in our taxi, the harder it rained and the mistier it got. At some points on the narrow, twisting, vertiginous hill roads, you couldn't see much more than a few feet in front of the car. I started to get those existential terrors that hit me in whiteouts. The fear of blankness, a kind of inverse agoraphobia, the fear of dissolution into nothing. Your mind wanders on a long trip up to the hills; conversation is non-existent; your driver speaks no English; and Tom and I tend to plug ourselves into our iPods. As we headed into the hills, I felt very like my British forefathers who, embittered and slightly unhinged, journeyed to Ooty for some R&R; for some sport; some milder weather; for some golf.

We were put in the former guest house of the summer palace, in quite simply the largest room in which I have ever resided. Apart from the television and electric fan heater, this room, its attached bathroom, and its furniture and trimmings couldn't have altered that much from the 1940s. The main building is an immense maharajah's palace on a hunting-lodge scale; it has a wonderful grand hall where I took tea every morning and read *The Times of India.* That we were pretty much the palace's only residents didn't bother us. We were getting used to feeling like we'd entered the Bollywood version of *The Shining* everywhere we went. That first night we ate alone in the huge dining room, in almost absolute silence, the only sound being the sharp bzzz-zap of the electric neon mosquito killer every time an unfortunate insect wandered into its vicinity. Indian waiters tend to take more time to serve you in inverse proportion to the total amount of customers they have to wait on. The quickest meals – and often the tastiest, and cheapest – are to be found in the 'veg meal' joints that throng each main street in every town. A bamboo leaf is whacked in front of you, several boys appear with a variety of curries and rice which they slop on to your leaf, and you tuck in heartily with your right hand. Left hand (the arse-wiping hand) is never used for food, of course, and is always to be found dangling limply on the lap, under the table.

In the long waits between courses at the palace, I wandered around its corridors – wooden floors and walls all covered with photographs of maharajahs past and present, their families, and parties and hunts going back a hundred or so years. The current maharajah's face appeared over and over again, fetishistically, walls of repeating Warhol-like images, the iconography of the self-obsessed. I sauntered into the beautiful (but closed) bar and saw tiger-hunt photos on its walls, with the huge beasts usually displayed lying dead at the feet of their slayers, a crowd of dignitaries and fellow sportsmen in the background, applauding the deed. We ate roast chicken, vegetables and chips, followed by chocolate sponge, all washed down with several bottles of Kingfisher beer and a couple of (awful) whiskies. Once we'd picked up our takeaway 70 per cent rum, we staggered out of the palace and decided to look for the hotel's golf course.

Even in the dark, and feeling a bit inebriated, it was soon clear that there was no golf course, couldn't be, couldn't have been – the land just wouldn't allow it. I resolved to have a good look in daylight, but I knew that we would not be getting out our three woods on this patch of ground. Once again online misinformation had triumphed over hope.

Ooty was being hit by a vicious whip of the monsoon's tail. Normally the rains would have calmed down by early October, but during our visit, there would be a monsoon downpour around lunchtime, and then persistent drizzle and showers the rest of the day, every day. The only time it didn't rain was at dawn so we resolved the next night not to get drunk but to get a good sleep and rise before dawn to catch an early rickshaw to the golf course. Fat chance. We had to get through at least two Indiana Jones movies first.

It's weird watching *Indiana Jones and the Temple of Doom* in India. Statues of Kali, the consort of Lord Shiva the destroyer in Hindu mythology – often therefore stereotyped by the West as being a dark, violent goddess of annihilation, with references to the Thuggee cult (where the English word 'thug' comes from) – are in every museum in India. Spielberg and Lucas's script is pretty anti-Indian, and no wonder Indira Gandhi's government refused the film-makers permission to shoot it in India in 1984, as they felt it would show the country in a negative light. Too right it does: corrupt maharajahs and courtiers, evil cannibalistic black magic death cults, savage diet (sheep's eyes, monkey brains, snakes etc), a supposedly contemptible religion (Hinduism) whose rituals are profane, and whose priests can beguile and hypnotize people into doing whatever they want. The only Indian residents coming out of the film with any credit are the wise old shamanistic village priest, the poor of the village and, rather bizarrely, the British Captain Blumburtt and his troops who save the day. Though what the Pune Rifles (as they are described) are doing in the northern Indian jungle/Himalayan borders is anybody's guess, with Pune being some 1,000 miles away. In the end the film was shot in Sri Lanka, whose government had no qualms about making its neighbours look like mad, superstitious murderers.

Spielberg's Captain Blumburtt of the Pune Rifles, and the regiment saving the day at the end of *Indiana Jones and the Temple of Doom*, made me remember a real-life member of this regiment whose story I had discovered in the vaults of the British Library.

During the summer before the trip I took up residence in Soho, in an apartment on the corner of Frith Street and Old Compton Street, right above Bar Italia and opposite Ronnie Scott's Jazz Club. Mozart had lived in this block (at 21 Frith Street) in 1764–5. It was here that he wrote his first two symphonies . . . before his tenth birthday. Even more relevant to me, John Logie Baird had performed the first public demonstration of television in these rooms in 1926. My father (b.1927) – a man who grew up as excited by television as my generation has adored the internet – was always so proud that Baird had also lived in his hometown, Hastings, from 1923 and had a laboratory on Queen's Arcade, which is still famous locally for the amount of times the crazy technologist blew up the building.

So this Soho building had pedigree. It was also the noisiest place I've ever stayed in. Twenty-two hours a day the roar of Soho revelry swamped the flat. It felt as noisy as central Mumbai, all the time. Yet I found it really relaxing. I would sleep with all the windows open, on a mattress on the floor. If I couldn't sleep I would stick my head out of a window and watch the party from my sniper's nest, enjoying the vicarious night out of the fourth-floor voyeur.

Every day I would cycle ten minutes to the British Library, where I found refuge, peace and inspiration in the magnificent Asian and Oriental Studies Room on the top floor. This space, unvisited by the hordes of young students trying to write essays while listening to their iPods, is a haven of

Asian scholarship. Sometimes I felt like a dilettante even being there. Other times I felt that I had found home.

Surrounded by the East India Company records, myself and an assorted band of mostly Indian and Chinese academics poured over our texts every day. It's the sort of room where if you turn your computer on and it blasts out that trilly 'hello' jingle, fifty old scholars tut, without looking up from twelfth-century versions of the Bhagavad Gita or Confucius.

The dress code was very much like that of an Indian library – polished brogues, smart slacks, collared shirt (neatly tucked in), belted jacket, reading glasses. Most of the room wore this uniform. There weren't many women present. This was a boys' club, and sometimes I enjoyed dressing smart to work there. It felt like an Oriental version of the Garrick's Reading Room, the Marylebone Cricket Club in the old days or the London branch of Calcutta's Asiatic Society.

I had found a bundle of letters and reports between the Rowan family of Poona (the British name for modern 'Pune'), the India Office, and several private individuals, all putting in a good word for the recently deceased Reverend Rowan.

Captain Revd T. Rowan, a volunteer in the 35th Poona Rifles, according to the official Army medical report, suffered an 'ingravescent apoplexy in the left hemiplegia' in 1919 while playing golf in Pune – presumably at the old Poona Golf Club course, the oldest in the city, still open today. This cerebral haemorrhage (as we would call it these days) incapacitated the reverend and he was shipped home, eventually dying on 7 March 1923 in Sevenoaks, Kent, at the age of fifty-one.

The archive charts the attempts by his widow Josephine to obtain a pension from the India Office. They were rather reluctant to offer one as they could not see how his death was related to the injuries he incurred as a volunteer soldier.

They were too polite to upset the widow, but the inference was . . . er, didn't he just drop dead on a golf course?

However, Mrs Rowan launched an impressive letter-writing campaign to gain support for her cause. There is desperation in her correspondence. She gives the impression that if the India Office does not cough up it will be the workhouse and gruel twice a day for her family. Whether this is insurance-claim hyperbole or an accurate representation of the plight of widows of serviceman in India who suddenly expire, I'm not sure.

The letter-writing campaign worked, and she eventually succeeded in procuring £100 a year from the Secretary of State for India (Peel) via the 'Officers' Families Trust'.

Peel was clearly being kind. The Military Department report of 21 August 1923 is sceptical that the reverend's collapse had anything to do with his military service, but it states that Rowan was 'seized with an attack of cerebral haemorrhage while playing a game of golf on 3rd January 1919 . . . eventually it was accepted that there might have been a connection between this service and the paralytic stroke, in so far as the service had weakened him and so made him less able to resist disease'. The report concludes sympathetically: 'it is submitted that the case should be dealt with on compassionate grounds' and the money awarded, especially for the education of his children. The correspondence gives a touching insight into the precarious position of the footsoldiers of the Raj, and how influence and connection meant everything.

***

So, typically, we had crawled into bed drunk at about three, and predictably had not slept much after that. I eventually took a sleeping pill to at least guarantee I got some shut-eye before the round. Obviously we slept through our alarms at six, and finally staggered out of the room at around nine, the drizzle already starting and that weird pre-storm tension in the air. We didn't talk. It was at times like this that I knew Tom resented me for dragging him here and I, too, had a sense of hungover gloom about me, as I tried to remember precisely why I was doing this. Which was the fun bit?

Ootacamund Gymkhana Club is the only golf club in India that hasn't been surprised that we've turned up to play. We had to go through no elaborate back-story, no meeting of senior club members, no questioning (and fibbing) of handicaps; we wanted to play, we could play, we had clubs, there were two caddies, so go play; they couldn't really care if we were there or not. Originally there were two golf courses in Ooty. One was set up by golf fan Colonel Ross Thompson, who arrived in Ooty from Bangalore in 1889. He put a few holes on a piece of land called Hobart Park. Writer Frederick Price was commissioned by the Governor of Madras in 1906 to write a history of the town. In it he rather surprisingly says that 'these pioneer links were used principally by ladies'. For some reason this course did not prove generally popular, and soon Thompson and friends had constructed a new eighteen-hole course next to the municipal rubbish tip. As the new 'Municipal Corner' course thrived, a Colonel Fane Sewell, then Honorary Secretary of the Blue Mountains (Nil-giris) Tennis and Cricket Club, rebuilt the old Hobart Park course. In his planning application to the council he states: 'The Royal and Ancient Game of golf is now become a very popular one in which the greater part of the [British] community is nearly certain to wish to participate.'

Meanwhile, the golfers at the Municipal Corner course were getting fed up with the foul smells from the rubbish dump that they had to deal with when trying to play a relaxing four-ball. They were also frustrated by the rough nature of the course and in 1899 moved it to its current site, the Nilgiri Golf Club. Price recalls the controversy when the new course opened: 'I can call to mind the outcry against the new links when they were started, and the abuse showered on one man – a Scot – who was at the bottom of the move, on the ground that the course layout, mainly at his suggestion, was exceeding difficult, and at a terrible distance from Ootacamund.'

However, Price modified his views after a few years, saying by 1906 that 'All, however is now changed. Golf has become the rage, and during every afternoon in the season the links are crowded with players, who think the distance nothing much, and very generally hold – possibly quite rightly – that Ootacamund possesses the best golf course to be found anywhere in the East, with, in addition, the fairest surroundings.'

I wondered why it was in the period 1870–1900 that India saw its first golf boom. Why not earlier or later? Many of the hill and rural courses were set up during this period, when the hill stations, and the concept of a season in the hills, was becoming exceptionally popular. Some of these golf courses were established by bored military men, but others were set up by tea men, many of whom were Scots. Much of the hill landscape, north and south, resembles the Highlands, and the hill courses there tend to feel like Scottish links, even today. They were exporting tea, but had imported St Andrews.

The first tea was planted in Ooty in 1833 by Colonel Crew, Commandant of Ootacamund, in the grounds of his mansion. Not only did these tea men and women import golf, they also brought to India lots of British plants – gorse, dandelion, pines, horse chestnuts and camellias – that still dominate the Ooty golf course. India could not look more like Scotland.

Our four hours on this McMasala course were a bit

hallucinogenic. I think the combination of the beer, rum, sleeping pill, late night, hangover, lack of sleep and horrible *avant le déluge* atmosphere had made me feel quite odd. The course is also at altitude (7,400 feet above sea level), which can affect your brain, your lungs and your legs. So, very unusually for me, I can remember little about the golf, even with photographic aids – except for the following:

We endured a bone-shaking thirty-minute tuk-tuk ride to the course over a million potholes and several small floods. This was even more fun on the way back as we were getting lashed by the rain and the driver had to put up the tarpaulin 'weather cover' sheets, which were mostly holes.

I hit a great straight drive on the first. Tom sliced his drive terribly and it shot over the road, bounced in the car park and ended up on the roof of the clubhouse.

It is one of the most beautiful, well-maintained courses in India. On its website the club rather immodestly describes itself as 'the finest natural golf course in the world'. Well it's certainly not far off.

I played really quite well. Wide, open, obstacle-free, British-feeling fairways always help.

There were no other players on the course. Not one.

As Tom drove on the seventh, his club head flew off the shaft and ended up a hundred yards away, nearly decapitating his caddy; my caddy couldn't stop laughing at this. Tom had only recently bought this club for £200.

For about thirty minutes, the sun came out, the course glowed and shone, and I remember feeling that golf doesn't get much better than this.

By the fourteenth it was drizzling hard. By the sixteenth it was a monsoon. Our caddies looked wretched, we decided to call it a day and dry off.

We saw no tigers on the golf course, despite the fact that on the course map on the club's website, by the sixth fairway is printed the legend 'Here There Be Tigers'.

Our altitude colds started here: blocked and snotty noses and thick heads. I originally put this down to general illness, but after two weeks of being around 6,500 feet above sea level it seemed conspicuous that our heads cleared and our colds went away every time we spent a night back down in the plains. In Ooty it seemed rather ironic that we were full of mucus but surrounded by the biggest eucalyptus trees in Asia.

11

The Cattle of Coonor

Among the Europeans opinion was divided. The older men said that I was right, the younger men said it was a damn shame to shoot an elephant for killing a coolie [Indian servant], because an elephant was worth more than any damn Coringhee coolie . . . I often wondered whether any of the others grasped that I had done it solely to avoid looking a fool.

George Orwell, 'Shooting an Elephant' (1936)

You feel closest to the British in India in their churches, their railway stations and their golf clubs. The triple needs of spiritual comfort, transportation and exercise exist as they did 150 years ago, long after the counting houses, the factories, the warehouses and the cantonments have been demolished or rebuilt. It's when you look at the British in their time off, when they are praying, travelling or hitting an iron that you can still imagine how they thought and felt.

Moreover, I found my reactions to India, as an Englishman now, felt perhaps similar to theirs; I felt this strong sense of historical continuity, the sense that the Raj didn't quite die, but was passed through our genes.

Ooty has splendid examples of all three parts of the Raj legacy – St Stephen's Church and its bewitching graveyard, the UNESCO World Heritage-listed, narrow gauge Mountain Railway and the Ooty Gymkhana Club.

I went back to St Stephen's Church for a third time, on my own, and, extremely rarely for me, I took my camera. I never take photos. I feel I have a very bad visual eye, but a very good ear. I hate the idea of stopping time to capture a moment on film that has already ceased to be. All photographs are images of the past, like the stars in the sky which are already dead, but we watch their death glow mistaking it for life. I like moving forward not stopping, framing and light-metering the past you have just seen. But I felt a strong urge to go back to the graveyard and photograph the gravestones.

I saw two graveyards in Ooty. The one behind St Stephen's is a magical place, spread over a bank behind the church, about half an acre in size, and it felt at first glance like a part of Highgate Cemetery that has been teleported into the Nilgiris hills. But looking closer I saw that the dense green overgrown foliage was tropical, the drizzle did not feel like at home, and always there was that dense muggy humidity that you never get on Highgate Hill. Amongst the foliage dozens of British gravestones, tombs and memorials rise out. There are few places in India where I have felt more that I belong. Amongst all the chaos, the noise, the pollution, the terrible poverty, there is this hillside where my ancestors lie, marooned in death, far, far from home.

This is a sad place. A preposterous place. A few new graves are scattered among the ancient British ones: Mary

Kuruvula (a doctor's wife, died age ninety-one in 2008); nearby, Rowena and Dennis Dique are buried side by side in an elaborate modern grave; Walter Frederick Daniel (d. 1998) has a handsome black marble slab, next to the very elaborate, garish grave of Victor 'Sunbeam' David (1942–2007). There are a few freshly cut and weeded patches with wooden 'reserved' signs stuck into them, like at a restaurant waiting for the night's customers.

But almost all the graveyard's residents are very British and very old. On the other side of town, as we rickshawed out to the golf course the next day, I noticed a much larger graveyard, spread out over a hillside; here there were no expensive tombs, no lush bush to soothe the souls of the dead and grieving, just row upon row of small blue wooden crosses. I realized this must be where Ooty's modern Christians are buried. A bleak, anonymous out-of-town field, the graveyard had the feel of a meadow in Flanders given over to the crosses of unknown soldiers. I couldn't help but think of my father's very modest grave with a wooden cross and a brass nameplate that we had stood around a few weeks previously. It was the first time I'd thought about this all trip.

As I walked among the Victorian ghosts of St Stephen's, I wondered who this cemetery was *for* anymore. And the longer I stayed, and the more I didn't want to leave despite the rain, I realized that this graveyard was here for me.

***

I wrote this letter to my father in 2004 when I stayed a few days in his home town Hastings. I meant it well, though I remember him being rather embarrassed at its content and not really knowing what to say about it. I was trying to connect with him, and my grandmother, but I think he rather didn't want to talk about it. I read it now and it feels like a young boy trying to impress his father, which I suppose in a way it was. But visiting my grandmother's grave was a very powerful experience. I also tracked down his boyhood house and rang him from outside it. As I gazed at the place from across the road, he poured seventy-year-old, pre-war memories into my ear. He loved to recall and reminisce about his youth and early manhood. It was perhaps, as it is for most of us, when he felt ultra alive.

Dear Dad,

Today I went to Hastings Cemetery and found your mother's grave. From the directions you gave me last Saturday I worked out that it was near Ore so I took the train there then walked uphill to The Ridge and then along to the cemetery. Only had to ask directions twice. Ore these days is quite a bleak area – grim-looking housing estates, unused caravans, non-tarmacked roads and dodgy looking youths hanging out on the streets. Once you get to The Ridge the neighbourhood becomes a bit more upmarket. The walk from the station I guess took about 30 minutes. By the time I got to the cemetery I was pretty tired and sweating considerably. I tried not to seem too intimidating to the rather gentle lady who helped me at the office. She found your mother's entry in the book of plots very easily – entered on the 9th August 1969.

Five minutes later I was in the area where she is buried. And I'm almost certain I've been there before, though you seemed to think not. The lady in the office had told me it was the third grave in from the corner of the section, but I couldn't see a name plaque on it. So I got on my hands and knees and started to weed a bit, and brush away layers of grass and dirt until finally I cleared away the whole plaque and I saw her name.

The grave itself is in pretty good shape. There are still a lot of the marble chippings there, and it's not too overgrown, though the front has slightly sagged into the earth – but all the graves nearby have done this too.

I sat down, and spent about an hour there, thinking. A few rows away was an old boy with a trowel maintaining a headstone. We both acknowledged each other's presence though politely kept our distance. He was nice to have for company.

Indeed the whole place feels very serene and appropriate – the long view of the distant hills adding to the tranquillity.

I wondered why no one has ever referred to Rhoda to me as 'my grandmother'. I would have loved to have known her.

I also realized I know nothing whatsoever about her, what sort of person she was . . .

I also thought for the first time about how difficult it must have been for you and Grandad in the time before she passed away.

I felt that I really connected with something today. Death is part of life and reality and I don't want Rhoda, who was so important to you, to not be a part of my life.

I'm writing this in my friend Pete's flat that's at the top of Warrior Square facing the sea. I think you said one of your great aunts lived in this block, so there's another link for you.

I'm going to walk into town now – it's 8.20 p.m. and find a bite to eat and maybe a drink . . . it's a beautiful evening here . . . one of the reasons I like coming here is that it makes me feel very close to you, to Grandad, and to my history . . . I was delighted when I found 43 Belmont Road, and sat outside it talking to you!

See you soon!

Love

Grant

***

I travell'd among unknown men,
In lands beyond the sea;
Nor, England! did I know till then
What love I bore to thee.

William Wordsworth,
from 'Lucy' (1800)

Three men leaning over the Kodanad View Point. Ranjit pointed to the jagged, gnarly, peaked rock formation ahead of us: 'In the British time, there were two plane crashes here. When the cloud is over, pilots thought that this was all flat plain land – the Rangaswamy Peaks can come out of the blue. For two guys, they saw it too late, and "Boom!"' He clapped his hands then threw them up in a circular gesture that suggested bits of airplane and human beings scattering for miles. 'One of these planes was carrying gold and coins – all the treasure of the Madras Presidency. When it hit the peaks, this booty was flung all across this area. News spread quickly, and hundreds of local villagers rushed to the scene to pick up some riches, before the British could get there and reclaim their money. But at that time this area was leopard territory, and many locals were killed and eaten while they searched for coins. You can sometimes see leopards from this point. The tigers, though, are long gone. The British shot them all.'

The Rangaswamy Peak is a conical structure at 5,500 feet above sea level. The hill on which it is situated is considered extremely sacred. According to Hindu legend, the god Rangaswamy used to live at nearby Karamadai on the plains but quarrelled with his wife and came to live alone here. Footprints on the rock not far from Arakadu village below the peak are said to 'prove' this. The Rangaswamy Pillar is found on the north-west of the peak. It rises in grandeur to a height of about 400 feet as an isolated rock pillar with vertical sides. With Rangaswamy being the holy deity of the Nilgiris, this shrine is visited by thousands of pilgrims every year.

While Tom climbed up a nearby cluster of boulders to try and photo some monkeys, Ranjit, Sanjay and I gazed at these monumental stalactites in silence. There was a gentle, warm breeze. This incredible 180-degree panorama demanded contemplation, respect, quiet. Our companionship seemed to enhance the power of the spectacle, and we knew that all humans would react the same. We all come here for the same reason: to look in awe, to lose ourselves in perspective. We looked down, across and all around the ancient vastness of the Mysore Plateau, punctuated by rocky, craggy mounds here and there, farmland and water. In the middle of the vista, the Moyar river soothingly trundles its course and to the right the new Bhavanisagar dam filters and tames the rains. But most of all the impression is one of immense flatness. I realized this is what the British struggled so hard to conquer. The central and southern Indian Deccan Plateau – of which the Mysore Plateau is the southern end – was the scene of some of the bloodiest conflicts between the native states and the British, as the latter fought to gain control of Hyderabad, Mysore, Bangalore, the Coorg and the fertile Deccan soil. Clive, Cornwallis and the Duke of Wellington slowly ground the local resistance down, culminating in the Mysore wars against Tipu Sultan and Hyder Ali at the end of the eighteenth century. The British had quelled the Deccan rulers. And yet this landscape is so huge, lunar, alien, beautiful, that the British could really never claim to have conquered this ancient land. It would survive long after the British had gone home. Their 300-year stay in India was just a flicker in the ancient history of this peninsula that has seen empires come and go four times a millennia for thousands of years. Limestone lasts. Empires always crumble.

Ranjit was a tall, portly man of thirty-five; he wore a big white-collared shirt and a vivid orange lungi (skirt) wrapped skilfully around his loins. He was a man, like many Indian men, who was comfortable with his belly. The English middle classes suck theirs in as middle age approaches; the new Indian bourgeoisie puff it out. He wore simple but smart chappals (flip-flops) on his feet, and the whole look was set off by some dinky shades and the obligatory thin moustache. Sanjay was more Western-looking – thinner, in blue jeans and black T-shirt, and younger by eight years, I would guess. Ranjit had a calmness; Sanjay had that frenetic edge that a lot of young Indian men have. He was a software programmer, he told me, and had recently moved back to Hyderabad after a year in Solihull. We then had an incongruous chat about nightlife and balti houses in Birmingham.

They asked me why we were here. I explained.

'You come all the way to India to play golf?' Ranjit looked at me incredulously.

I explained some more. The more English I became the more they forgave the eccentricity. In fact, Ranjit, an accountant, had recently taken up the game himself, he said. He had been having lessons and using a range in the nearest city, Coimbatore. This place, like Bangalore, Mysore, Chennai and Hyderabad, is revelling in the Indian economic boom, and I had heard that its golf course – only founded in 1977 – was thriving. When I briefly stopped over in the town on this trip, I was struck by the energy, the optimism, the forward-looking feel of the place. Bangalore and Hyderabad may be the headline cities, but there are dozens of satellite towns that are in the second wave of the economic thrust. Coimbatore, perhaps, is the new Solihull to Bangalore's Birmingham of the Industrial Revolution.

Ranjit, however, had reservations. The game was very expensive to play. This is true: a set of golf clubs in India can cost more than they do in a pro shop in Britain, and whilst green fees are low, membership is very pricey – up to 1,000,000 rupees (£15,000) for life. To obtain club membership, not only do you need a series of recommendations and introductions, but often your bank accounts are checked by the club to see how wealthy you are. He also told me that it was still seen to be an 'upper-class' sport, and suggested that the nouveau riche and the new young aspirant middle class like himself and Sanjay still found it hard to be accepted in these institutions.

Then Ranjit asked me an odd question that I heard a lot on this trip: 'Have you ever played with Tiger Woods?' I looked at him to join in the joke, then I realized that he actually thought I might have done.

We had spent a few days seeing one spectacular viewpoint after another, all of which had entertaining names – Lamb's Rock, Dolphin's Nose and the local suicide point, Catherine Falls. These dense green, steep, foresty valleys can seem very Caledonian – the cloudy, generally overcast skies, the mist and the low temperature amplifying this. And yet you are looking at jungle. It's as jungly as anything in Bengal – jungle with elephants and tigers, leopards and pythons prowling – it just looks like Aviemore.

***

The whole area smells of tea, in the way English brewery towns – my mother is from Burton upon Trent, home of Bass – reek of hops and beer. Tom and I visited a tea plantation, Broadlands, and saw how the crops were processed – often using ancient equipment – into 'British' brews. Without this tea plant, and without our taste for the beverage, there would have been considerably less golf in this part of India.

The origins of Wellington Gymkhana Club, just outside the hill station of Coonor, are slightly different. It was founded in 1873 on the site of the nearby garrison's recreation ground (and sometime racecourse), though it wasn't until 1916 that it adopted its current name. The course land is still owned by the military, and golfers have to walk through the neighbouring Army base to reach the back nine. The tenth tee is right next to the officers' accommodation block. When I teed off there one generalissimo was shaving his beard with thick lather on a balcony, barely ten yards away, minutely inspecting my slapdash swing.

Hacked out of reclaimed jungle, 6,000 feet above sea level, Wellington is quite a secluded and exclusive place. There is a helipad in the middle of the first fairway and it is the only golf club in India where we have been refused admission to the clubhouse to get a refreshing drink after our round. Believe me, we tried everything, and every door, but ended up having a 10 rupees cup of tea from a vending machine in the pro shop. Otherwise the members and caddy staff made us feel very welcome.

The club's setting is outrageously beautiful. The course is spread out over three separate sections of land. The main section in front of the clubhouse is about 900 yards in length, and is framed on one side by a gigantic, steep-raked bank with tea crops piled high into the sky. It is one of the most beautiful settings for golf I have ever encountered. I just wanted to look at the place for hours. The thought that we would be amongst this amazing scene, hitting a ball around, was mouth-watering; as I would discover at Naldhera, the British found the view, then built the course. The difference here was that they'd found some flat land to build half the course on.

We turned up as instructed by the Caddy Master at 9.30 a.m. the next day and once again the view took my breath away. I've rarely played at a course – Kalimpong is perhaps the other – where all I want to do is just stare open-mouthed at the hugeness of the scenery. That morning the sharp bank of tea fields facing the clubhouse was being harvested by dozens of women all in multicoloured saris, covered with thin transparent waterproofs to protect them from the inevitable morning rain.

We were clearly the last pair out for the morning, and had been put behind an old-lady twosome, and a thirty-something woman on her own playing pretty neat golf. It struck me that I had never seen so many ladies on an Indian course. Also, this was by far the busiest course I had seen in India – even though it was one of the most remote. Playing in Ooty, Gulmarg, Shillong or Kodaikanal (which we were just about to visit) feels like playing on empty, beautifully maintained ghost courses. My caddy was about thirteen years old and called Purash. Tom's caddy, Anu, was a little older and with a thin moustache that made him look like a Puerto Rican gangster's apprentice. I wasn't convinced we were going to get the best shot, club, yardage and line advice ever, but they seemed nice boys so we went along with it.

We both played rather well. I am a walking barometer. And I have worked out that I play golf better in absolute proportion to how cool is the climate. In the Himalayas and the hills, I played decent golf; whenever we played early in the morning on the plains or the coast, I played decent golf; in the cities in the noonday sun, my golf is terrible. The Coonor climate is so very English, it feels like playing golf in Kent or Sussex. Your body relaxes into the familiar drizzle, mud, sharp wind, patches of sunshine, wearing three layers and holding an umbrella between shots. It feels like home.

I drove consistently well and bogeyed the first three holes, which pleased me on a brand new course, and this was pretty much the standard for the round. By the fourth there was a queue building up at each tee, so Anu suggested we freestyle the hole order a bit. This was fine but it meant us going back and forth across the main road that divided the course several times, as we drove high over rickshaws, scooters, schoolchildren and the ubiquitous golf-course cows that were tethered and grazing on each fairway, tended by old women in rainbow-covered sari farm gear. In the club's official history minutes I found this amusing reference to the start of this practice, and the wiliness of our Caddy Master's predecessor in the 1920s:

> After a long and heated argument Mr Butler is permitted to graze his three cows on the fairways provided they are tied and do not go onto the Greens. The large fairway in front of the Club House was and still is a multipurpose area, being used when required, as a cricket pitch, a ground for mounted sports, a polo ground and a race course . . . The Caddie Master is brought to book and is ordered to start paying the club 20% of the charges he receives from members for cleaning their golf sets. He is also told to stop forthwith his avaricious practice of taking a fee from each caddie for the sand paper used for cleaning and the club decides to buy the sandpaper and issue it to the Caddie Master.

Sometimes one of these large cows would be grazing right in front of your ball, with no intention of shifting. You had to take a loftier club than you might normally, aim high, and hope you didn't thin it and whack the holy animal in the guts.

This is not a new problem.

In the British Library Archive I chanced upon a collection of Raj writing, collated by one R. V. Vernede, called *British Life in India*. This was published in 1995 by the Oxford University Press, after Vernede died. It has the splendid subtitle: *The Itch to Write – A Disease of the British Empire*. It's a very whimsical nostalgic collection of writings on all aspects of Raj life, and includes two poems about golf in India. Both are written under the pen name 'Momos' (a form of Tibetan dumpling that are eaten in India's Himalayan areas). After some research I found that Vernede was stationed in Garhwal, a princely state in the Himalayas, so perhaps he is the author of these charming, excruciating pieces of doggerel.

Indian Golf

If links were sometimes grassy
and the Indian suns less hot
then golf might be enticing.
If I could leave off slicing
with driver, spoon or brassy,
and play a decent shot,
if links were sometimes grassy
and Indian suns less hot.

If golf were more like hockey,
and I could hit the ball,
if 'browns' were much less bumpy,
and nerves were not so jumpy,
and fairways never rocky,

I'd not complain at all,
if golf were more like hockey
and I could hit the ball.

If cows did not distract us,
and drives required less aim
if golf balls cost but little,
and clubs were not so brittle,
and courses free from cactus,
then golf might be a game;
if cows did not distract us
and drives required less aim.

Golf in India

Little clumps of cactus,
little grains of sand,
make the local golf course
in this arid land.

Little hills and nullahs
little slabs of stone,
give the local golf course
features quite its own.

Where you least expect them
little holes and ruts
thwart your best approaches,
stop your straightest puts.

Cattle on the fairway,
donkeys on the 'brown',
help to send your score up
and your spirits down.

Little caddies standing
just where they should not
make the soundest player
miss a simple shot.

Little palms that blister
little pores that drip,
spoil the golfer's temper
and his Vardon grip.

Little pulls and slices,
little fuzzled drives,
in the tropic sunshine
shorten human lives.

But these little worries
only after all
make you play with caution,
make you watch the ball.

Little drops of whisky,
little lumps of ice,
when the game is over
make it worth the price.

At another point in his book, Vernede makes interesting general comments about the tribulations of hitting golf balls in the subcontinent, most of which rings true to this day:

> The rules, with some variations to meet Indian Conditions, were much the same as in England, but because of the terrain it was a very different game from golf in England. There were 'browns' instead of greens, it was impossible to construct

> proper fairways and even the best players hitting down the middle where the fairway ought to be might see their balls kick off at a tangent on landing. There was no way to keep the course free of unwanted visitors, the odd cow or a small boy driving goats. It is known that a tiger once walked onto one golf course to see for himself what was happening. Of golf courses in the Hills I have very limited knowledge, but by hearsay they were to be compared with golf courses in England rather than with courses in the Plains of India. One grew cunning on a Plains course after a while, and this made it a less frustrating and more enjoyable game.

Wellington's fifth hole took us across the main Coonor-Kotagiri road – which the British built to link two of their most notable hill stations. As we ascended to the sixth green we were aware that a vintage Lockheed Lightning fighter aircraft was staring at us. After we holed out, we then had to walk through the Wellington Regimental Centre Army base to reach the seventh tee, with soldiers drilling and marching all around us.

Then it got really good. You tee off high above the 225-yard par-three eighth, and even though Anu and Purash were begging me to use my five-iron (probably because it was working well), I overruled them and took out my three-iron.

I hit the best iron tee-shot of my life. From the moment I struck it, I knew it was good. I managed to get the swivel of the hips, the flick of the wrist, the push of the follow through and the maintenance of a straight line exactly right. It felt physically beautiful, a perfect orgasm, all the muscles and organs working in beautiful momentary harmony. Purash and Anu, standing a hundred yards away to watch the ball land (as the green is partly obscured from the tee) jumped about excitedly. I walked down, resting the three-iron on my shoulder like a satisfied hunter with his shotgun after a pleasing tiger kill. All around me were spectacular pine trees and I felt the opposite of my Chittagong despair: this is why I play golf, I thought. For a few seconds, I can touch God. When I reached the green I saw why the boys were excited – I had landed five feet from the hole. I was elated.

Of course, I two-putted, and then was so cocky that I didn't focus on my next tee-shot and duffed a five-iron a hundred yards along the floor. Still, I played a great lob wedge up to the high green, and putted in for a four, so no disaster. At the par-four ninth I parred very tidily: great drive, good pitch in, two putts. I was on a mini roll. It got even better on the tenth. Oh boy.

I hate long par threes, and this was about as long as you can get – 234 yards, all downhill from a very high tee position. I can't hit three or five woods off a tee, so in this situation I usually take an iron and aim to play the hole in four shots. Tom and I looked at each other. We were both feeling confident and we decided, what the hell, we'd both take a driver. I struck it beautifully. A great drive is almost as good as scoring a goal or bowling someone out. It will be all you can think about that night in bed as you make love. You will remember it all your life. Time elongates, the moment becomes super intense. I saw the ball bounce just before the green then lost it due to the sightlines. Tom stepped up and hit a similarly fantastic-looking drive. As we walked down to the green, both balls gradually became visible and our smiles widened. We had both landed plum on the green, with mine eight feet from the hole and Tom's twelve feet. We took a photo of both balls. I do not think I will ever play a better shot. My control over the club, my body and the ball was as good as Tiger Woods. Once a year I can be that good.

Halfway down the thirteenth fairway, we stopped for

some refreshment. We sat in a cage taking tea off fine porcelain and tablecloths whilst monkeys hammered and rattled the lattice structure around us. It is an inverse zoo: the monkeys watching the humans eat and drink.

By the fourteenth, I was getting tired, and was starting to lose concentration and hack away at shots without much thought and with frustrating results. The drizzle had been increasing, as well, and halfway down the monster 590-yard par-five seventeenth, the rains came with aggressive venom. We were drenched instantly and decided to call it a day. The four of us, now the only people still out, shook hands in the middle of the vast plain in front of the tea fields and forest backdrop, then bolted for the clubhouse.

We were meant to give our caddies 80 rupees (£1) for the four-hour job – carrying our bags up and down steep hillsides. Tom gave them 300 rupees (£4) each for their labour. As we left in our air-conditioned taxi we noticed there was a squabble going on between Purash, Anu and some of the older caddies as to how to distribute this windfall.

***

My father was delighted when Margaret Thatcher handbagged into power in 1979. He hated the unions and socialism, and was the sort of aspirational, property-owning, lower middle class, suburban middle-management man that the Tories courted throughout the 1970s. I always felt he most hated that which he might have become were it not for a mixture of hard work, luck and charm. Being a boy throughout the 1930s gave my father a horror of unemployment, food shortages, bread queues and social unrest. My grandmother (b. 1905) still feared the workhouse to her dying day at the dawn of the Blair government; a generation down and it was the threat and shame of the dole queue that terrified Dad. He had entered into Harold Macmillan's property, goods and standard of life casino, built around petit-bourgeois debt.

Twenty years later, Mrs Thatcher seemed to represent the apex of this post-war shift of the economic empowerment of the white-collar social climber. What Thatcher brought in, however, was a recession almost as bad as the one he had known as a boy. Rather than soar, his own career plummeted in the initial years of the first Thatcher government and would never recover. He had been let down by the promises made by upper-class Tories, carried through aggressively by people from his own background like Thatcher and Norman Tebbit. He lost one job, walked out of another because he didn't want to be a travelling salesman and resigned from third after realizing that half the company was involved in serious criminal practice. Following this, he collapsed and was bedridden for several weeks. He was diagnosed with pneumonia but refused to take any medicine. Apart from when he was dying it's the only other time that I saw him seriously ill. The doctor told him bluntly that if he did not take his pills, he would die, so he relented and made a rapid recovery. I remember him triumphantly playing football with my friends and me in 1982, just two weeks after he was bedridden. It's only recently I realized that what he'd had was actually a 'breakdown'. In 1997, for the first time in his life, he didn't vote Conservative and opted for Blair.

12

The Roast Chicken of Kodaikanal

During the hottest months of the year, when the air is close and still, the nights are often passed in restless slumber; the system is depressed, and the body bathed in perspiration . . . Restless nights unhinge the nervous system, affect the general health, and render one unfit for the ordinary duties of the day. When night after night is passed in unrefreshing rest, as they often are by those who have lived an unbroken residence in India . . . a change to the hills or some cool station must be taken.

E. C. P. Hull and R. S. Mair,
The European in India (1878)

Even though it is only a hundred miles or so as the crow flies from Coonor to Kodaikanal, the logistics of the journey were deliciously complex. First, we boarded the famous

Ooty toy train (I wondered how many British golf bags have been loaded underneath those seats in the last hundred years) and breezed gently down the Nilgiris hills (maximum speed 30 mph) from cool, damp English weather to the burning plains below. The usual phalanx of monkeys followed us and, in well coordinated squadrons, hassled the train's passengers for food whenever it stopped at a signal or station. In a country where so many people are well below the breadline it seemed odd to be throwing biscuits and bread to these creatures. As I gazed at the scenery I once again thought how Scottish and familiar the landscape looked, and then was shown by the guard a memorial stone by the side of the track dedicated to a railway worker who had been crushed to death recently by an elephant.

By the time we reached Mettupalayam in the plains, the sweat was back. We had moaned about the cold, the rain and the mud in the hills; now we were complaining again about the heat and dust. Perhaps the Raj needed something to grumble about, too. Stropping about the weather is fundamentally British. Well, *English.*

Another (more modern) train took us to Coimbatore, the IT and industry feeder city for the Bangalorean metropolis. Tom called the station 'Clapham Junction' and we stayed overnight in a hotel nearby, lushing out on hot showers, room service, lager, Indian Premier League cricket and deluxe toilet roll. The next morning, we persuaded someone to drive us four hours up through the Palani hills to Kodaikanal, whose name means 'The Gift of the Forest'. The British in the south used to call it 'The Princess of Hill Stations', presumably deferring to the north's Darjeeling, known as 'The Queen of the Hills'.

We drove across the vast, utterly flat Deccan plain, heading southeast. It felt like a tropical Cambridgeshire. This endlessly level yellow valley is punctuated by one small but magnificent hillock, which is visible for miles in any direction. This is the spectacular Hindu temple of Palani Murugan, precariously perched on top of the hill like an austere Franciscan monastery above remote Italian cliffs. On one side of the hill a cable car slowly climbs its way up to the summit, taking pilgrims to worship at the feet of the statue of Murugan, the Tamils' favourite Hindu deity and God of War. We stopped for tea here, feeling the shadeless blaze of the sun lasering our necks.

From there we ascended into the hills up to Kodaikanal. With iPods blaring out prog rock we were surrounded by spectacular views: mutant hills pockmarking the plain, a huge flooded lake, dense green cropland, towns and higher mountains in the distance enshrouded in mist. A bit like a Yes album cover, in fact. The temperature started to drop as we climbed, the rain came in and the landscape became jungle.

It is thanks to Tipu Sultan that these hills became developed. Villagers from the Palani foothills fled into the Kodai hills to escape from his oppressive rule. Kodaikanal as a hill station was actually set up by American missionaries, though the British soon joined them. In the 1860, the first church was built, and soon summering Raj officials from Madurai and Madras were heading up to Kodai for its cool climate, wonderful views and, eventually, its golf.

We thought that Kodaikanal Golf Club was going to be one of the hardest in India at which to get a game. It was founded in 1895 and is situated on 'Golflinks Road', close to the popular tourist attraction 'Suicide Point'. Its website was intimidating and gave out the impression that strangers were not too welcome. We rose at dawn after four hours of horrible sleep and tried to find breakfast. This town bans eggs and booze. Our stomachs were particularly delicate at this point in the trip, and we simply couldn't face anything involving cumin, coriander, turmeric, garam masala, chillies, fenugreek seeds, cardamom pods . . . in fact, anything remotely

Indian. It just wasn't worth the am-I-going-to-make-it sprint to the loo and the sphincter pain a few hours later. So we had 'vegetable sandwiches' – cucumber and tomato on sweet white bread; then we shaved, smartened up and, like good actors, warmed ourselves up in a way that would have made Stanislavski proud. We were out to make an impression.

This was going to need a performance, I thought, a blag. This was going to need accent and class. This was going to need a better jacket than the one I was wearing – a very cheap, light black one nicked from my father's wardrobe on the day of the funeral. I felt a little spivvy, a bit Wizard of Ozzie, as though if anyone looked too closely they would see through me. But damn it, I thought, all I want is a game of golf because I love it. I'm not trying to pull off a bank job. Then I thought of how my father would always put on a 'posh' accent whenever he was on the phone to a stranger in some kind of authority. I used to cringe. 'Received pronunciation' opened up doors for us Brits for decades. Now we sound funny and anachronistic. Only in India, where the local version of English is often positively Edwardian or Wodehousian, do we fit in still, a race of Cholmondley-Warner's and Joyce Grenfells.

I had the nerves of an actor before his first entrance on opening night. I had heard you needed to have a handicap card or they would 'give you a lesson' before you started to play. The logo of the club, resplendent on its daunting gates, is a snarling tiger with the catchphrase 'Play the Game' on it. Am I 'playing the game' by conning these people a bit? I mused on the inadvertent double meaning in the phrase: the British had played the game – that is, shot big game like tigers – so much that the beast was nearly extinct. My stressed, manic brain bubbled away with word games like this. All I was really thinking about were Orwell's words, 'Every white man's life in the East is one long struggle not to be laughed at.'

My negotiations had a bad start. I strode into the clubhouse and was stared at with hostility by an office guy who said that I couldn't possibly play without a handicap card. He looked me up and down, assessing my wardrobe. Probably thinking, 'What a cheap jacket!'. I embarked on my familiar spiel about my mission. At the end of this moving speech he looked me hard in the eye then jerked his arm in the direction of an inner office. I'd got past Cerberus.

Inside this cupboard-like space I found the charming Mr Serendeshekar, the Administration Officer, who, once he discovered we had brought our own clubs, couldn't have been more courteous. He showed me around the impressive modern clubhouse, which was rebuilt in 1995, in Raj-era style. I learned that he plays off a six handicap even though he only has a round twice a week because of the job. Late forties, he had a bad limp and the air of being middle-officer class – a captain, maybe a major.

Describing himself as an 'agriculturalist', he told me that Kodaikanal is 'the only organic golf club in India'. The club was concerned about the pesticides they used to smarten up the course infiltrating the water supply that is used by the surrounding (very poor) villages; so in an impressive (and, for India, very unusual) initiative they changed to organic pesticides a few years ago. Mr Serendeshekar said it's not expensive but people need re-educating. The method they use, he said, is an 'ancient science', and they only spray and cut the crops in relation to strict cycles of the moon. A conference on this subject had just been held at the club. They were expecting sixty delegates from other golf, leisure and farming institutions; 150 came. I pondered that this was all a very Indian mix of ancient astronomy, cutting-edge science, eco-awareness, money and sport.

Then he said the most beautiful thing anybody has ever said to me in India: 'After your round, would you care to join us for lunch? Today is Sunday, so we are having roast chicken, roasted vegetables and garlic bread.' I'd barely eaten in two days. My stomach sung Hosannas at these words. Real hot English food . . . a Sunday roast . . . *garlic bread.*

***

Leaving the clubhouse, in the lobby we passed a magnificent giant wooden statue of a cobra, around which hung pictures of past club captains going back to Independence. The cobra is rearing up, on the offensive, not aggressive as such, but certainly confident and territorial. 'Guardian of the Jungles' was inscribed on a small plinth at the base of the statue. Apparently, it is rare for anyone to see a tiger on the course anymore (though the sixth hole is called 'Tiger Hole'), but there are bison and boar. Around each green (well, 'fast bumpy browns' really) there is a ring of four-foot-high blue plastic mesh fixed to the ground by tough wooden stakes. To play your putt you have to dip under the mesh. If your ball lands around the netting your caddy will hold it up for you whilst you delicately attempt to chip in. In the rules printed on the scorecard, under 'immovable obstructions', 'Fresh Excreta' is listed. One can 'gain relief from interference' here. That is, move the ball out of the shit without a stroke penalty. There is a sense at Kodaikanal that the course was borrowed from nature, and that the club is keen to give back, too. On the ninth fairway my caddy picked some magic mushrooms and handed them to me with a grin. 'You'll play better golf after these, sir,' he said. Then he asked me how much these are to buy in London. I guessed a probable figure. He was very impressed. We chatted about omelettes.

On the long par-three third I was standing by my ball on the green, contemplating my par putt, and was casually gazing over towards Tom and his caddy who were in light rough the other side of the green. Like many holes on this course, it was fun to play – you either go for a long drive and try to get over the stream and grazing cattle in one, or you lay up and chip on to the very uphill putting surface. This course isn't the prettiest one in the hills but it feels very *real.* Like eating rough granary organic bread rather than Kingsmill white-sliced. The golfer can feel that they are part of the gaia principle here. I felt a deeper paradigm of aesthetic beauty at work beyond the superficial thrills of modern course design.

The morning sun was out, there was peace all round. I felt good, in tune with things.

Suddenly there was sharp movement at the corner of my eye. With a loud 'Woah!', Tom and his caddy Regina had leapt away from the spot where Tom was about to chip from. Brandishing his nine-iron like a sabre, Tom was backing away slowly.

'There's a snake on my bloody ball!' he hissed.

A cobra in the rough, perhaps? Perfect. I ran over and joined Tom and Regina a safe-ish three feet away from a large, coiled, yellowy-brown serpent that sure enough was sitting on Tom's Titleist.

'Python,' said Regina and, being the most cool-as-a-cucumber caddy in India, pulled out Tom's pitching wedge and started prodding the snake to move it away from the ball. After all, Tom was two up and in danger of losing this hole. The snake looked up at us unconcerned, as though something was tickling its toes. Its forked tongue flicked in and out slowly and repetitively. Regina shoved harder at the snake's considerable body and slowly, reluctantly, it started to slither off, uncoiling its ten-foot-long body lazily through the grass. It disappeared into the deeper rough, in a huff.

'You can now play your shot, sir,' said Regina brightly.

Tom moved the ball as far away from the snake spot as he could before I would claim he was cheating, then chipped on to the green.

I had a good first eight holes: one or so over on every hole and in a fine mood. Golf seemed easy, the climate was lovely. I hit a splendid drive on the 496-yard ninth, then a fantastic five-iron into the rapidly incoming mist that left me a pitch onto the green. One well-judged shot, I thought, and I could be in for birdie here. The green was ringed at the front by a brook, to the sides by small bunkers and at the back by a fifteen-foot fence that cut it off from the 'Golflinks Road' behind it and the chai, samosa and drinks stalls. Just under a hundred yards to the hole – perfect pitching wedge distance. Better hit it reasonably full to ensure I got over the brook.

I struck it beautifully. Too well. And as the ball was in flight I realized that the mist had made me totally misjudge the distance. It was more like 60 yards. Bugger. Thoughts of a glorious birdie at the turn became panic-filled thoughts about who I was going to injure as the ball carried high over the fence, over the road and down into the groups of people around the snack shacks. Bugger bugger bugger. I lost sight of the ball as it came down and primed my ears to give me a clue.

CLANG. CLANG. Clang. Clang. Clang. Clan . . . cla . . .

'Hey! Hoi!' followed by shouted curses in Tamil.

The ball had hit the roof of a minibus, thankfully causing no casualties. I found the ball, found the owner of the bus, apologized profusely, shook his hand, then slowly walked up the hill to the clubhouse as the mist came down.

I grabbed a bottle of Coke at the bar and sat on the steps of the clubhouse looking out over the course. In the last ten minutes the conditions had gone from England in July to Scotland in November. The skies were grey and drizzly, and thick fog had descended so that I could barely see thirty yards in front of me. I realized gradually that it wasn't actually mist but, in fact, *cloud.* When you are in the jungle it is easy to forget you are as high as the Alps. It felt surreal and slightly frightening. Perhaps I was picking up on an ancient fear in these hills of hidden wild animals ready to pounce from the gloom.

My mind drifted with the clouds, back to the previous year, to what was already seeming a long time ago. I wondered what my friends from Cruse were doing right now.

***

When you are grieving, especially for the bewildering first time, you seek out others who have grieved. You huddle like shifty smokers or recovering alcoholics in corridors, in doorways, at the back of buildings, in car parks, often hugging each other, usually crying together. Old enemies can suddenly become partners in grief at this point, your spirits unified by the shared sense of an understanding of what has been lost, of that disorientation, that horrible vacuum of love, while your best buddies who have never grieved seem like clumsy children when they try sympathetically to relate to you. Non-grievers gave me sympathy and offers of pints and golf, but they couldn't really understand. I ended up feeling like I'd got a contagious form of cancer that they were worried they might catch, so I tended to ignore them and seek out fellow members of Grievers Anonymous. Grief was utterly unlike anything I'd ever felt; indeed, I started to think it doesn't really exist as one single feeling you could label as 'grief', but really is a catch-all term for the twenty or so different shards of gloom, loss and despair that you go though.

I found myself continually asking the already-grieved, 'How long does this hell last? How long will I feel like this?' I couldn't sleep, I could barely eat and I was, above all, SO ANGRY. I was furious with the world and with everyone in it for taking him away, hurting those closest to me with my rage, those who will forgive you anything at this time. The only chance we get to behave like an emotionally chaotic child again is when a parent dies. Everyone gives us a grace period to relive that childishness before stepping up into the dead man's shoes. It's the sweetest maturity rite around.

And when I would ask the experienced griever 'How long will it last?' they would look at me sadly and sympathetically, and usually say, 'It never goes away but you start to feel better in a year.' A YEAR? I would scream inside . . . how can I live with this pain for that long? I will surely explode. I feel like a star about to go supernova, red hot, white hot with fury at this crime against nature, this sundering of the natural order, this death.

Even after a few weeks I sensed – perhaps because I was putting on such a good show – that people thought I was OK. I remember turning up at a barbecue with my closest friends, one summer's night, and felt that they, for the first ten minutes or so, were all taking a step back from me, observing me, letting me talk, being an audience, assessing me, considering me to be *coping*.

But privately I was a mess all summer, sobbing until I was dry and my diaphragm ached, finding obscure corners of Elstree Film Studios where I could sit and wail for an hour at a time. The disabled loos on the third floor of the George Lucas Building were a particular favourite. (The other use of these loos was as a cottage for gay *Big Brother* editors to ease the boredom of nightshifts together.) I became obsessed by a video game called *Zelda – The Phantom Hourglass* on Nintendo DS. This beautiful, jolly, cartoon-like fantasy world of gentle puzzle-solving was a wonderful escape. I would play it on trains, buses, at work and long into the night; it made me forget myself, forget the agony, forget Dad not being there.

I was on a train with Tom one day and had handed him *Zelda* because I was stuck in a labyrinth and asked for his help. He too couldn't see the way out. At about midnight, and after a day of huge stress and strain, Tom texted me: 'Mate. Well done on getting through the day. Please don't kill yourself. If you do you will never know the secret of how to get Zelda out of the labyrinth.' I didn't, and I finally worked out how to get out of the labyrinth and escape.

So we build around ourselves a grief-circle, who we know will understand. But grief, unlike other depressions, is really something we can only deal with on our own, in a natural space of time. Talking helps in the sense of knowing that we're not going mad, and that not only are there others out there who have experienced this, but that there is something in this awfulness that is fundamentally human; primal.

There are also no pills we can take, and no way we can rush it. We have to sit with it. There will be good days and bad days, and there will be times when we think we're over it. There will be horrible occasions when we might wish our other relations would die soon, so we can get all the grieving done in one go. The thought of having to go through this again and again obsesses us. But maybe, like love, the first time is always the most intense.

I threw myself into researching and arranging the India trip, and this, for some of the time, made me put the grief to one side. But the moment my brain was unoccupied it would be there. I would wear shades all the time – even though this was late autumn – and would push a shopping trolley up the aisles in Asda while weeping behind them. Sometimes I would stop in the middle of a remote aisle (Baking or Kosher Goods, say), and stay still for up to ten minutes, overwhelmed by the tsunami of grief inside me, which could only dribble out in this public place. I was lonely as hell and living a deliberately solitary life. Was this me giving time to allow the natural flow of grief to emerge? Or was this me being self-indulgent and masochistic, allowing myself to be romantically consumed by something that needed distraction rather than navel-gazing? I would summon up enough self control to take my shades off to interact with and pay the till girl, and then would trundle down the seafront towards home, snivelling.

Grief does not attract people. And it was no surprise to me that I wasn't overburdened with visitors during this period.

After a few weeks I turned up at Cruse.

***

I smile at Agnes as I shut the office door and go down a flight of stairs to the gents. I walk up to a urinal and reach for the zip of my fly. Without thinking I start to fumble for my cock, but then stop. I place both hands high and wide above me on the wall behind the urinal, and stand like I am being searched by an American cop. My head dips slowly until my chin rests on my collar bone. I can feel it coming, rapidly shooting up from my guts like molten vomit. My body contorts a little, I twist my upper body muscles to allow through this force; all the points are changed to allow the intercity express through. As it nears expression I don't know if I will throw up, have a stroke or wail.

I wail. Sobbing up the blackest shit that has been lodged in my guts for months.

And I don't know if this is my grief or the absorbed grief of others much worse off than me. Or rather, perhaps better able to express it without embarrassment.

Six of us sit in a circle. Agnes is our leader, seventy, sweet, instantly wonderful, maternal but tough. She gives the impression that she has gone through hell and survived, that nothing you say will surprise, that all is forgivable, that the normal politenesses don't matter here.

Richard and I share backgrounds and so we click. He's a forty-three-year-old barrister; or rather was, until his mother became ill several years ago and he devoted himself to her care. He gave up his job to look after her, is furious with his siblings that they didn't help out and, since she died a year ago, has clearly fallen to bits several times over. He talks eloquently, coherently, in that logical way lawyers do, until he is seized by sudden rage and pain, and breaks down in front of us, sobbing his grief out, his red hair and red face pockmarked by the colour of pain. We let him cry and then he resumes his story. Sometimes he becomes self-conscious and guilty that he is doing so much talking and not enough listening so he throws a question out to another member of the group; but his tone is of a barrister cross-examining a witness and makes us shrink away from him a little.

Everyone here is grabbing their five minutes to say their story. Because no one else will listen to them. It struck me that I have twenty people I can ring this instant who will listen to my moaning and care for me. The people in this room have no one. Or they are the most self-indulgent of grief-o-philes, having a vampiric urge to feed off others' pain.

Andy is a tall, thin Scot of my age and looks like a corpse. A year ago he found his mother hanging in her house. His life fell to bits after that. His thick Glaswegian accent is punctuated by swearwords, each of which he apologizes to Agnes for using. He stinks of sweat and alcohol; he has a junkie's eyes and gauntness; he tells us he's on a large daily dose of an anti-depressant; he says that this is the first time he has left the house in weeks; that there is a dent the shape of his body on his sofa as he has spent months just lying on it watching daytime TV. We listen to him. I'm not that bad, I think. I may have had the odd day on the sofa, but not a year. The decision to cope or to slip is such a subtle one.

Dave works in the Debenhams warehouse in Hove. He is in his late forties, a working man, who lost his mother one month ago. He seems a normal, straight, responsible guy whose simple life has been schismed by his loss. He feels utterly unable to talk to anyone about how he feels. His wife is getting annoyed with him, his kids don't want to hear him talk about their dead grandma, and it's not the sort of thing the lads at work discuss. He says several times how grateful he is that he can share his feelings with us. A group of solipsistic strangers, who perhaps are only pretending to care in order to have their go.

Molly is a twenty-five year-old single mum from the rough Whitehawk estate, who also lost her mother one month ago; she can barely say two sentences about this without crying; we all tell her it's all right, take your time, let it all out.

All these dead mothers. Is it only me that lost a father?

MY NAME IS GRANT AND I AM A GRIEVER.

Agnes doesn't so much run the session as sit back, be present and, through her seen-it-all solidity, silently inspire the rest of us to create the circle of discussion. The odd thing is that I find I don't actually want to talk much. I feel that if I did join in I would be inventing feelings. I try to work out whether I am just being reserved, self-conscious, embarrassed and a bit too English, but I think it's that I have nothing to say. The others do try to involve me and encourage me to open up, but instead I find myself being the questioner and, after a few minutes, running the session. At times I feel like a Dimbleby, bringing people into the discussion, linking themes, encouraging the quieter ones to come forward, shaping the meeting. Agnes lets me do this. Clearly I am not stepping on her territory. I feel anal, I feel like the HR guy and yet I think I'm doing good here. Something in me cannot bear the Babel-like chaos that would exist in this swamp of tidal emotions if I didn't shape it.

I have nothing to say. Either I've said it all to my friends over the last few months or I am so repressed and the grief is so buried that it has rendered me silent. I don't know. I recall the 'Responsibility Pledge' of Alcoholics Anonymous: 'I am responsible. When anyone, anywhere, reaches out for help, I want the hand of AA always to be there. And for that: I am responsible.'

For once I am away from my own pain and using my experience of it to pull someone else out of the quicksand. And I also think, crucially: 'I am really not that badly off compared to these people.'

And so at the end of the meeting, after we finished our weak milky teas, nibbled on a few Co-op digestives and put our pound coins in the donations box, we all agree to meet the following week. I have this urge to take Richard out for a drink to talk more, but it's probably too soon to cross that kind of boundary.

Now, at the urinal, I am crying out all their absorbed grief. I have to be careful. I need to look after myself. And, after all, maybe in comparison I really am OK.

OK.

Haven't felt that for months.

The following Wednesday, I nearly didn't go. I forced myself without really knowing why. I felt no urge to be there and when I examined my motives for attending, I realized I was going *for the others.*

This session progressed like the first one and ended in a similar way, too, with me vertically prostrating myself on the wall above the same urinal, sobbing my empathic tears.

I wouldn't go back. I couldn't put myself through this every week, just to be an unpaid session leader; besides, I couldn't honestly say I felt much grief anymore, certainly not compared to my fellow CRUSE grievers.

Maybe – whisper it – *I was starting to get over him.*

I sustained myself with this for several weeks, ignoring the sudden emotional breakdowns on buses or in supermarkets, the inability to really connect with anyone, the increasing dourness of my tone and the crippling loneliness.

I'm OK.

It was later, when I had to clear out my father's garage, that I realized how not OK I was. Perhaps by throwing away his stuff, it was the first time I'd had to admitted to myself fully that he was gone. Forever.

***

The chicken was tough as hell (it always is in India), but it was the best and most unlikely Sunday roast ever. Our empty, sore, infected stomachs adored us again for familiar tastes and textures rather than intestinally challenging local cuisine.

After lunch a beer was put in my hand and I was introduced to a retired businessman, Mr Arun Uday, and a friend up from Bangalore Golf Club. We chatted golf, golf courses and about Nottingham, Tom's hometown where Mr Uday's daughter was studying. The club bursar appeared and asked Mr Uday how his round went.

'OK,' he replied.

'Well at least it's BTS,' said the bursar.

'BTS? What the shit is that?' said Mr Uday.

'Better than sex!'

They bellowed with large manly laughter. So did we. The bar staff grinned politely and silently. Backs were slapped. Here, we can be boys. Mr Uday's friend told us he got a hole in one on the seventeenth recently. Mr Uday muttered in my ear that he wants to get one of his friend's clubs and 'shove it up his ass . . .'

We said goodbye to Mr Serendeshekar, who told us that the membership secretary was sorry he was unavailable to meet us. The club would love more tourists. I told him that their website was not that welcoming, to which he sighed, agreed and admitted that he'd only just inherited the web side of the business.

As we were driving away in our rickshaw – two big men with two big golf bags sardined as usual into the backseat – Mr Serendeshekar stuck his head in and said: 'By the way, that snake you saw – it was a rat snake. Totally harmless.'

13

The Tea Hills of Munnar

You don't know how much you are to me and it is so hard having to go away from all that is dear to me to that hard frontier life again – still it is noble work. Oh! Mrs Douglas it will be a terrible wrench going away from you my dear, dear friend . . . I struggle against depression but I do need your sympathy badly . . . I do appreciate so much your wishing to call me by my Christian name and letting me call you by yours.

From the letters of Sir Francis Younghusband to Mrs Nellie Douglas (1892)

It is New Year's Day, 2011, and Graeme McDowell, the hero of Europe's Ryder Cup triumph at Celtic Manor, has been appointed a Member of the British Empire. That long putt on the sixteenth that effectively finished off Hunter Mahan's challenge – and therefore that of the United States – coupled with his brilliant US Open win have bagged him the gong. Westwood, Poulter, Donald and Casey may brood and wonder why they aren't going to shake Her Majesty's hand, too, but it is Major wins and heroic nerve-holding putts that mark out the great golfers.

The rather silly British Empire honours are a relatively recent invention: George V created the different categories of Order of the British Empire in 1917 as a way to honour the First World War brave who weren't upper class enough to be catered for by the established honours system. As well as the various anachronistic-sounding medals with which we are familiar, there is the British Empire Medal, withdrawn from British life in 1993 but still awarded in obscure parts of the Commonwealth, notably the Cook Islands. This feels like a sort of Colonial Stockholm Syndrome gone crazy.

My dad spent his adult life bewildered that the myths of British global supremacy he'd been taught as a kid in the 1930s had proved to be false. He would complain to me that 'Britain is no longer "great" anymore; we used to have an empire, now we have nothing.' He felt short-changed somehow, denied the glorious birthright he'd been promised. This generation were taught to feel racially superior to everyone else. When Britain was clearly in an economic mess in the 1960s and (especially) the 1970s, people like my father couldn't square this reality with the glorious myth of the endless Britannia-Reich that was in their DNA. He could never get his head round the fact that the Empire's greatest triumph – beating the Nazis – was also the beginning of the end. He lived in a pre-Suez political world until the day he died; his subtle discomfort with immigration was always a signifier to me of how collapsing empires can, like in Germany, create an anachronistic, extreme nationalism based on racial purity and supremacy.

Like my father, the golf establishment has been slow to adapt to the new world order. Tiger Woods's genealogy is the sort that would set my father's head spinning; to my father – who admired him greatly – Tiger would simply seem 'a black man', though Tiger describes himself as 'Cabilnasian' – an abbreviation of Caucasian, black, American Indian and Asian. Only going as far back as his grandparents, Tiger has African American, Chinese, Native American, Thai and Dutch blood in him. Perhaps this helped his acceptance by the conservative US golf establishment – a sort of Obama effect, in that uncomfortable whites can reassure themselves that neither are actually 'too black', but a colourful modern hybrid of several familiar cultures. However, I remember the awkwardness at Augusta when Tiger won his first Masters in 1997. He had not only won the tournament at twenty-one but had smashed every record in the book. As Tiger took part in the semi-Masonic ritual of receiving the winner's green jacket from our own Sir Nick Faldo, the previous year's champ, the faces of the Georgian golf establishment nervously shifted around him. For a moment, they looked like they were watching a kid from the cotton fields become CEO of the plantation.

***

I've failed for the army and navy,
The church and the law so you see
The only profession left to me – my last hope –
an assistant in tea.
You may not believe me but I'm chockful of brains
The one thing I can't do is think hard.
But I'm sure I'll love tennis and polo and golf,
I can work hard, and play hard and drink hard.

'Distant Lands Enchantment',
old Indian tea planters' song

I enjoy observing how we English are perceived by Americans, and tea drinking is such an obvious point of difference. It links us directly to India, China, Japan and the old dominions, while coffee culture in the United States has no real connection with, say, Brazil, Indonesia or Ethiopia where the beans originate. Coffee is Starbucks or the perennial pot on the bubble in the kitchen all day, which the first person up puts on. Tea is a connection to empire, or perhaps to the happier, fluffier slightly phoney bonds of Commonwealth that supposedly link us together like the trick wires in a magician's levitation act.

My father adored tea. Though India produces a quarter of all the tea in the world – nearly a million tonnes of the stuff in 2008 (India is also the sixth biggest coffee producer in the world) – my father had no interest in its place of origin. Tea was his life force. And it was absolutely British. Whereas really it is as exotic and 'Asian' as sushi, dhal or a Vietnamese steamed goat. In a similar way, in the last twenty years curries have ceased to be 'Indian' or 'foreign' and have become a distinctly 'British' dining experience – an alternative to fish and chips or jellied eels.

I never saw my father drink a glass of water or even take a sip. He survived on tea, maybe eight cups a day. He rarely drank alcohol, which perhaps means he was never particularly dehydrated so his body could get enough H_2O from his eight cuppas to keep him going. Say he started drinking tea at the age of ten in 1937. That means he had seventy years of drinking eight cups a day. That's 200,000 cups of tea in his lifetime.

I have inherited his tea-love. I never touch coffee. It makes my hands shake, spreads day-long halitosis, and is rich, bitter and pretentious. My first thought every morning is to work out where I am and where is the nearest tea source. It's conditioned, Pavlovian stuff, I know, but I am not me without tea inside me. When I'm in the United States

I drink tea first thing in the morning and feel delightfully different and old world. In India my first cuppa connects me with the country, with our shared history, with myself.

It may have been my father's obsessive tea drinking (and years of inadequate hydration) that triggered the failure of his kidneys; a dehydrated mouth and an increased inability to swallow food or liquid were the first signs that something was wrong. Increasingly anxious about his condition – though at this stage he could still function pretty well day-to-day – he became fixated on trying to find drinks that were smooth enough to force down his petulant oesophagus. The gloopy syrupy fruit drink sugar fest that is a bottle of J_2O was found to be the most suitable, and so for a while the fridge was full of the stuff in all it garish flavour options. When even this miracle panacea started failing to work, my father went to a doctor, who prescribed him . . . beer.

This was perhaps the most quirky piece of advice any doctor has given a patient since that time in the 1950s when family doctors encouraged people to smoke cigarettes as a stress reliever. Having faith with whatever a man in a white coat told him to do, my father started to drink two or three pints of Bass a day – far more alcohol than he had ever consumed on a daily basis in his life. Now he was more dehydrated, more sick and slightly sloshed every day. After he died I found a fridge in his garage still full of cans of Bass, which I polished off in a couple of nights' worth of mournful staring into space amongst his things.

Bass beer is brewed in Burton upon Trent in Staffordshire, my mother's home town. My strongest memory of the town as a child is the smell: hops. The whole place reeks of heavy damp hops, hanging over the town like an alco-smog. In Munnar, high in the hills in Kerala, the smell of tea has the same effect. It is unavoidably in your nostrils 24/7. For a tea-lover like me it's sheer bliss. I went around the Munnar hills deliciously intoxicated. Tom didn't feel this, but told me he reckoned he'd feel the same way in the Kronenbourg factory.

When we were shown around a tea plantation I was absolutely thrilled to see the process. I even felt the urge to do what I rarely do: take some photos. The machines looked so beautiful, and I felt I was somehow at the source of something that means a lot to me. This was my inadvertent Hajj.

Tea was one of the East India Company's great success stories. At first sourced from the Chinese Qing Empire, by the late eighteenth century it was the Company's premier trade, with a vital market in the American colonies. However, gradually the British felt frustrated by having to rely on Chinese tea farmers to produce the crop, and started to explore tea growing potential in its own emerging empire.

The genesis of the Indian tea trade, and the enormous profits it would bring, is directly linked to the success of one of the Company's more dubious products: opium. The acquisition of Bengal in the mid-eighteenth century brought with it the province of Bihar, where the best opium in the East was grown, and the Company quickly assumed monopoly control. Although its import was officially banned by the Qing Empire, opium was the one contraband product for which the Chinese were willing to pay, generating enormous revenue, much of which was used to source the valuable tea crops. From just 2,000 chests in 1800, over 50,000 chests of opium a year were being smuggled in during the Company's final years (the 1850s). This illegal trade in a notorious narcotic in turn brought about the bloody Opium Wars of 1839–42 and 1856–60. Not the British Empire's finest hour.

In the 1840s, India experienced a 'Tea Rush'. By the turn of the century, Assam was the leading tea-producing area in the world. Tea came thirty years later to Munnar. The area's tea industry would remain in mostly British hands until 1983 when the great Indian Tata corporation took it over. It would be this new mega-company (which also now owns Tetley, that quintessentially English brew) that would cause us the most golf grief we experienced in India.

***

Twenty-nine miles outside Munnar, near the village of Kundale, lies the centre of Tata Tea's Keralan operation. Perched on the peak of a hill, called 'Top Station' locally, is the multinational's regional base. And it has a golf course attached. We had to play it.

Sometimes our trips to weird golf locations were feeling like exercises in Blimpish arrogance. All the people we spoke to about playing this course said it would be impossible – the nice couple who ran the guest house, the guys in the restaurant round the corner, any rickshaw driver to whom we spoke and especially the cabbie who had been summoned to drive us. It reminded us of the conversation in Darjeeling when we were trying to persuade the local taxi and hotel fraternity that a golf course existed up a hill nearby, when it clearly didn't. This time our local friends were happy to admit that there was indeed a golf course up a hill two hours' drive away, but there was no way we were going to be allowed to play on it without permission. And there was no way anybody was going to give us permission on a weekend. I could see it in their looks and guess from their muttering to each other in the local Kanada language – 'What a couple of English idiots!' would probably be about right.

I was interested in seeing how far a benevolent Raj-era Englishness – my role model here was the liberal schoolteacher Mr Fielding in *A Passage to India* – could still get you in India. How much of the dynamics of our shared colonial relationship still permeates, if you press the right triggers? And how much could you be accepted in high social circles merely as a result of this – and an ability to talk a good game of golf and not embarrass yourself on the course. I often felt like I was hoodwinking people on this trip – from the taxi drivers to the posh old geezers in Bangalore with whom I would later have such fun. I was showing them one side of me; an exaggerated, clubbable bit that I had learned at school; a 5 per cent of me performance that was enough to convince people that they were seeing the whole. I was a lower middle class boy, like many British people in India before me who went to the subcontinent to be accepted in circles they could not reach at home, to reinvent themselves and to make some money; much like Clive of India himself.

India still gives the opportunity for a Westerner to be who they say they are or want to be. No wonder the ashrams of Rishikesh, the beaches of Goa and utopian communities like Auroville near Chennai are full of Westerners seeking a restart. British people used to come to India and work incredibly hard to reinvent themselves; now they come to chill, take drugs or meditate. This is the end of these decadent, post-imperial times. As India takes over the world, these truth and rebirth seekers will seem like sad former princes in exile – small-time Shahs of Iran or Wallis Simpsons, eking out a grandish existence on the remains of old money and a residue of deference.

So, in the boggy overcast drizzle of Munnar we headed up the hill. Nowhere yet had ever refused us admission; nowhere had refused us a game; and nowhere had flung us out.

Today that was all about to change.

The higher we drove, the better the weather. As we drove across the top of the Mattupetty Dam and through the small gathering of souvenir and refreshment stalls fringing the pretty Kundale Lake, our spirits lifted for the first time in days. The rain had really got to us – the oppressive atmosphere, the blackness of the skies, the sense of hilltop doom hanging in the air, vague hints of God's wrath, walking in mud, and non-stop drizzle. If the homesick British came to the hills to find some familiarity, then the rain must have helped; how wonderful to put on some wellies, fire up your umbrella, and maybe even don a sou'wester. Much nicer than sweltering in the heat and dust of the plains. However, 6,500 feet above sea level, the sun on Kundale Lake's gentle water and surrounding hills not only pulled me out of my bedrizzled gloom, but actually made me want to play golf.

We kept climbing, now up a tiny, potholed stone and dirt road that zigzagged its way upwards. When the bumpiness of this part of the ride was even starting to annoy our driver, he turned to us and said: 'OK. You will not be able to golf today; you need permission; we go back, yes? Do sightseeing? Excellent viewpoints all around.'

I nearly snapped haughtily at him, but bit my tongue; By God, I was going to play golf today. I insisted that all was fine and that we should proceed. Eventually, after crisscrossing the hill in crab-like fashion for fifteen minutes, the road opened out and we were surrounded by lush green vegetation. We were faced with a tea factory in front of us, with the Tata logo on it. No one seemed to be around, except the security guard at the gate who insisted there was no way we could play golf without permission, and that we should go back and maybe see some of the splendid viewpoints for which the area is famous. I insisted – trying to use Obi-Wan Kenobi-like Jedi mind control – that it would be fine for us to play golf today, so could I see the boss please? The security guard looked at our cabbie, then they both looked at me with scorn mixed with deference. The guard said sure, you'll find him in his office on the first floor.

So, dressed for golf we walked into the Tata tea factory.

It was deserted. We looked around the concrete Soviet-style 1970s building, shouted a few speculative 'hellos', and 'namastes', vaguely tried to find the boss, and generally snooped around a bit. I thought how I wouldn't be able to do this at Tata's UK Tetley plant in Greenford, Middlesex.

The place was run down. The office corridors adjacent to the factory floor were bare and whitewashed; thin crimson carpet had been placed on the floor, but not tacked down. The ceiling was made of chipboard, and bulged and sagged with the weight of the years and the rains. Someone had put up four small posters of the nearby viewpoints presumably to make guests like us feel welcome. They didn't. We felt like we were in a ghost factory in an abandoned town in the Wild West.

We eventually found a door with 'manager' on it and, after a few unanswered knocks, decided to enter. The room was almost empty apart from a couple of office chairs, a desk with a few bits of paper on it, a mug of cold tea and some framed certificates on the wall, proclaiming the factory's tea-producing excellence. I took one of my business cards from my wallet and went through my story in my head.

The subcontinent loves business cards. Every rickshaw guy has one and you are asked for yours all the time: it is a sign of status; it is a self-definition; it *individualizes.* I looked at the card and remembered the ease with which one can access places and people in India when you have a BBC News pass. India is the county of the 'no', a place where you are forbidden to do things by every jobsworth at every point in the day. However, unlike in Britain, these 'nos' should not be taken at face value, rarely mean 'no' per se and should be seen as an opening gambit in a longer term conversational barter whose basic gist is 'make it worth my while to turn this no into a yes'. There are two ways to do this. One is by offering baksheesh, the only slightly under-the-surface, gentle, black market that operates in every transaction every day everywhere in India, from asking directions to sorting out who gets billion rupee IPL contracts. The other way is by pulling rank, so that your co-haggler starts to think he will get into trouble if he persists in his 'no'. In India, I feel the words 'BBC News' could get me into Prime Minister Manmohan Singh's bedroom. However, on this trip I couldn't claim to be working for them and, not wanting to lie, I had to use the only card I had that represented who I was and what I did at that point. Sort of. All this to get a game of golf.

I was staring at the card, going through spin options. It said this:

> Junk Food Studios
> London's Newest Music Rehearsal and Audio Recording Space
> Grant Gordon
> performer – producer – radio – online

I'd packed up the studio a few months before, but being too tight to make new business cards, and because I wasn't actually quite sure how to define myself, I was still using these. Not got much to do with golf, or writing or the BBC, or anything much unless you want to record a demo in Camden. Still, this would be a good test of the power of the business card and I rehearsed the speech that I would give the factory manager (if he turned up and, of course, if he spoke English). I knew we would come across as strange, frivolous, slightly pompous and unhinged, and I suspected I'd only have a few initial seconds to capture his interest before he called security or politely told us to go and see the famous nearby viewpoints.

And as the bewildered manager walked into his office to find two large Englishmen taking photos and snooping around, I thrust a card into his hand, and without allowing him time to respond with as much as his name, started my stream of consciousness jabber about why we were here.

Mr Venkatesan spoke excellent English, invited us to sit down and very calmly explained how it would not be possible for us to play golf today. We would need an invitation. This we might be able to get from a Mr Rao, at the Tata HQ back in Munnar, two hours away. Today was Saturday, the office would be shut on Sunday, and we were meant to be out of Munnar on Monday. Damn.

I persevered, using all the arguments that usually worked – we had played all over the country, at prestigious courses in Delhi and Calcutta, across the Himalayas, even in nearby Ooty and Coonor, but nothing moved Mr V. This was a wall of 'no' and it was made of thick concrete. As I kept going with my rhetoric he looked slightly pained, until he said, 'Look, I would like to let you play golf, but it is not possible. I am the factory manager. I am not a senior man here. Please go and see Mr Rao and obtain permission, then you can play.'

I stopped my persuasive efforts, feeling slightly ridiculous, and sorry that I was hassling this guy who was just trying to do his job and was in fear of his superiors. I thanked him and we headed back down to the car.

'No golf?' our cabbie asked.

'No golf today,' I confirmed. 'We need to get permission.'

He looked me in the eye and didn't bother suppressing the grin of I-told-you-so triumph that spread across his face.

As we drove back down the hill, we caught a glimpse of the top of the small clubhouse – the course was founded in 1918 by British tea planters – and the tops of the trees down the opening fairways. The sun was out, the temperature was like early June in England and I felt devastated I wasn't hitting a golf ball.

***

High Ranges Golf Course was not only back in Munnar, but was about 300 yards from our guest house. Our cabbie pulled up in a scrub area, one side of a creek, with a narrow footbridge across it.

'There is High Ranges,' he said, pointing to a clump of buildings the other side of the water. 'You go talk to boss there, I wait here with clubs.'

My spirit started to sink again – why did he not drive us to the front door? What does he know that we don't? So we walked across the creek and into the clubhouse. We followed a sign to the 'office' where three startled men stared at us.

'Yes?' asked the most senior, most middle-aged and most rotund one.

'Hello, we'd like to play some golf please, could we?'

'Sorry, course is closed.'

'Ah, that's a shame, we have our own clubs with us in the car.'

'It is not possible to play today.'

'Oh but we have played all over India – in Delhi, Calcutta, across the Himalayas; yesterday we played in Kodaikanal, and they encouraged us to visit your famous course.'

'Tough luck. The course has been closed two weeks. It is overgrown. You can't play golf on it. It reopens in February. Sorry.'

'Could we just hit a few balls around a couple of the holes?'

'No!'

He was snappy and irritated now. I knew I must back down. 'OK. Sorry to bother you. Could we have a quick look at the course?'

'A look?'

'Yes I'd love to see the layout . . .'

'OK, you can have a quick look, please come through.'

So we walked through the clubhouse and on to the course, which you could barely distinguish from the jungle from which it had once been carved. It was utterly unplayable, the grass being knee high or higher around most of it.

I surveyed it for a few minutes and enjoyed the look of this easy, flat, short, nine-hole course. I had a chat to one of the groundsmen about the work he was doing – replacing soil that had been washed away by the recent late sting of monsoon. The sun was out now and it would have been a beautiful few hours hacking round this place, but for the second time in a day, it was not to be. Probably too many cobras in the rough here, as well.

As we chatted to some of the staff in the clubhouse and took photos of the place and its framed pictures of local tiger hunts, the portly office man re-emerged and was clearly keen for us to go. He seemed to be suspicious of us, even though we couldn't have been dressed in a more serious-about-golf way.

We'd been kicked out. Twice. Munnar had defeated us. The sun went in and the early evening rain suddenly streamed torrentially from the sky, soaking us within seconds and presumably washing away all the good work the groundsman had done that day.

14

From Palolem to Eternity

In the address I delivered at his funeral, I mentioned that my dad was a lifelong roadie to my mother and me. That for nearly fifty years he had been picking one of us up from theatres, concert halls, pubs and studios in which we were performing or recording. My mother was an accomplished semi-pro choral singer, a member of the Royal Choral Society and frequently sang at the Albert Hall, on recorded oratorios or at BBC Maida Vale studios for broadcast. After taking a break to bring me up she joined the local amateur operatic group and sang twice a year in Gilbert and Sullivan or Rodgers and Hammerstein shows. In the 1960s my father would drive my mum from gig to studio to home. When my mother sung in the G&S shows he would become the front-of-house manager. He would dress in a dinner jacket and bow tie, and sternly deal with any ticket controversies or misbehaving children. He adopted his 'officer' personality. Disciplined, austere, no nonsense, haughty, chilly.

When I worked in a department store with him during

university vacations I realized that this is how he came across to his young staff members. Some of the boys loved him and joined his smoking circle. These were the ones who would have enjoyed National Service, I think. Others disliked him and found it awkward relating to me. He could be sharp, almost cruel, in a professional setting though I never once saw this side of him at home. He hated ill discipline, laziness, tardiness, sloppiness, skiving, backchat, corner cutting. Above all, he worshipped customers. They were ALWAYS right. And could always be sold something if you were courteous and patient enough with them. Sometimes I would lunch with Tony's group in the staff canteen. It felt like a gathering of minor Ealing Comedy gangsters, all chain smoking, reading the *Mail* or the *Express*, eating fry-ups, talking shop, slagging off the bosses. One man – Charlie from Accounts – never said a word but would spend every break obsessively completing *The Times* crossword. I was welcomed in as the guvnor's son, and I enjoyed their 1950s barrack-room, mildly misogynistic banter.

While he was showing old ladies to their seats at the opera I would try to flog them a programme – which he had designed, using his 1960s newspaper ad copywriting skills. I liked working in his team, and I thought he was a very impressive, authoritative, tall slim figure in his smart black and white outfit, swooping down to ensure all were seated and happy by curtain up.

My life changed when I was fourteen when my father bought me my first guitar. I had seen two boys play folk songs at the church hall one night and had this incredible urge to do that, too. I loved their two-part harmony singing, the simple repetitive melodies and the narrative in the lyrics. Before that night I had never thought about being a guitar player. Now I knew that it was my calling. From then on, every week I would look in the small ad sections of the *Surrey Herald* and *Walton and Weybridge Informer* to find a guitar and, eventually, I saw one. I fell in love with that battered acoustic guitar the moment I saw it. The vendor wanted £19 for it; my father, to my embarrassment, offered £17, which they accepted. The axe was mine.

From that moment on, music became my obsession. I had already learnt how to hit the drums, and started to form and play in loads of bands at school and in Walton. My father would drive me to all rehearsals and gigs, and the sight of the white Sierra at the end of a show was as reassuring to me as ever. Even in my twenties my father would drive me, a drum kit or a boot load of amplifiers around London and Surrey. I think he liked being 'crew'. I'm sure he appreciated the time to himself, and the packet of cigarettes he could devour.

Then, in his mid-sixties, something unexpected happened. Like the moment when the lifelong roadie becomes the new lead guitarist in the band, Dad started to act a bit. At the same time that my mother had decided she'd had enough of performing, Tony took up the baton and enjoyed a late blooming of performing talent. He would appear in the male chorus of the local opera group for their big shows, and in little pre-war comedy skits for charity events. He couldn't sing much and had two left feet, but he adored being on stage and making an audience laugh. Eventually the show directors would create comic cameo parts just for him and insert him into random bits of *HMS Pinafore* or *Anything Goes.*

Usually these characters would be old, incoherent drunks, shuffling around the stage delivering a few sozzled gags and generally getting in the way of the dancers. My father was never drunk in his life, but he acted it well. In fact, during one performance of *The Pirates of Penzance* he had immersed himself so much in his drunken role, that he forgot how close to the edge of the stage he had reached. In pirate costume, with an eye patch and a wooden leg, he took one method-acted drunken step too many, slipped and fell headfirst into the orchestra pit, crashing into the percussion section with an almighty bang. Half the audience gasped; the other half laughed uproariously. From amidst the rubble of drum kit, glockenspiel and cymbals, Tony hauled himself to his feet, kept acting drunk and dazed, and, bringing the house down with mirth, exited through the audience.

***

> *The newly arrived European in India requires no alcoholic beverage whatever; that is, if he comes to India, as he certainly ought, full of life, vigour and energy . . . The idea that beer, wine or some alcoholic stimulant . . . is necessary to counteract, as is fancied, the depressing effects of the climate, is a delusion and too often a snare. It is the rock on which more lives have been sacrificed than from any other cause. The climate demands no such thing . . . Beer drinking between meals is pernicious in the extreme.*
>
> E. C. P. Hull and R. S. Mair,
> *The European in India* (1878)

After an exhausting journey down from the tea and rain hills, we arrived in the Goan beach village of Palolem in the south of the state. We were there because it's one of the areas of Goa to which I had never been, because so many people we had met in India had recommended it, and most importantly because it was where Matt Damon and Franka Potente hid when they were on the run from the CIA in *The Bourne Supremacy*. Bourne, as I always knew, is more of a man than me. As off-the-map places go to hide away from the most powerful security agency in the world, Jason made a poor choice. Globally, it's really not that remote: Violet and Bernie, my recently retired Scouse package-tour friends who I chatted to on the train from Cochin, had done Palolem last year, and were advising me about the best bars to go to. It was a hippy haven in the 1980s, becoming a junkie's paradise in the 1990s, before finally settling on a very Goan mix – relaxed, and open to the backpack and grown-up tourist communities alike; online access, burger and chips, Pepsi Cola and lager are everywhere.

Best of all, there is satellite TV.

We had chosen possibly the worst time in the golf calendar to be *en passage*: every two years the Ryder Cup grips the American and European golfing worlds. During the first two days of the event we would be in some sort of vehicle en route to our beach paradise. I thought maybe on the third and final day we could hire mopeds, scoot to the nearest five-star luxury intercontinental mega hotel, buy some ludicrously priced lager and find a TV showing the event. Imagine a football fan booking a flight that lands on the day England reach the World Cup final. It felt like that.

We arrived before dawn with not a soul around, the only sounds being the slowly ascending cacophony of birds and insects as they cleared their throats for the impending dawn chorus, and the hissing and growling of Goa's ubiquitous street dogs, snarling at territory encroachers.

We camped outside a decent-looking hotel for an hour until someone appeared and showed our weary bodies into a pleasant enough room, which we took without hesitation. I sat on the bed and started the ritualistic flick through the hundred or so channels you find in any Indian hotel room. Half of the channels show cricket – any cricket; one channel is devoted to showing over and over again Sachin Tendulkar's finest centuries. I hit the jackpot with Channel 54 (Ten Action): extended highlights of yesterday's Ryder Cup action from the nouveau riche upstart Celtic Manor course near Newport in South Wales. Oh, bliss. As our scrambled, up-for-too-long brains gently pieced themselves back together, we lay on our double bed (no twins available), ceiling fan whirring rapidly, emphysemic air-conditioning unit groaning at max, and watched the always amusing sight of Tiger Woods in a thick sweater and heavy rain gear hack a ball miserably round a wet, terse, British golf course, clearly hating it.

***

It was a terrific final round that saw Europe triumph. For the first time since 1927 the competition was extended into a fourth day due to the appalling South Wales weather. This suited us just fine, as the rain delays had meant we hadn't missed that much. Each night we stayed up until the early hours watching the action live with the heavy late monsoon cloudburst intermittently spattering our windows. Each morning we tuned into the highlights show just in case we'd missed anything the previous evening. Our room was on the ground floor of the hotel, fronting on to a pleasant monkey-, kingfisher- and snake-inhabited lush courtyard, and more importantly, next door to reception, where there was a fridge filled with Kingfisher lager. We emptied it during the Ryder Cup. The Sunday of the tournament was nearly a disaster, as it was 'Gandhi Day' throughout the state, which meant that no booze could be sold, in honour of the great man's militant asceticism. Tom got round this by convincing the young boy on the reception desk that 'Bacardi Breezers', which the fridge also amply contained, were simply flavoured fruit juice. We ordered twenty, and sank them, drifting slowly away into a syrupy, Essex-girl-on-a-night-out, alcopop high.

A friend of mine once told me a great story about the European captain Colin Montgomery. It's a bit shaggy, but I hope it's true. A friend of his, Jack, is an academic and a keen golfer. Jack went up to the University of Hull to meet a more senior fellow academic with whom he had corresponded with a lot on email but never met. He went to the department and was shown into the Hull man's rooms. To break the ice, the Hull man showed Jack some ornaments on his bookshelves and explained their significance to him. As Jack half listened to the commentary, his gaze strayed upon a photo, framed on a shelf next to his host's desk. It seemed to show the Hull man with an arm around the shoulder of Colin Montgomery, with both giving strained grimaces to the camera.

'Oh!' said Jack, delighted that he'd found a fellow golfer and could establish some conversational common ground, 'I didn't know you were a golfer! What a great picture of you and Monty.'

There was a long awkward pause. The Hull man looked at his feet before saying quietly, 'The other person in that photo is my wife.'

Monty is one of those sportspeople I find it difficult to like; a man so wrapped up in his own self importance that he fails to see quite how grumpy he can come across. I like my sportspeople to be entertainers first, and to have some degree of gratitude to us, the spectators who at the end of the day pay their bills. Yet with Monty, and Paula Radcliffe, Cristiano Ronaldo, Kevin Pietersen, the whole Chelsea team and Andy Murray, there is a sense that they really don't give a hoot about us, and we are there to admire their brilliance and tremble at their wrath. Their levels of self obsession are at such a pitch that they cease to connect with me. If you are a genuine genius like Tiger – a man who is on such a Mozartian higher plane it's as though he doesn't even know how to communicate to the rest of us, and we don't mind – you can get away with it. Though you can't get away with infidelity and a fixation on cocktail waitresses, it would seem. Maybe the problem here – our disappointment with Tiger and the moral cyclone that has hit him – is that he has shown himself to be *human*, to be just like us. We need our gods to be gods, and we will slaughter them if they seem, in the end, as human and fallible as us.

***

At five the next morning I was wide awake; more awake than a man on a cocaine and Red Bull binge. So of course I lay for one hour in the pre-dawn light trying to return myself to sleep. I had only slept for seven hours in the last forty-eight. I was clearly approaching a sort of exhaustion.

By six I knew I had to get on the scooter and drive through the villages as dawn rose. So I slung on some clothes, and sped off on the blue Honda Dio moped I'd hired the day before. As a non-driver, there are only two situations where I am allowed to experience the thrill most of the rest of mankind gets every day: in a golf buggy and on a scooter in Goa. It is stupidly easy to get hold of a machine in this state; go into any shop or hotel and there'll be someone there who'll happily hire you his own machine out for about £5 a day, no questions asked. I have never had to show anything resembling a licence. On my first ride on a scooter in Goa in 2005 I lost control of the bike at a T-junction and sent me, my girlfriend and the bike spinning into a roadside ditch. A few cuts and bruises, some ripped clothes, a highly pissed-off girlfriend and some scratches on the moped were all the damage, but I could easily have destroyed it and us by my rookie handling.

It was a lovely ride. I went into the narrow lanes that wound through villages clustered around the two small bays where fishermen were heading out to sea in tiny boats. I reached Patnam, Palolem's little brother resort, and walked up and down the sand as the sun rose. Barely anyone was awake. Unlike anywhere else in India where people rise, are active, working and praying at or before dawn, Goans have a more Caribbean attitude to early rising. The only other living beings were the ever-present snarling dogs that are a Goan speciality. This is Goa, the waves were softly saying, what are you doing up? Go back to bed! Chill out! Relax! But I couldn't really relax, couldn't quite lie down on the beach, drink it in, feel that release, that wonderful feeling of soul-calm I always get in Goa. I still couldn't stop. I was still too ill at ease with myself. Only at 20 mph on the scooter, with the lush bush and beaches whizzing past me could I find a sort of peace, so I kept motoring, sometimes pushing the speedo past 30 mph into the 'economy zone' when the engine would make a contented, stretching out its legs moan, and my carbon footprint improved momentarily.

The guards at the Hotel Intercontinental's huge security gates seemed mildly surprised to see a man dressed for the beach roll up on a moped at seven in the morning, asking if he could see the golf course, but happily let me through. As I motored up the preposterous, grand driveway, I was aware that I was driving through the golf course. On each side of me there were holes from one of the most beautifully maintained, florally abundant, exotically planted and bijou-lavish golf courses I'd seen in India. It was all a bit too perfect, really; like a Disneyland approximation of a golf course. It also looked a lot of fun. Then there was the topiary. Two life-size topiary elephants each side of the driveway guard the course, their trunks resplendently shooting pretend topiary water from the water features before them.

I was seized by that familiar urge, perhaps inspired by Graeme McDowell's splendid gusto in the Ryder Cup the night before, to play it now; especially as the weather was mild, there was a pleasant breeze and I knew that by ten this place would be a furnace. I chatted a bit to the bleary-eyed golf pro, found out that we would be welcome to play, then scooted back to base (maybe even touching 32 mph) to wake Tom and force him to go round with me.

By the time we returned, washed, shaved, kitted out and golf-bagged in a deluxe air-conditioned taxi it was 9.45, and scorching hot. There was still no one on the course, and the rich, strong sun had made it look even more enticing and more plastic. We both drove well off the first tee – over the river, over the ninth green, above two topiary pachyderms and the grand maharajah-style drive, and on to the fairway the other side of the concrete. If you sliced your drive here you'd end up smashing one of the deluxe hotel's deluxe front-facing windows. It was tempting.

The course was fun, pretty, short, flat and relatively easy. The par-three third tee is right next to the gates of a small Hindu temple, so your gentle six-iron shot is watched by distracted worshippers. Fluff this tee shot and you might hear the derisive chuckle of Kali.

The fourth was one of the most magical golf holes I've ever played; and certainly the longest. From tee-off to putting out it took us forty minutes. That's because we had a beach break in the middle.

It's a 332-yard par-four, but it was hard to tell where the flag was as the green is downhill and three-quarters protected by a thick spinny of tall bare trees. The fairway too is narrow, so we just hit a driver and waited to see what happened. We both struck decent long shots, which veered off at two o'clock towards a large patch of wiry bushes on red earth scrubland, with the next hole's fairway beyond. We headed towards this further fairway, as we assumed the balls had carried over the scrub. As we walked gently downhill and past the scrub, we suddenly saw the beach, in all its immensity.

Bordering the next fairway, it was a beautiful, long, deserted, tropical stretch of sand – I later found out it was called Galjibag beach – with the Arabian Sea ever so gently licking its shoreline. Coconut trees, palms and casuarinas bordered the seashore, and now and then in the near distance we thought we saw turtles scuttling over the sand. We forgot about looking for our balls, or golf, and instead, still wheeling our golf trolleys, we walked as one creature, mesmerized, on to the beach. We looked out to sea in silence, filled with the wonder of the place, which was doubled as it was so unexpected. It was so hot. We were hungover and tired. We looked at each other cheekily. The water looked so inviting. We checked up and down the long, straight beach. There was no one around. We were the only players on the golf course. A local wooden fishing boat far out on the horizon was the only connection with the rest of humanity. With a whoop, we stripped off in a frenzy and threw our very white, very naked English arses into the water, flopping into the sea with a mighty collective floppy splash. There was barely any tide, and no current of which to speak, so for once in Goa we could actually have a good swim, as opposed to a tumbling lark around which is *de rigueur* on most of the beaches. I could feel the midday sun burning harshly on my neck and shoulders as I swam, but it felt so good and the water so fresh.

After ten minutes or so we headed back to shore, and lay on the sand after having dried ourselves with our tiny golf club head towels . . . I lay there with my six-inch square green 'The Open, Muirfield 2002' towel covering my manhood like a fig leaf; we sunbathed for a few minutes, drinking in the rays, overdoing it with the sun as tourists do in their first few days.

I shut my eyes, the sunlight playing ping-pong on my retinas, and I drifted off, and thought how much this course oddly reminded me of the local short, flat, holiday-camp course my father and I played on for years. It was only a short memory jump for me in my sun-dazzled state to think about him, and about the day of the skip.

***

The skip arrived at eight in the morning, and I was already freaking out. Grief is a pernicious, sneaky set of emotions that always catches you by surprise. Slight triggers can pierce the over-inflated balloon of your grief-resistance, and cause a mini unexpected trauma release all over again. This morning it was his golf shoes.

Some men look great in golf shoes, the finishing touch to a smart golf clothing combo that embodies their aspiration to belong, to impress, to aspire and to rise. Golf fashion is now big business. Ian Poulter is often criticized for putting too much time into his clothing business at the expense of his golf. He is also further lampooned for wearing items from his garish range at every golf tournament in which he plays. He is golf's kitsch, loud peacock. He says his quirky dress sense was inspired by his mother who managed the Letchworth branch of Dorothy Perkins. His most famous pieces include trousers featuring a pattern of the Claret Jug, worn at both the 2005 and 2006 Open Championships. Commentating for the BBC, Seve Ballesteros jibed that this was 'the closest [Poulter] would ever get to it'.

The other legendary pair of Poulter pants are his Union Jack trousers that he wore at the 2004 British Open, which were a masterpiece of Poulter showmanship. The golf world tends to hate this. But what balls, what spivvy entrepreneurial spirit, what Bowie-esque sense of himself as a work of art. Poulter will never earn a tenth of the money Tiger can through sponsors begging him to endorse their products (until recently). But he has made himself his own shop window for Brand Poulter. He is his own Chief Executive and

Supermodel – a brilliant union of talent, initiative and gall. What a plonker.

He is also an obsessive tweeter, his hundreds of thousands of followers proof of his brilliant mastering of the new technology to self promote. In recent BBC coverage of the Open and the Masters, even commentators Ken Jones and Sam Torrance were heard mentioning Poulter's tweets in their commentary. Nothing like having a sales pitch reported on the extreme front line.

Ian's most brilliant moment though, was a quote he made in the March 2010 issue of *Golf World* magazine: 'Don't get me wrong, I really respect every professional golfer, but I know I haven't played to my full potential and when that happens, it will be just me and Tiger.' This is one of the most brilliant and hilarious statements of hubris and undeserved arrogance that has ever been uttered. Tiger barely purred, hardly raised that famous eyebrow of his. In the same magazine Poulter posed naked for a photoshoot, with a golf bag strategically preserving some modesty. The old guard can't stand Poulter, but I think he's rather magnificent. A poor boy from Hertfordshire who battled to carve a career in an expensive, class-ridden sport; that he exhibits Thatcherite and *Dragon's Den* tendencies makes the bastions of old money curl their lips snootily. Poulter is brash, cocky new money, and new golf. He deserves to be mentioned in the same breath as Tiger only because they are positively changing this game. His passionate performance at the Ryder Cup in 2010 (and in 2004 when it was his putt that won the cup for Europe), and the crowds' raucous encouragement of him, is testament to his appeal. As the players teed off each morning on the first tee, the biggest cheer was always for Poulter, not for his more successful colleagues.

Long may he look stupid.

Some people look good in golf shoes; my father did not.

Today's golf footwear is as groovy-looking and high-tech as the best Nike trainer – and as expensive. My father had the same pair all his life, being the frugal son of a Scotsman that he was. They were really low black brogues with old-fashioned, vicious metal studs in them. They were set off by a strange white leather tassel flap that covered the laces, as though they were embarrassing. I always thought they made my father look a little like a faded Spanish guitar player in a mariachi band.

They were in the green carrier bag on the hook on the left side of the garage wall as always. Underneath them on the same hook hung his blue Dunlop golf trolley (I never once saw my dad carry his bag on his back). When I was a kid and used to play my mates, it was a real treat to borrow this trolley and wheel it around like it was mine. Resting nearby was the enormous green, yellow-and-white striped golf umbrella with a Sony logo on it that some sales rep had given him in the early 1980s when he worked selling expensive hi-fi systems to yuppies. And next to that was his simple, unpretentious brown golf bag that he bought when we decided to take the game a bit seriously and play on proper grown-up courses when I was eleven. I looked in the bag and there was the normal grubby potpourri of tees, ball markers, balls, mouldy gloves, tatty bits of score-cards from games we had played over the last few years, and kitschy items of stocking-filler golf paraphernalia that my godfather had bought him – plastic distance estimator, ball cleaner, tee and pencil carrier, etc. His clubs looked sad, old and distinctly charity shop, a selection of random woods and irons cobbled together over thirty years.

I looked round the garage – which was his den, his smoking room, his workshop, his place of solitude and reflection. Nothing had been touched since he had died. Neither my mother or I had thrown away or moved anything. It was a shrine. In the ashtray there were cigarette butts that he must have smoked shortly before he died. I couldn't throw them away. I couldn't throw them because I thought *his lips have sucked on these fags* . . . it was a direct physical connection with his body, or rather the remembrance of his body.

Whenever I came to visit my mother after he died, I would find time to sit in his garage and think about him. I would sit on his old stool at his workbench surrounded by his and my grandfather's ancient tools, and look out at the view that he saw to calm him. I would sit, drink beer, listen to BBC Radio 3 (for me the only radio station in a crisis), look through some of his magazines or papers, feel him, and cry. This was his shrine, in a very Indian sense. It was the tomb of my dead ancestor, a Taj Mahal. It was the first time in my life that I realized the point of such places.

I never really wanted the garage to be cleared of his stuff. It was here that I felt him most. It was here that I felt most like him, his son, a younger version of him, a feeling so much stronger than any I had when I was with him when he was alive. I felt like his flesh and blood, him but me; it was a beautiful feeling; I felt like my life should be a tribute to him; I felt like a man, maybe for the first time; gradually I was becoming ready to step into his shoes.

So months after he died, the skip arrived; the skip into which my friend Will and I were going to throw my dad's life. I had felt fine, had thought I'd dealt with all the grief four or five months earlier. Work was good, life was good, I was achieving what I wanted. Looking back I realize I was deluding myself, that even though I'd patched up the surface to function well, grief was still ruling me. The unbearable feeling of epic loneliness hit me every day; a loneliness I'd never really felt before. Much worse than losing a lover.

The skip. I'd said goodbye to my Brighton friends on the previous Saturday. I felt fine. I couldn't understand why they seemed concerned. Yes, I will be clearing out my dad's gear, but I'm over the grief, I said, it will be a good thing to do, a moving on, a catharsis. A magpie part of me was excited by how much of his stuff I could loot and use for myself. They looked at me funnily, gently sceptical. I could sense them biting their tongues. The next day I travelled across from Brighton to the New Forest. It was a beautiful, sunny, early summer's day and I boarded the train feeling buoyant and businesslike. I had to change trains at Havant and had nearly an hour to kill. So I walked round the rather grim new town, thought about sitting in a pub but in the end bought a sandwich and some crisps, and sat on the station platform in the sun.

It was then that it began to hit me. It started as a dim but persistent sense of unease and discomfort that I couldn't shake. I wasn't able to concentrate on the book I was reading. There were no specific thoughts, just a feeling of being hyper, brain working too quickly, unable to anchor itself on anything. Over the next few hours, this feeling worsened and I resolved to drink myself out of it. So after dinner I stayed up and knocked back a few whiskies from a Teacher's bottle I remember my father buying.

I slept badly, my rest disturbed by whisky dreams. The second I awoke at 7.30, I knew I was in trouble. I instantly felt the urge to sob with horrible force. It was like when you suddenly know you have to vomit violently and immediately. I pushed it back and forced myself out of bed. If I can keep busy, I said to myself, I won't have to feel this stuff. I washed, I breakfasted, then I went to the garage and waited for the arrival of the skip guys. The skip arrived, the metal open coffin that we were to dump eighty years of my father's life into. I looked at his golf shoes. I looked at the skip. And I broke down.

Will arrived and we cleared the garage. Once we were working I forgot to feel anything, and busied myself with the physical labour and the practicalities of how to dispose of what.

Eventually, in the evening, Will left and my mother went out to dinner with a friend. I was alone in the house. At last. I went to the bathroom, turned on the extractor fan to cover up the noise, knelt down as if to pray, and wailed and sobbed until my guts burnt.

***

When the moment came that the sun on Galjibag beach was just too intense, and when we reverted to English type and were a little embarrassed by our Garden of Eden state, we silently got dressed into our golf togs, and wandered back on to the fairway to find our balls. These turned out to be in the middle of the scrub, in a dense cluster of spindly leafless desert bushes. I had no time to worry about any snakes that would be slithering around this kind of land (king cobras are prevalent in Goa), as these bushes were home to swarms of giant dragonfly that, attracted by our sweat (and maybe the sea salt on our bodies), surrounded and nipped at us as we tried to play our shots out. Taking a three-iron, I attacked the swarm, beating them back, and had just enough time to aim and hit a very low short shot through gaps in the bushes on to the adjoining fairway. By the time I completed the shot, I looked like one of those Japanese endurance guys who make beards of wasps on their faces, except I was covered in buzzing, humming dragonflies the size of my hand. I ran out of the scrub, aiming a few last wild air slashes with the three-iron in their direction.

Not only was I now on the wrong fairway, but my line into the green was completely blocked by the small wood protecting it. Damn it, I thought. Hit high. I took my nine-iron and gave it all I had. Ooh. That felt good. I'd hit it really well, and I actually thought it was going to clear the tallest tree, but it caught it at the top and ricocheted off somewhere I couldn't see.

As the green and flag came into view I was struck by two beautiful sights. The first was the view of the estuary of the Talpone River. There was a small fishing boat harbour and lovely views of the hills on the other side of the estuary. The second glorious sight was my ball, resting four feet from the pin. It seems the ricochet had done me a favour, and I putted in for a very unlikely par after completing the longest and most enjoyable golf hole I have ever experienced.

15

Help Me, Obi-Wan

We were booked on a midnight train out of Goa, travelling from the remote one-platform, Wild West station of Canacona north for a thousand miles to Delhi. As it turned out the train did not arrive until 3.30 a.m. and we spent the night sitting on the balcony of the station, lit mosquito coils battling off yet more squadrons of insects determined to nibble our flesh. Our playing of computer games was interrupted with breaks while Tom sent frequent, lengthy and amorous texts to his very new girlfriend back in London.

We had spent the evening before this on the beach at Palolem one last time. Feeling like Dennis Hopper and Peter Fonda in *Easy Rider,* we revved up our mopeds and headed into the village to catch the sunset. I loved my moped. By this final evening, I was pretty confident, and had only nearly crashed once – two nights previously after three litre bottles of Kingfisher lager I had shot out of a T-junction, misjudged the parabola of the turn, then mistook the accelerator for the break, and came within an inch of smashing into a gift shop selling plastic Ganesh and Krishna ornaments for tourists.

The ride took ten minutes and we pushed it as we wanted to find the best place to get the money shot, the Jason Bourne shot, the main reason we were in Palolem in the first place. We adore the Jason Bourne trilogy, and have watched the movies together over and over. In Kashmir we watched all three films on consecutive nights.

Tom and India were never easy bedfellows. Tom's Nottinghamshire accent and inflection puzzled every tuk-tuk driver with whom he tried to communicate, and if – as in the UNESCO World Heritage-listed village of Mahabalipuram – the choice of activity was seeing 1,200 year-old Dravidian temples or lounging on the beach for a few hours, he'd always opt for the latter. I got to know his tastes: he doesn't do architecture, temples, palaces, tombs, Indian art or chats with the locals; he does do mountains, hills, big views, beaches and Aussie backpackers in bikinis. The Bourne connection with Palolem was one piece of bait to get him to India, and he took it. Now we just needed the photo to cap the experience.

It's a big, wide, rolling beach in Palolem and at the last minute I grabbed my sand-iron and a couple of balls, and scootered with the club between my legs, thinking that I might get in some bunker practice as the sun set.

Goan sunsets can be dazzling. Years ago I would sit on the beach at Benaulim, twenty miles north of here, along with the other sunset-chasers. We would gather silently – Indian and Western – find a spot in the sand, and gaze above the sea like it was some natural drive-in movie theatre. Often, we would remain there for an hour or so as the reds, yellows, pinks and oranges cascaded across the sky, as though God was playing with the brightest, warmest paints in the style of Jackson Pollock. It's the best free entertainment on earth.

In Palolem the sunsets had been pretty good, though the overrunning monsoon had meant lumpen, unpredictable cloud preventing the best spectacle most evenings. Tonight though, the skies were brewing up nicely, like an orchestra tuning to A and shuffling their scores before launching into Beethoven's *Eroica*.

We walked up and down the length of the beach, ditching a bloke who wanted to take us out on his boat to Butterfly Island, dismissing another guy who wanted to sell us some weed and quietly stalking two Scandinavian-looking blondes in skimpy swimwear who had come for the show.

I found a quiet spot and started practising chips and sand play. I am appalling at bunker shots. To play them correctly, you have to think counter-intuitively. Golf is for the most part an incredibly logical game of yardage, windspeed, club length, force and timing. To play a bunker shot, however, you have to angle your body forty-five degrees away from what feels like a natural stance, slice into the ball rather than hit it full on, aim for a spot an inch or so behind the ball rather than the bottom of the ball itself and, most of all, do a full swing and hit it hard. This is the toughest bit, mentally. Your brain is telling you that with a full swing you will send the ball 100 yards, whereas because of the friction the sand creates, you will in fact chip it out ten or twenty yards on to the green. If you hit it well.

It is impossible to hit, kick or throw a ball in the subcontinent without people wanting to join in or see what you are up to. It's great fun. Walk along any beach in Goa and there will be a game of football, cricket or volleyball going on that you can talk yourself into. Nothing gives a subcontinental cricketer more pleasure than bowling an Englishman out. I was walking the backstreets of Dhaka with some friends and we came across a wide alleyway behind the main street where some teenagers were playing cricket, using a battered oil barrel as the wicket. We joined in and soon there was a huge crowd all waiting to see these large, overweight, middle-aged English oafs make fools of themselves. When I went into bat I felt more pressure than at any other time in my cricket-playing life. If I'd just walked out at Eden Gardens in front of 100,000 screaming Calcuttans I would not have felt more nervous. I remembered my batting mantra: play straight, play late, play on the back foot, play down into the ground, keep your head down. This has got me through numerous matches over the years, occasionally turning out for friends' teams, batting at nine and fielding somewhere between fine leg, long leg and the car park. After thirty years of being bored sick fielding, I worked out that the way to cope with a dull few hours in the deep outfield is to have a nice glass of claret positioned the other side of the boundary ropes, which you sip on between overs; the ennui passes much better then.

The thing about Indian street-cricket is that the bowling contravenes every possible ICC rule on chucking. Street-bowlers make the controversial actions of Lasif Malinga and Muttiah Muralitharan seem conservative. The run up is the same as a Jimmy Anderson or a Shoaib Akhtar, but at the point of delivery there is no balletic leap then a beautiful elegant windmill of the bowling arm before releasing the ball at the zenith of its momentum arc. No, street-bowlers charge in then hurl the ball at your face with all their might like an angry baseball pitcher. If Douglas Jardine had encouraged Harold Larwood to bowl this sort of bodyline, there really would have been war, and Donald Bradman would have needed plastic surgery. After the first zinger of a ball, which I swipe at and miss (ignoring my defensive mantra), a stupid, old-fashioned part of me wants to shout out how unfair this is, how illegal, how unsporting, but I bite my tongue as I look at the forty or so Bangladeshi faces laughing at my humiliation. Even my mates are having a giggle. So I think, bugger it, imagine you are in the IPL, and the next ball I back slightly away to leg, charge down the wicket, and swipe it at full toss height over the heads of the bowler, the crowd and into the street behind. There is a boomy clang as the ball lands on a truck, followed by some muttered Bengali curses aimed in my direction.

So as I chipped and gently pitched in the sand at Palolem, and Tom furtively paced the beach looking for the ideal angle for a sunset shot, two twelve-year-old boys came up to me and watched me practice. Their names were Mingel and Joki, and they seemed puzzled by what I was doing. I realized this was because it looked a bit like cricket but clearly wasn't. I handed Mingel the club and showed him how to hold it and the basics of a swing. I put a ball down, and he tried to hit it in the way Virender Sehwag dispatches a cover drive to the boundary. He even did that characteristic flick of the wrist that great Indian batsmen do. I persisted with my lesson, but eventually they created a game where Joki bowled a golf bowl at Mingel, and he tried to hit it with the sand-iron as far as he could. So that would be cricket then. Or golfket.

The sunset had begun, and I chipped a few balls with my back to the sun, sea and island for Tom to get some pics. Mingel and Joki became our official ball boys as I lobbed balls around the beach, and also unofficial coaches – 'bad shot sir', 'slice shot', 'head too high' were the sort of comments they threw at me after every scuffed hack. I realized how hard it is to play a decent golf shot and make yourself photogenic at the same time. Hats off again to Ian Poulter, who has mastered this.

Tom was happy with the set up, and the sun was sinking low now. We knew we had only a few minutes left to get the Bourne shot, so we swapped roles. I took the camera, Tom disappeared to 100 yards away, and sprinted towards me.

The trick was to try to catch him as close to the camera as possible, in the most macho mid-jog pose, with eyes open, perfectly framed in the gap between island and shore, with the resplendent dying red sun's rays shining through him as if he was a stained glass saint on the west window at Chartres Cathedral at noon, the sun epiphanizing the space with the holiest light.

With the light nearly gone, and the boys becoming increasingly bewildered by our behaviour – though I remembered that whatever weird stuff you are doing in India there are millions doing weirder stuff than you – I got the shot, and Matt Damon's Jason was re-Bourne.

As we turned to go, I chucked one of my golf balls at Mingel and told him to keep it, but that it was for both him and Joki to play with. We headed to the nearby beach-front restaurant, and found a table facing out on to the water and the Valhallan dusk skies. When we were already nearly through our first Kingfisher, Mingel and Joki appeared at our table, their hair scuffed up. 'Please sir, we need to ask – whose ball is this? Did you give it to him or me?' They scowled at each other. If they'd been tiger cubs they'd be snarling and growling with dripping saliva hate. I realized they'd spent the last fifteen minutes squabbling and fighting over who had ownership of the golf ball. And that it had come to blows. I gave them another ball, and told them to go and play some golf, and not to fight anymore.

'Golf is a game for gentleman, boys!' I shouted as they ran off.

Tom went to an internet café to have a titillating MSN chat. I said I'd wait for him here. I was quite happy to sit, watch the gathering dark, stare out to sea, eavesdrop on the beach walkers and drink Kingfisher. I gazed into the waves thirty yards from me, and watched the foam lightly crash on to the shore. I heard that lovely, soothing, noisy-calm sound of sea rolling in and rolling out, scraping on sand and stones as its rip-pulls it back out. There was a gentle hubbub of conversation around me in the restaurant, and the place was lit by red lamps that cast a pleasing glow on the gloaming. I looked at those waves, and in the trippy space between awake and dozing, thought of Barton-on-Sea.

***

I look out on to the waves crashing against the cliffs thirty yards below at Barton. I am sitting on a wooden bench just off the cliff-top footpath with my father, facing the sea, with the golf course behind us. This part of the coast suffers from serious cliff erosion. All along from Bournemouth, ten miles to the west, out to Henry VIII's Hurst Castle, which signals the start of the Solent at Keyhaven to the east, England is being reclaimed by the sea that enabled it to build the biggest empire in history; the waves are now ruling Britannia. It looks like some giant surf monster has taken hungry bites out of the cliffs in this area, leaving jagged, rocky, tooth marks, vast walls of exposed chalk and Outback-red quarries of vertical sand crumbling into the surf below. This coast – my father's territory – is dotted with Martello towers, built to ward off the Nazis, and older fortifications like Hurst Castle, which was to be the first line of defence against possible invasions by the Spanish in the sixteenth century and, later, Napoleon. My father was born and bred in Hastings, where British history officially started in 1066. He even lived for a time in the village of Pevensey Bay, near Eastbourne, where the Norman Army first disembarked on to the English shore. I remember that stony, groined expanse well from childhood trips. The ruins of the Norman castle are still there, and I have reels of Super 8 cine film featuring me playing in the water on the very spot where the version of British history that I was taught commenced.

This thousand-year, imperial cause-and-effect narrative is coming to an end; from Pevensey Bay to the cliffs of Barton, England is imploding like a supernova, falling in on itself, slowly disappearing under the oceans like a modern-day Atlantis. In 3,000 years the British Empire will be as significant as that of the Assyrians, or the Persians, or India's Vijayanagar. I suspect that India's modern empire, whose birth we are witnessing at this moment, will be strong though. We are in a new imperial age where the East is rising again. Bangalore is the constantly momentous tip of this new expanding universe. It is inventing itself as it heads endlessly forward at light-speed; nothing is closing there; Bangalore is the new Nineveh, the new Alexandria, the new Athens, the new Rome, the new Byzantium, the new Vienna, the new London, the new New York.

As always it is gusty on these cliffs. It is early October and even though there are patches of autumn sunlight, we feel chilly and windswept as we huddle into our coats and scarves, looking towards the French coast, like Englishmen here have done in fear for a thousand years. Between us rests my father's elegant cane with its handle shaped like a golden tiger, and the cheddar and Branston sandwiches wrapped in foil that my mother hastily made up for us when we announced we were going for a drive.

Side by side, we look out to sea, like two old sailors on the prow of a tea clipper looking out for land; throughout our lives we have often sat like this. Most often in his car – on those long drives up the A1 twice a term when I was at university in Durham. Driving for him was his escape, his release, his relaxation. He invited only the chosen few to accompany him in this internal combustioned reverie. On the last day I will ever see him, I will sit side by side with him in bed; him drifting off into sleep now and then, waking up disoriented, or mumbling semi-coherently; we will sit like that for a few hours. I will know that I am silently saying goodbye to him as he starts the only journey that I cannot accompany him on.

But at Barton, six months previously, it was him helping me.

I'd crash-landed at my parents the previous day. I'd spent the previous three weeks in a sort of 'nervous exhaustion' hell, where I'd been unable to work, read, watch TV or sleep, and had been plagued by crippling headaches after lunch every day, which rendered me bedridden. I was having serious panic attacks throughout the day and night; taking a cocktail of sleeping pills, anti-depressants and paracetamol that was making me spaced out and nauseous; and seeing a psychoanalyst four times at week (at eight in the morning) to talk this all through. I was fucked. My anger, sorrow and stress all came out in a weird back-door way, masquerading as physical symptoms, which I'm sure looked to the outside world like hypochondria. Day after boring day rolled by with me lying on cushions in the sitting room listening to the radio, forcing myself out now and then to meet the odd indulgent friend for a cup of tea in the café by the canal before retreating back to the house with migraine thumping, hyperventilation and a sense of the world imploding on itself.

My parents were bewildered by my condition. As I chatted to my mother she commented how normal I seemed; how she couldn't tell there was anything wrong with me. And she didn't know the effort I was putting in to force down my hyperventilating lungs, maintain focus on what she was saying, attempt to stop the room from spinning, suppress the urge to scream. They were baffled that I didn't want to watch TV as we usually did as this was the other great lifelong hobby of my father and me. Any TV, as much as possible, all the time. I was brought up in the 1970s when being a goggle-eyed couch potato was not seen as being bad – it was just a way to relax, for the family to come together around modern technology. In a few years such addiction to TV would seem as immoral as smoking when pregnant. Which also went on all the time in the 1970s. And drinking.

It wasn't that I didn't want to watch *Inspector Morse* or *Midsomer Murders* with them; it was that I couldn't. The screen was too bright, I couldn't focus on John Nettles's super-chilled, sunbed face without the room spinning, my heart racing and my head pounding. My father and I had been huge fans of his Bergerac so I knew it wasn't his fault.

So I'd gone to bed early, pumped myself with pills, and had the usual hellish night's sleep filled with panic attacks, nightmares and nausea. In the morning the first thing I did after I awoke was run to the bathroom and throw up, violently retching up the combination of chemicals and my mother's chilli con carne from the previous evening. I realized I had properly hit rock bottom. But at least some deep honing instinct had propelled me home, to my parents and my ancestors; back to the gene pool. All through these days I became obsessed with photos of my family, of my past, of my parents and great-grandparents. I think I felt so splintered that I needed to piece back together who I was; my daily fear was of whiteout; of nothingness; that I would implode, in a reverse Big Bang, back to a vacuum, to nothing. Looking through the photos slowly helped remind me who I was, and how I had become; how I was a sum of all these people's personalities, sprinkled with the glitter of my own experience.

After I'd thrown up, flushed and cleaned up, my mother looked at me hard and sympathetically in that war generation way. She said simply, 'I think you should throw away those pills, they don't seem to be doing you any good.' I muttered something about how does she expect me to sleep without them. But I knew she was right. How could it be worse?

I staggered downstairs and forced down a cup of sweet tea, the back of my throat twitching at its milkiness and threatening another session 'driving the porcelain truck', as Billy Connolly once so brilliantly put it. My father was sitting in his armchair, looking at me with concern.

'Put some clothes on, mate, we're going for a drive,' he said.

I looked at his kind face, and thought, why not? What have I got to lose? I didn't care what I did; I just wanted to surrender, to sleep; if I was truly done for then bring on whatever there is to come.

We drove down the familiar country lanes. I didn't care where we went. I didn't care about anything. I just felt awful, and wanted him to drive, in silence, for hours and hours – maybe to Durham, stopping off at the McDonald's near Giggleswade aerodrome on the way and the service station just past Doncaster for tea and chips.

We drove between the fields of Hordle Lane, down past the nursery, to the Milford Road junction, and the old Royal Oak pub. From there, I was dimly aware of driving through the outskirts of New Milton, then a bit of Old Milton (which looks newer than New Milton) then we took a left at the crossroads where the Army and Navy Stores and the Taste of Peking takeaway sit, marooned on a nondescript corner. I knew then we were heading to Barton. And I knew that what was in his mind was not 'take him to the seaside' but 'take him to the golf course'.

We must have made a pathetic sight as we both hobbled from the car: an eighty-year-old man with chronic sciatica bent over a stick, wincing as his feet failed to grip on the uneven ground, and a seemingly fit but deranged-looking thirtysomething in dark shades concentrating on putting one foot in front of the other as the too bright, migrainous world spun around him.

Barton-on-Sea golf course is smart but unspectacular; what makes it a great course is its location and the views. Several of the holes are perched precariously on the edge of the cliff, a narrow public footpath and cycleway separating them from the plunge. As the sea has forced itself into the land over the last few years some of the holes have been redesigned to lie more inland. This is a golf course (like many of the great cliff-top sea-links) with built-in obsolescence. Similarly the Bangalore Golf Club (BGC) is holding out, but against the rampant property-market needs of the monster of aggressive capitalism. That ancient club (founded 1876) might well have to move soon from its century-old site in the middle of the city, because the value of its land is too great in this new Xanadu. The club rents the land off the government. The only thing stopping the government from selling this land is that some of them play golf there. The BGC is besieged by the quicksilver economic forces that its members themselves have created by being so successfully entrepreneurial. Barton-on-Sea Golf Club however, is fatalistically holding out, like Cnut, against the very waves themselves.

It was wonderful to stand on the footpath with my father and watch the (largely male and OAP) golfers hit a few balls. For the first time in weeks I felt a tiny flicker of calm and an old, more anchored sense of self than I had felt in weeks. Like two Dickensian cripples we walked up the side of a par-five and followed a fourball. All the players were over sixty, none could hit it far, but they were so accurate with their little seven and nine wood shots that it was comforting to watch. They'd be scoring one over on most holes; neat, efficient, flairless but honest old-man golf, the sort I hope to be playing in thirty years, when macho and competitive urges have been tempered by the soreness of old muscles and the amalgamated complaints of a battered nervous system.

The Barton golfers were something external to me I could focus on, and I fell in love with the game again. The beauty of a neat swing, the perfect effortlessness of a well-timed shot, the tactical brilliance needed to navigate around the hazards of a hole, the simple prettiness of the course, the impressive backdrop of the cliffs, the sea and the Isle of Wight looming in the distance; the wonderful truce between posh-private and prole-municipal land – the course is littered with public footpaths, so this course means upstairs frequently meets downstairs. Most of all, I love the arc of a well-executed shot, especially the beauty of a pitch. I think this is the main reason I play golf, to carve out beautiful shapes in the air with the invisible sine wave trajectory of a golf ball; then to hear the ball hit the ground and – if you're lucky – watch the delicious (usually unintentional) few seconds of back spin before the ball settles.

Golf is the most beautiful of games. The fact that on a good day I can tee-off on a par three and make a ball curve through the air for 180 yards and land within a few feet of a hole just two inches across still fills me with wonder. I'm still not sure how I do it. It's a mystical mix of intense muscle memory, being in the right relaxed brain zone, and being able like an artist to paint a gorgeous ball picture in the sky. Even the dourest golfers – the John Dalys, the Colin Montgomeries – or the trendiest – the Ian Poulters or Justin Roses – are sublime artists. Tiger is Picasso, Bach, Shakespeare and Jesus Christ all in one.

I suddenly really wanted to play: to feel the flow as I swing, to hear the wonderful thwack of a well hit ball, to ache in my legs a little after walking eighteen holes. But not only was the £50 green fee prohibitive, I told myself to be sensible – I could hardly walk, how did I expect to play golf? So after watching the golfers a bit more we rested on the bench, with our backs to the course, looking out to sea, both lost in our own thoughts, unable to find a common ground in dialogue, but content in each other's company.

That night I tried to sleep without sleeping pills for the first time in a month. Predictably, I barely slept at all and was hit by the familiar panic attacks, usually at the very edge of sleep, as though I didn't trust myself to surrender to it or I didn't trust that I would wake up again – and so my subconscious triggered a panic attack, shooting my body with adrenaline to fling me back into consciousness to deal with the emergency that had never existed. It was a night of a hundred false alarms of body death; my internal wiring had become severely crossed. Somehow I dropped off around six, then woke at 7.30 with the world spinning and more nausea in my guts. Another sprint to the bathroom and another hurl. I stared at my puke, still clutching the sides of the loo, my face dripping with sweat, my heart racing, my legs and arms shaking, my chest sore due to the volcanic vomit that it had violently evacuated. I couldn't see a way out of this. I was in hell, and there was nothing I or anybody else could do about it.

I had only one urge: to get out. I threw some clothes on and started walking, I think initially just to get a bit of fresh air, but I couldn't face returning home so I kept going, and kept going. At any moment I thought I would collapse, but didn't. After a few minutes the world would spin and I wouldn't be able to breathe, but I managed to keep going. And slowly I started to feel ever so slightly better. The countryside calmed me, the quiet and the animals – for the first time in my life I stopped to talk to and stroke a horse who put his inquisitive head over a gate. I thought: I will keep walking; when I can't go on, when I am on the point of collapse, I will call my father to pick me up in the Escort.

But I didn't collapse. I kept walking, following my nose, and heading down footpaths when I could. Suddenly I emerged from one of these wooded paths and found myself facing Barton-on-Sea Golf Club. This time I took one of the footpaths that criss-cross the course, and again felt that surge of 'I want to play' build inside me. I said hello to a few golfers, watched a few holes and started walking once more. But this time I had a mission: I was going to get my father out of his armchair, into the car, and on to the golf course.

I walked all the way home, via the cliff-top path, then through Keyford-on-Sea, up the long hill home. I must have walked about seven miles and seemed to be alive. I hadn't eaten anything, had barely slept and yet felt the best I'd felt in four weeks. 'Best' being a relative word denoting 'slightly less unbelievably shit', but still, progress.

I'd been gone for four hours and my parents were concerned – I had, after all, officially proclaimed myself a pretty much bedridden invalid – and were angry with me, clearly fearing that I'd had enough of the world and had lain down in the path of a combine harvester and been mashed up.

'You all right, mate? We were getting a bit worried about you,' said my dad.

I looked at my father moulded into his large soft armchair with a thick multicoloured patchwork woollen blanket draped over it, either for decoration or as a dust-cover.

'Want to play some golf?' I said.

He was up from that chair before I'd even finished the question.

We hurried to the garage, grabbed the clubs, jumped in the car and screeched out of the drive.

As we drove to the par-three course attached to the mobile-home holiday village at Bashley, we discussed our separate physical issues, and how that would affect the round. Mine was simple: could I hit a golf ball when I couldn't even focus on a page of newspaper or the TV, when daylight hurt my eyes, and when the world would suddenly lurch into a spin without notice? Dad's was more physical: with his chronic sciatica, he couldn't walk far; he certainly couldn't walk uphill, which seem to trigger an agonizing neural paralysis of his buttock muscles.

I found inspiration in a scene from *Star Wars*, when young Luke is struggling to use a light sabre while blindfolded. Obi Wan mumbles, 'Use the Force, Luke,' and Luke quickly uncovers the mystery of being a master sabre-wielder. Recently England batsman Kevin Pietersen has scored a hit on YouTube with a clip showing him, blindfolded, hit six after six. KP is clearly a young Jedi, too. I reckon KP would join the Emperor's Dark Side if the pay was good enough, though. Indeed, Darth Vader's hotchpotch platoon of renegade bounty hunters, enlisted to hunt down Han Solo, has the feel of an IPL squad, hastily and expensively assembled for one season only, with high rewards for all.

So I decided to find my inner Jedi. I would use the Force to hit the ball.

Dad's problems were less philosophical: how were we going to get him round the course with the minimum amount of pain? The first solution was that I would carry both our bags. Irritating, but a happy sacrifice if it would make him enjoy the game. This meant that he could hobble down the fairways hunched over his stick, while I brought his clubs to his ball, and caddy-like hand him the appropriate club. The second solution was that we decided Dad would not play any holes that involved going uphill. So we constructed a route for him whereby he played the first five holes, skipped out six, seven and eight whilst I dashed round them, then met me on the ninth tee for the final hole and the 200-yard walk slightly uphill to the car park.

And so, unexpectedly we found ourselves on the first

tee, next to the tennis courts, near the children's play area. I had never imagined I would be playing golf with my father again – it had been two years since we last played, and his walking had become so bad that we had tacitly admitted that he'd probably reached the end of his links career. And I had woken up only five hours ago in the same state of psychosomatic, hypochondriac, insomniac, nervous-breakdown hell that I had been in for the last month. Usually it was a big expedition to reach the kitchen to make a cuppa, and now here I was, after a seven-mile stroll, ready to tee-off.

I focused on the familiar pre-shot rituals. For the first time since I had left the house, I took off my shades and recoiled at the daylight that assaulted my pupils. I found a small green tee and a Titleist ball. I put another ball in my pocket for lost-ball emergencies. I found a small IKEA pencil in my golf bag, and marked the scorecard with the date and our names. I encouraged my glove on to my left hand and snapped its velcro shut; 120 yards, flat, straight, no hazards. I took out my thirty-year-old seven-iron, and just concentrated on swinging well, not trying to whack the ball, just feeling the rhythm of the swing. My practice swings were already the most exercise my body had undertaken in a month, and I could feel the migraine monster start to rouse at the base of my skull. I will pay for this later, I thought, but I can get through this game.

I swung back, half thinking about the twenty-point checklist all golfers have embedded in their semi-conscious routine as they progress through their swing: head still, feet still, bend the bottom, move the hips, slow backswing, pause fractionally at the top, smooth down, play through the ball, flick the wrist on impact, keep your line as you strike, bend your legs through the shot, don't think about sex.

I hit the ball. My God, it felt good. It felt like the first useful, rewarding thing I'd done in four weeks. It wasn't a great shot – a rather limp low chip that dawdled a hundred yards in the gentle rough to the right of the green, but frankly I was happy to have hit it at all. I put my shades back on. It was safer that way. Dad (using a driver!) played pretty much the same shot as me – which for him constituted a beauty – and so we hobbled and staggered up the fairway both feeling triumphant, but looking like the bewildered, huddled survivors of a terrible air raid.

Not only did I have the golf to focus on, but I also had to make sure my father was OK and the physical demands of my caddying duties to perform. My brain was busy, occupied, outside itself and I was feeling fine. Dad, however, managed the first hole and then started to struggle. We had a long break on the second tee as he chain-smoked two Mayfairs, massaged his leg and arse, and reassured me that he was all right.

He wasn't. He could hit the ball fine, and swinging a club gave him no pain at all. It was walking from one shot to the next (usually about forty yards) that rapidly caused him severe agony. After each hole we stopped for longer and longer smoke-and-rest breaks. He complained that his arse was becoming numb. I told him to take his time and chatted to him whilst practising edge of the green chips with my sand-iron. I didn't care if we were here all day. Life had lost its shape, I was assaulted by stress on all sides. At least here I felt a few moments of calm. Also, suddenly I was the carer and he was the invalid. I felt responsible for him.

We stood at the fourth tee and looked down the fairway. 'Oh God, it's so long,' he said. The hole was the longest on the course, but it was barely 230 yards. I realized how small my father's world had shrunk to as a result of his gradual physical impairments and general old-age perspective on the world. We used to play 500-yard holes together frequently. That's long. In India, Tom and I played 600-yard holes. That's really long. If you hit a good drive on the fourth at Bashley then you're one good chip away from a very decent par three. The hole was also slightly downhill, and I knew my father was also thinking 'Oh God, I've got to climb back up that hill if I play this hole, and it's gonna hurt.'

He didn't complete the hole, but almost crawled to the fifth tee to have a sit down and a smoke. We agreed to stick to the plan, and as I bustled around the next three holes, he tortoised up to the ninth tee, inch by inch. While I nearly sprinted around the holes I was tracking him at a distance as he edged his way up the gentle incline. He was a tough man and must have been in severe pain. After he died six months later of kidney failure, I wondered if he had been misdiagnosed all along, whether this 'sciatica' and 'neural pain' was really the first rumblings of a pervasive renal problem that would shut down his whole body. Rather than sciatica, perhaps on that golf course I was witnessing the first stages of my father dying. At the very point when he was saving me, making me regenerate, re-find who I am and piece me together, he was on his final journey. He was Obi-Wan to my Luke; maybe deep down he knew that he was destined to die soon.

Why does Obi-Wan stop fighting Vader? He lets Vader strike the fatal blow, after significantly catching Luke's eye. Why? Does the old generation need to martyr itself, to be sacrificed for the new generation to prosper? Of course, Obi-Wan is only a demi-father to Luke. Vader is his real father. Perhaps the old man sacrifices himself so as to rid Luke of the comfortable surrogate and enable him to face the horrible truth of his blood-father's identity? Then he has to slaughter his father, Greek style, after first having a moment's reconciliation before Vader's heart beats its last.

Maybe there was an element of Obi-Wan sacrifice in my father's behaviour those few days. Perhaps he knew that his last significant act would be to rescue me from my wilderness and bring me back. And the way he did that was through golf. Perhaps he'd saved up enough life-force to do that. To play a final round with me, like some great old Classical warrior, fighting through the pain, even when the death urge is commencing; an aged Leonidas fighting to the last at Thermopylae.

I could hit a ball fine. I was even experimenting with some of my father's forty-year-old clubs, using his clunky five wood off every tee – something I never do. When I rejoined him on the ninth tee, he looked abysmal, but still insisted we play the last hole. It took forever for him to walk up the fairway. It took twice as long to get from the ninth green back to the car. We were almost pausing after every step, with him wincing and grimacing in silent agony as the pain jabbed through him. When I used to play this course on my own it would take me forty-five or fifty minutes to get round the brisk nine holes. Our round that day took two-and-a-half hours. He putted in from three feet on the ninth green, using the putter he had played with ever since our very first beginners' games thirty years before. The ball plopped into the hole. I reached in, pulled the ball out for him and placed it into his open palm.

It was the last golf shot he would ever play.

For the next few days I followed the same routine: I'd force myself to get up, go for a long walk through the fields, lanes, coastal paths, and via Barton golf course, have a light lunch then persuade my father to drive me to the Bashley course. He didn't play, but was happy to sit in the car, smoking, thinking, reading the *Daily Mail*, until I turned up an hour later having sped through the nine holes on my own. Each day the migraines lessened; each day I felt more me, less ill, more confident; for the first time in four weeks I was able to sleep without sleeping pills. I was able to read again and then suddenly found that I could watch television without the world spinning. Within three days I felt 75 per cent normal, ready to face the world. Golf had saved me, home had saved me, my father had saved me.

'Help me, Obi-Wan, you are my only hope.'

16

The Cobras of Delhi

In India there was always an unnatural tension, and every man who pursued the physical aim of sexual relief was in danger of developing a cynical hardness . . . of those who tried sublimation, some chased polo balls and some chased partridges, some buried themselves in their work, and all became unmitigated nuisances through the narrowness of their conversation.

John Masters, *Bugles and a Tiger* (1956)

We took the train to Delhi, as a first stop on our journey up to the mountains in Kashmir: fifty-one hours in a second-class compartment, most of them spent lying on my berth, swatting cockroaches and watching the fields and plains of Karnataka, Maharashtra and Madhya Pradesh pass by. Our stomachs were suffering at this point, and it was actually quite pleasant to not have to do anything for a while. The other six berths in our carriage were taken by a group of enormous Sikh accountants, returning from a boys' trip to Goa. They were in giddy spirits, and shared food, card games and chat with us. They were very proud that India's No.1 golfer, Jeev Milkha Singh, is a Sikh.

Centred on the Punjab in north-western India, the Sikhs under Ranjit Singh had built up a formidable territory by the beginning of the nineteenth century. When he died in 1839, political chaos came to the region, and the British, tempted by the lush arable lands (the Punjab is known as 'The Garden of India') moved in with full force. Sikhism is the world's youngest mass religion – it's founder Guru Nanak Dev created the faith in the early sixteenth century. Sikhs are generally big guys – much taller and stronger than most other Indians. The British found them formidable opponents, and loyal strong troops after the Punjab had come under their control. More recently, in 1984, the assassination of Prime Minister Indira Gandhi by her Sikh bodyguards, in revenge for her authorizing an attack of the holiest Sikh temple in Amritsar, sparked an anti-Sikh pogrom. Thousands of Sikhs were massacred all over India. India is a vast country where all the faiths of the world are gathered, and get on with each other mostly harmoniously for long periods of time. Then, almost out of the blue, something sparks a period of the most savage brutality between former neighbours. And all returns to normal again.

***

So we arrived in Praharganj, the dossy budget-traveller centre of Delhi. Tom thought it was a 'slum'. It really isn't. The streets are thriving, lined with shopkeepers who seem to be doing a roaring trade. No cars can enter this warren; there's just too many people crowding the narrow bazaar streets. There's space for furiously honking tuk-tuks and milder, sweatier, bumpier cycle rickshaws, otherwise it's a pedestrian zone. And a cow zone. They wander around freely, getting in everyone's way, sleeping, eating the remains of people's lunches and shitting holy poo everywhere.

I suspect we were the first Englishmen to each drag a set of wheeled golf clubs up the Main Bazaar and into the tiny side alley where lay our hotel, the elaborately and inaccurately titled Supreme International. I wanted to break Tom in gently to Delhi, and thought I'd booked a nice mid-range number. I was expecting a boutique Holiday Inn. We got a dump. Dark, damp, and with air conditioning that would asthmatically clatter for hours in the middle of the night then switch off, causing the heat to become intensely claustrophobic. But it was a friendly dump. Prakash, from the hotel's restaurant, spotted we were up for a lager or two, so he would send one of his boys out to the liquor store to procure us India's ubiquitous watery, fizzy beer, Kingfisher. He then decanted the beer into a teapot, and served it to us in small china tea cups and saucers. Apparently they had no alcohol licence and this was a way to beat the system. We were also delighted that we could watch live England–Australia cricket on the Ten Sports Channel in our room. Prakash kept supplying us with tea caddies of lager whilst we followed the games into the early hours, until we had to tell him that we were drinkers, not alcoholics, and enough was enough.

The following morning we marched out again into the Praharganj heat and headed for Delhi Golf Club (DGC). The British built the course on land that used to situate one of the great Mogul emperor Akbar's palaces. Akbar was the grandfather of Shah Jahan, the man who built the Taj Mahal for his dead wife in the most narcissistic, sentimental gesture in history. The British kept the ruins of this palace and built a course around them. The Moguls were non-Indian invaders, like the British, establishing their empire in 1526 and ruling much of northern India until the British formally took over in the nineteenth century. Like the British at their best, Akbar had a very secular attitude to religious tolerance, and rather than ostracize the native Hindus, would involve them at all strata of government and society. So on this golf course, the last two imperial rulers of India had their pleasure grounds. When planning the trip, these thoughts captivated me and I would drool over internet images of the course. Tom started to call it my 'Indian golf porn'.

I think we were the only people who'd ever arrived at the DGC in a rickshaw. The car park was a sea of big silver cars and 4x4s. Private drivers huddled in a corner of the area, smartly dressed, smoking and, presumably, slagging off their bosses. The club itself has some very arcane systems. The first person you meet at the gates is the Caddy Master as you have to secure a caddy before paying for anything else. They then subtly follow you around – from driving range to pro shop to restaurant – for hours until you want to play, when they pop up to carry your bag. Before this trip the only other time I've ever had a caddy was on my stag golf day, when Andrew my best man (a brilliant academic but a non-golfer) carried my bag for me and plied me with a fine malt in between shots. His shot advice sucked but the whisky didn't. After securing a caddy you have to see the Starter by the first tee. He asks you your handicap, then asks you what it really is, gives you a time slot, then sends you back out of the gates into the car park to a grubby little office where you pay for your round. Here you also pay for your range balls. He gives you a token to take to the Range Master.

We walked to the range, past wonderful red-brick Mogul buildings. On top of the palace of the greatest Mogul emperor of them all, the latterday imperialists built a quintessentially British golf course. What a gesture, what symbolism from the new colonial rulers. At the very moment the Empire was about to collapse.

The range looked like a jungle. Very lush, green and tropical, with exotic vines and branches hanging over the boundary fences like natural reminders of the ephemeral nature of any empire. Behind each bay was a huge electric fan aimed at the back of the practising golfer. It was noon. It was incredibly hot. There wasn't much air to breathe. My brown shirt was already black through sweat. I took out my pitching wedge, chucked a ball down and did a very satisfying 100-yard pitch on to an imaginary green. The only other person on the range was a short Indian man in his late fifties whose caddy, as we had seen on other courses in India, put a new ball on the tee for his employer to hit after each shot, so that he didn't have to bend down.

After fifty balls each we were exhausted and drenched so we decided to head to the restaurant to rest and drink several litres of liquids. The veranda bar/restaurant is wonderfully perched by the eighteenth green, and would have a lovely view were it not for the thick netting that covers the course-side of it. Presumably too many over-hit green-bound pitches had found their way into members' lunches or had caused injury, so Health & Safety had decided this was safer, if much less aesthetically pleasing. Another arcane system here: you can't pay for anything at the restaurant using cash. You have to walk back out the gates, into the office in the car park where you paid your green fees. You then buy books of 100 rupees coupons that you can spend on your lunch. The books look like a bunch of raffle tickets from a 1960s church fete in the Cotswolds. Of the 100 rupees tokens you can only spend 80 of them, as the other 20 is apparently a 'surcharge'. You then go back to your table, and pay the waiter, who will give you change in coupons. Which you can then take back to the dingy office to convert back into rupees if you really want. Big signs say 'No Tipping'. This seems to be a club that really doesn't trust its staff to handle money.

During this trip I realized what a luxury are the long wide fairways in England. Indian fairways are usually narrow and surrounded by threatening rough. You have to play straight in India or you're stuffed.

In Delhi I also started to appreciate why we had caddies. They have three roles here: bag carriers; motivational coaches – 'Come on sir, head down, beautiful swing sir, nice follow through . . .'; and, most importantly, ball finders. These men know their course so well that it is extremely rare that you lose a ball. If they ever can't find your ball they look mortified, however much you tell them it doesn't matter. They look sad and mumble disconsolately, 'Sorry sir. Ball lost in jungle.' One caddy I had in Naldehra knew the place so well that he located balls by sound. You hit the ball. It sailed towards the deep forest rough. The caddy politely asked for silence and listened as the ball fell to earth. You might hear branches, leaves, a rustle then a plop or a splash. Then he would inevitably find the ball.

However, it seems the main reason to have a caddy in Delhi is as an anti-snake device. The rough throughout the course is writhing with cobras apparently. Sometimes they will saunter across the fairways. Just as in a Raj tiger-hunt when coolies were sent forward to find and lure the tiger back to the British huntsmen on elephants, so the caddies at the DGC plunge into the rough to find balls and avoid cobras. Sometimes they ask for a nine-iron as a weapon. Ibrahim and Sien, our caddies, loved a device in Tom's bag we call 'The Tool'. It's a long extendable rod with a ball-shaped hook at the end, designed for fishing balls out of water. Tom carries it around everywhere with him. The caddies thought this was great. Not for finding balls, but as a way to ward off and even trap irritated cobras who were sleeping on Sir's ball.

Walking to the third, I saw the other famous fauna on this course: peacocks, the national symbol of India. I was worried I might not see one; that like pandas, they may be shy, few in number and prefer to lie hidden. In fact, the peacocks are everywhere. On the tees, the fairways, the greens, often watching you as you putt, and quite annoyed if they are sitting in the line of your putt and you want to move them. They are handsome creatures. All the males are a deep exotic blue; they strut around haughtily, magnificently overseeing their golf course. At home we get excited if we see a rabbit or even a squirrel during a round.

I played some good golf. In fact, in retrospect it was probably the best round of the trip, card-wise. Perhaps the thrill of wandering amongst the ruins, the peacocks and the lush fairways inspired my tired mind to ego-free hitting.

By the end of the round the four of us – me, Tom and the caddies – were working as a smoothly oiled golf machine, bringing out the best in each other, spurring each other on. Both Tom and I parred the final hole, we all exchanged hearty handshakes, then Tom started to ask the caddies whether they would like to join us for a drink in the clubhouse. My India caste snobbery antennae immediately quivered frantically with the scale of this social faux-pas. I realized Ibrahim and Sien hadn't understood what he meant, and hissed at him about the inappropriateness of his kind offer. There is even a sign on the veranda saying 'No caddies beyond this point.' I felt myself a snob, brutally complying with the Indian master/servant, caste-based dynamic, perhaps even behaving like a prejudiced Britisher thinking of uneducated Indians merely as servants. We gave the boys double their fee to assuage our guilt. So for the four hours they spent with us in the terrible sun, carrying our heavy bags and battling snakes, they received £3.50 each.

We returned to the veranda. Unusually for a golf club in India no one seemed that chatty; certainly the members seemed utterly disinterested in us two big, sweat-drenched Englishmen. Perhaps word had got round about Tom's social near calamity and we were being snubbed?

***

Unable to sleep on the train from Delhi to Simla, I jotted down my father's top 20 favourite things:

Formula 1
Roast beef and Yorkshire pudding
Telling a funny story
Listening to a funny story
Making model boats
Watching television
Driving
Golf
Walton
Performing on stage
The RAF
Mountbatten
The Andrews Sisters
The 1950s
Cameras
Dogs, esp. Ruffles, our Afghan hound
A good tune
Whiskey and ginger ale before bed
Radio Times
Planning a route with a motoring atlas

. . . and ten things that made his blood boil:

Cheese

Garlic
Unions
Bad drivers (especially female)
Hospitals
Indian food
Chris Tarrant
Digital technology
People telling him how to fix things
A poor performance from the England football team.

I also dug out the notes I made on another train heading toward my father's funeral. Clutching these subject headings, I had made my semi off-the-cuff speech in the church. Now, listed, these notes seem like an indexed poem of his life:

Thank you for coming
Hastings, Uckfield
Dad v. good at telling stories
RAF
Simla '47
Planes
Film soc
Mountbatten – Avro York – Edinburgh VE Day projector
Rank – Powell & Pressburger
Elstree Studios – Focus Puller
Fixing televisions for the Krays
Technical mind – could fix anything
Hi-fi
EMI-HMV – Sixties – Beatles
Sanders Music Shop – 1963–81
Piano salesman – Brixton Riots

Knocking over Princess Diana
Doctor Who convention
Bentalls/chain smoking
Chris Tarrant – hatred of
Golf
Operatic Society
Lifetime chauffeur
Love of performance and showing off.

17

Snake Temple at Naldehra

Now India is a place where one mustn't take things too seriously. Too much work and too much energy kill a man as effectively as too much assorted vice or too much drink. Flirtation does not matter, because everyone is being transferred and either you or she leave the Station never to return.

Rudyard Kipling, *Plain Tales from the Hills* (1888)

Naldehra is probably the craziest, most surreal, split-your-sides-laughing golf course in the world.

It is situated twenty miles outside the British summer capital of Simla, 8,200 feet above sea level, with glorious views of the Himalayan foothills all around. It's tremendously beautiful, like playing golf on top of Ben Nevis in high summer and being able to look down into the amalgamated glens of a hundred shires.

I'm standing on the sixth tee, my breath taken away by

the gorgeous panorama of Himalayan magnificence in front of me, my body shaking through mirth. This hole is pure golf course design comedy. A 170-yard hole, you have several obstacles to overcome to get to the green. At seventy yards you have a large pond-cum-cesspit whose sludgy greeny-brown water looks toxic. Then there is a ten-foot tall wire fence, then the main road into Simla, with cars passing – and often stopping to watch. This strip of road is used by the men who run pony rides to rest, feed their animals and generally while away the day waiting for punters. If you clear these fellows and their ponies, there is another ten-foot fence, the green of the twelfth and finally, at the back of all this, the third green. We stood on the tee and giggled. This is seaside crazy golf on an epic scale with the risk of human and animal casualties. In such a vast country they crammed a golf course on to a postage stamp. I shout 'fore' . . . *before* I hit the ball to scatter the numerous random fairway dwellers. I had used my usually reliable six-iron, but didn't get hold of it properly. Normally the ball would settle down on the fringes of the green. In fact, the ball landed on the road, narrowly missing an ox-pulled cart, then rocketed off the concrete high into sky, clearing the second fence and landing twenty feet from the pin.

When the British built this golf course, I think the heat had got to them.

The story goes that one of the most dynamic viceroys, Lord Curzon (1899–1905), adored this beauty spot at which he and his family used to picnic. So much so that he named one of his daughters 'Naldehra' after the place. It is called 'Naldehra' after Naldeo, a Hindu snake god who is popular around here. Beside the seventh green today is a snake temple, devoted to this deity, where worshippers pray and chant whilst golfers whizz balls into the green, trying not to overhit and disrupt the snake-rites in the temple compound.

It must have been a very pleasant two-hour drive out of town along the road we took, which winds round the hills on a permanent bend. In the clubhouse there are pictures of the location from 1903, showing the view pretty much as it is now, but empty of all hint of civilization. The British loved their 'viewing points'. They could look down on what they owned.

Curzon was a golf man and after a few visits thought that Naldehra would be a fine spot to build a course. These links have amazing views, it's true. But there isn't enough room here for a nine-hole golf course, let alone an eighteen-hole one.

I was exhilarated. The height, scenery and preposterousness of the place were making me feel unburdened for the first time in ages. I was standing on top of the world with a golf bag. The vast blue mountains ahead of me shimmered in the noon sun. I looked down on ectoplasmic cloud drift; beautiful tall green pines surrounded me; it felt like there was barely a soul around for hundreds of miles; finally, after all these hard months, I had found an ephemeral sort of peace.

***

The British came to Simla to escape from the heat. We would make the same journey on our way to play at Naldehra. Delhi – always entertaining – was becoming hell. The temperature was in the mid-thirties centigrade, the humidity rocketing, and the noise and congestion reaching a point that had ceased to be thrilling and was now starting to rankle. I remembered those Kipling characters who went mad in the heat of the plains and I started to see why. The heat, noise, congestion and chaos can trigger a strange urban claustrophobia. Even getting anywhere was becoming a mission. After walking up a flight of stairs my shirt would be sodden. It was time to go, so we dragged our bags to the central rickshaw point in Main Bazaar at Praharganj, where the tuk-tuk wallahs wait and watch for the unwary tourist. It was decided by rickshaw-guy consensus that, as we were only going a mile up the road to New Delhi station, we could go in two cycle rickshaws. We protested that we had very heavy gear and it would be unfair to make a chap pull this using only the strength of his legs and the nineteenth-century engineering of a bike. We lost the argument, and headed to the station through the tiny medieval backstreets of Old Delhi with our clubs jutting out into the street. We were a wide load for these ancient narrow alleyways, riddled with potholes, burst drainpipes and aggressive oncoming traffic. Twice the clubs nearly fell off, and twice my driver whacked someone in the face. Neither the victims nor my driver seemed bothered so I wasn't.

We reached New Delhi station only to find after half an hour of persistent enquiries that, despite what everyone had told me, we were at the wrong station, and in fact it was Old Delhi station that we needed. We piled into a taxi and urged our guy to drive super quick as we were now in danger of missing the train north, and therefore our connection to Simla. A pacy, sweaty, cramped hour through Delhi's finest traffic and we made it. I tipped the driver for his celerity. He thought it wasn't enough.

There followed a nine-hour sweaty, humid, almost sleepless train ride to the mountain gateway town of Kalka, arriving at 4.30 a.m. Then a two-hour wait whilst very enjoyably watching the sun rise over the hills in this refreshingly cool, England-in-May climate, before we boarded the famous narrow gauge 'toy train' for the five-hour hop up the mountain to Simla (or Shimla as it is now known). India is famous for the engineering masterpieces that are their mountain railways up to the former Raj hill stations. Three have been granted UNESCO World Heritage Site status (so joining a list that includes Stonehenge, the Great Pyramids and the Great Wall of China): the Kalka–Simla route we were on; the Ooty–Mettupalayam trip in the south; and the most famous one – the Siliguri–Darjeeling steam train in the north-east that runs on track only two feet wide, and still uses the engines the British brought over when the railway was established in the 1880s. Our journey to Simla had felt arduous, but was nothing compared to the miserable journeys the British took to reach their vacation retreats before the railways were laid. According to a contemporary account by a W. B. Gladstone:

> Until 1878 the route from Calcutta to Darjeeling was by rail from Howrah (Calcutta) to Shaibganj, then by steam ferry across the Ganges to Carragola, thence by bullock cart to the river opposite Dingra Ghat; after crossing which, again by bullock cart to Siliguri, whence the ascent commenced via the Pankhabari road to Kurseong then Darjeeling. The whole journey took 5 to 6 days and was about as exhaustible and uncomfortable a journey as will be imagined.

The British built Simla to be like home. The town's a poem of homesick longing. The main purpose of the town was to stop the women going mad in the cities during the hot season. The male administrators of Empire mostly stayed in the cities to sweat and rule, and sent the memsahibs and the kids north to cool down. This, of course, had the effect of turning these hills stations into dens of refined gossip, scandal and debauchery. As Kipling slyly writes in *Plain Tales from the Hills*, extramarital affairs were common, especially as Simla was the town of choice for R&R by dashing officers in the northern Indian regiments. The women were bored and often still very young. It was not uncommon for rich greying civil servants to marry women fresh off the passage from England, twenty, thirty or more years younger than them. Once a year new girls arrived from Britain on the P&O ferries, specifically to look for husbands. These girls were called 'The Fishing Fleet'. Finding their still burning young passions unsatisfied by their absent ageing husbands, many of these very proper English gals turned to Sandhurst's finest to get through the night.

The figures are staggering. At the peak of the Raj's success – around 1880 – about 1,000 British bureaucrats, backed up by a white British Army of 20,000 men, governed a country of 300 million people. And the Viceroy ruled this empire from a remote village in the mountains. The gall. The cheek. Gandhi commented that this was 'government working from the 500th floor'. That they got away with it for so long – and I am no Raj apologist or glorifier – is historically astonishing.

And the homesick Brits wanted to make this mountain sanctuary as much like home as possible, so they recreated the Home Counties. Mock Tudor cottages nestle in the bush at Summer Hill; Christchurch, which dominates the central market place, wouldn't look out of place in Saffron Walden; the Gaiety Theatre, beautiful home of Raj amateur dramatics, still stands; the main strip looks typically rundown and Indian but if you examine the architecture underneath you can see the remains of a Stratford-upon-Avon facade – a sort of historical recreation of what England was or ought to have been; a Disneyland or Vegas version of the Kent Weald, with monkeys wandering round freely and China visible on a clear day. All this is epitomized by the architectural horror that is the Viceregal Lodge. This grey-stone Scottish baronial castle was where the Viceroy and the upper echelons of the government of India decamped. Three miles outside Simla town centre, it is a fantasy of the lost Scotland of Ivanhoe, so out of place and yet so much the defining symbol of the surrealism that this clash of cultures produced. The tragedy of India's Partition was mapped out here.

***

I hole out for a four on the sixth and contemplate the uphill seventh – the snake temple hole. Naldehra is addictive. I've always had a fantasy of building a full-scale crazy golf course, and this is the nearest I've found to it.

No one else is playing the course. Indeed, I get the feeling that Naldehra is often deserted apart from the strolling Indian tourists. A twentysomething holidaying couple suddenly appear as I'm teeing up. They insist on taking a picture of me, in the way people in a zoo snap a rare species of wildebeest. They seem to find it amusing that there I am, dressed in golf gear, playing golf on a golf course.

After I putt in, I leave Tom and walk over to the temple and startle a group of worshippers who have just pulled up on ponies. I make out I am looking for a ball and let them pray uninterrupted. When they have gone I return to the temple, hoping – as in those other snake temples in south Asia – that it will be full of writhing serpents, like the pit in *Raiders of the Lost Ark*. But there aren't any, just a few paintings of the beasts and a lit fire. It's the first religious building I've entered since my father's funeral, and I spend a few moments thinking of him and what he would make of this eccentric golf course. I feel closer to him here than ever.

There are no snakes out on the course either – though there are armies of hissing, snarling monkeys. In fact, for a spot so devoted to the slippery critters, it is distinctly un-serpenty.

Few of the holes are particularly visible from the tees. It's not that they are clever dog-legs, more that right in front of you as you tee off there is a bank of sixty foot pine-like deodar trees. You have no idea where to hit. There are no maps on the scorecard or at the tee-side, so you just . . . guess. Or ask one of the assortment of green-keepers, children and caddies that lope around the course doing not particularly very much but point you roughly in the right direction. Then they laugh at your shots in gently sarcastic Hindi. So you five-iron it over the trees, over the jungly ditch, back over the road and just sort of hope. Of course, when you get to the other side of the road it's very difficult to find your ball, as you haven't see it land, natural hazards abound and the lie of the land is pretty rough. In fact, there aren't really any fairways as such. The whole bank of hill has been mown so that it all has a sort of light rough feel. Then you reach the green where the rough is slightly lighter. At this point we often discovered that we had been aiming for completely the wrong green. In the end we just made it up. Never have I had to hit the ball so hard on greens, and never have I lost so many balls reaching them. Perfectly good tee shots are lost as the ball could have landed, well, anywhere in a fifty-yard radius. It's fun, but slightly expensive fun.

While I am sitting on the clubhouse veranda, enjoying the blissful view, Rohan, the office manager, comes up to me and goes through my clubs. He likes the look of my Texan sixty-degree lob wedge (£15 on Amazon), so I let him try it. I'd seen him play yesterday with one of the caddies. He was great. Clearly knowing the course better than anyone, he rode it like a master rodeo star taming an unruly mule. He spends a quarter of an hour making exquisite chips with my club, and then spends the same time with my putter. I can't even remember which branch of Save the Children I bought it in. Rohan loves the lob wedge, and we talk about club prices, how you can get golf gear in India and the course in general. He really wants a fifty-six-degree lob wedge. Rohan has something about him of the pioneer in a remote area who has a passionate hobby that the savages around him can't begin to comprehend.

We take tea together and look out on the view, exactly as Curzon saw it a century ago, and dream our golf dreams.

18

Adwaita, the All-Seeing Tortoise of Madras

Sandown Park racecourse in Esher, Surrey, was where I first learned to play golf properly and fell in love with the game. After seeing my interest in hitting a white ball with a stick develop through South Coast Crazy Golf sessions, and a few goes on a pitch-and-putt at a hotel in Peebles, Scotland, my father decided to take us up a notch. At the age of nine or ten we started to go to the driving range at Sandown, then we progressed to their pitch-and-putt course; after a while he judged me proficient enough to have a go on its par-three course, and I was hooked. As I would find in Chennai, the golf area was encircled by the vast grandstand of the racetrack. The best bit of each trip was that after we'd finished our golf we would head to the clubhouse. Here, I'd be in paradise – Dad would buy me Coke and give me a handful of old 10p coins that I could ram into the Space Invaders machine. I was in high-tech heaven, consumed by intergalactic mega-blaster fantasies, and I never wanted to leave. When I ran out of 10ps we'd look round the pro shop and sometimes, if he was feeling flush, he'd buy me a second-hand club for my slowly developing bag. The thrill of getting a 'new' five-iron was marginally less than spending ten minutes zapping aliens, but it was still pretty good. I still love pro shops – especially the immense wish-fulfilment golf shops in the United States, where there is a club made for every possible golfing need. I also still love golf-club bars; I think in an odd way I feel at peace in them; perhaps I feel connected back to our Sandown trips.

Now the whole golf complex at Sandown – they also manage to squeeze in an eighteen-hole par-five course, too, within the circumference of the race track – is a great practice facility, but holds no great pleasure or challenge or aesthetic appeal to most golfers. I was very disappointed that this was exactly what I felt when I looked out over the Madras Gymkhana Club course.

***

Pathos, piety, courage – they exist, but are identical, and so is filth. Everything exists, nothing has value.

E. M. Forster, *A Passage to India* (1924)

Delhi never changed its name. It just became 'New'. Calcutta became 'Kolkata' but no one uses this dyslexic version of the original – except for the Kolkata Knight Riders IPL cricket team. Bombay became 'Mumbai', but in India about 50 per cent of the population still thinks of it as 'Bombay' . . . young and old, the city's identity seems tied up in its Bombayness rather than its Mumbai-ity. 'Bollywood' will never be referred to as 'Mumbywood'. Bangalore was rechristened 'Bengaluru', but you'd be laughed at if you used this word to refer to the IT metropolis. Even the IPL team ignores the PC name change and opts to be called 'Royal Challenge Bangalore' – a seeming endorsement of both British and Mogul empires in the most forward-looking city in the world. Even the airport – that stunning new Gateway to India – goes by the cumbersome title of Bangalore-Bengaluru International Airport, as though they know no one is going to take the name-change seriously. Almost all the major cities have changed their names in the last fifteen years to rid themselves of any anglicization attached to their monikers. The results have been mixed.

'Madras', however, is dead. That most beautiful of names – a shortening of the fishing village name of 'Madrasapattinam', near where the East India Company set up a trading post in the seventeenth century – is buried. I have never heard anyone in India refer to 'Madras'. Indeed, the only reason we are all so familiar with the sound of the word is because of the medium-hot Chicken dish you find on every curry house menu in Britain. No, old Madras is dead, and new Chennai has risen. And it is booming. And it sucks.

The city is India's second largest exporter of software and information technology. A major chunk of India's car manufacturing industry is also based around the city – Chennai accounts for 60 per cent of the country's automotive exports. There is a huge Korean automobile presence. Most of the top honchos' wives play golf every day.

Every Chennaite I met in the hills was so proud of their city . . . sure it was hot, they would say to me, but there is so much to see, it is a beautiful city. I was recommended several times to check out the shrine of St Thomas (he of doubting fame), who is alleged to have died there in AD 72. Go see the 'bleeding cross', they told me – apparently a cross that the Apostle clutched as he lay dying, and which periodically still bleeds in that Catholic miracle way.

Every Indian non-Chennaite I'd ever met was always less enthusiastic about a visit to the east-coast city. It's too hot, too busy, too polluted, too noisy, it's hard to get around and it has no centre, I heard over and over again. The Western-oriented guidebooks echoed this: don't go there unless you have to. But I went with an open mind. I'd been to so many subcontinental cities that I thought I could deal with anything Chennai could hurl at me. I was wrong.

The heat sent me mad. We were staying in the wonderfully incongruously named Hotel Himalaya (the nearest Himalayan peak being 1,000 miles away – a bit like calling a London hotel 'Hotel Urals'). Whenever we could we spent as much time as possible lying, semi-comatose, under our ceiling fans with the smelly, clanking air-conditioning unit on full blast ('high freeze' setting). Just to go to the nearest restaurant a hundred yards away was a massive effort; we would arrive there drenched in sweat, our showers of five minutes previously counting for little; I had a throbbing headache at the base of my skull for four days; I couldn't sleep because of the heat; and if the heat didn't keep you awake at night, then the TARDIS-like wheezing, groaning noises of the air-conditioning unit's ancient parts did the job instead.

Chennai really is a city with no centre: a collection of suburbs all loosely stuck together, but with no sense – as in Delhi, Mumbai or Calcutta – of a metropolis cored around a central point that gets increasingly 'more Chennai' as you move towards it. It is also the first time in an Indian city when I found it impossible to move around on foot. One of the pleasures in Mumbai, for instance, is simply strolling around the island. Sure, there are far too many people, but you can still move; there is still something resembling a sidewalk. In Chennai, pedestrians, cars, trucks, rickshaws, motorbikes and cows all compete for the same narrow roads; or else the roads are vast new superstructures designed solely for cars. It's like LA crossed with the Souk in Marrakech.

But the city does feel vibrant and successful; it's the only Indian city where I've never seen a beggar and never seen a slum. Though I'm sure they exist, they seem invisible to the casual eye, unlike in Mumbai or Calcutta, say, where the slums are an inescapable part of the urban experience. It is clean; the gigantic work-in-progress cricket ground of the Chennai Super Kings rises like a half-completed Death Star above the city. Even incomplete it packs in 70,000 fans for every match. Lord's in London, the rather smugly self-titled 'home of cricket', seats 28,000. And at the end of our road the vast new local government building similarly ascends into the sky in ultra-new, nearly finished architectural glory.

***

I stand astonished at my own moderation.

Robert Clive (1772)

Robert Clive came into my life very early. I remember vividly how we were taught history at my prep school. There was no History at all until you moved up to the Fourth Form at the age of eight. This was my historical learning's Year Zero. Here you were handed a text book about Stone Age man; once you'd worked through that for a few weeks, you got given the one on the Bronze Age, then the Iron Age, then the Romans, then the Dark Ages. As you progressed through the school, you became closer historically to the present day and indoctrinated by a constant narrative stream of mythologized British imperial history, a version of history at which Churchill would have swooned. This long laborious chronological journey through history (Why start at the really dull bits? Why not kick in with the Tudors?) was structured around two things: the great historical folk myth events (the Spanish Armada, the Gunpowder Plot, the Black Hole of Calcutta) and 'great' men. This was being taught to me only thirty years after India had gained its independence. It was still a pink-bits-of-the-map, British imperial version of events that saw global history – certainly from 1066 onwards – as the actions of a few great Englishmen who spun the axis of the globe.

One of these Englishmen we were taught to revere was Robert Clive, the man who tamed India for British trade and whose presence still lingers in parts of Chennai. I lapped it up. We who grew up in the 1970s inherited the befuddled, disbelieving post-imperial hangover of our fathers; many of them hadn't come to terms with the loss of 'greatness', the rapid diminution of the Empire after the war. And we, their children, were still being taught the anglocentric history they had learned. Britannia, as far as I was concerned, really did still rule the waves. That I thought this during the Winter of Discontent in 1978–9, when I can vividly remember power cuts, the four- and three-day week, rubbish not being collected and the miners' and gravediggers' strikes, says an awful lot about the power of the stories we tell our children, even when they are in such stark contrast to the actual world around them.

So Clive of India was joined by Wolfe of Canada, Gordon of Khartoum, Cecil Rhodes, Scott of the Antarctic, Francis Younghusband, Lawrence of Arabia (this assisted by my father's love of the David Lean film) and the rest of the deeply flawed, often tragic, bunch of repressed right-wing psychopaths we were told to admire. Perhaps Lawrence is an exception here – more disturbed than any of them, but a man who was certainly motivated by more than the profit principle or imperial glory.

When I was a child we frequently went on Sunday afternoon mini-rambles. Ostensibly we went to walk the dogs, but also because I loved playing in woods, and at that point my parents still seemed to enjoy trekking through the green-belt hinterland. There was a great choice of woods, forests and heaths near us, and so twice a week we would end up at Oxshott Woods, West End Lane, Claygate Woods, Esher Common or down by the rivers Thames or Wey. One of the other places where we went was the grounds of Claremont House, near the commuter stock-broker haven of Oxshott. This is a large, impressive eighteenth-century Palladian pile, with expansive grassy meadows around it, and pretty, more formally landscaped gardens, replete with lakes, follies and flower features. Years later when I played cricket and hockey for my senior school, I would often find myself back at Claremont, which since the 1920s has housed a Christian Science public school (Michaela Strachan and Joyce Grenfell are the most notable alumni). Even as a young boy playing cricket I remember how appealing, how nostalgic, how *English* those days at Claremont felt. I recall once having completed my innings and lying on my back behind the boundary, the sun creating psychedelic shapes on the insides of my closed eyes, waiting leisurely for the rest of my team to bat out their overs. I felt content, filled with a sort of old reassuring British Ready Brek of the soul.

The house belonged to Robert Clive. He bought it in 1768, enlisted the services of the great Enlightenment designer Capability Brown to redesign it and its pleasure gardens, and reputedly spent £100,000 on its redevelopment. The scheme was so ambitious that Clive never saw it completed – he died in 1774, just before the house was fully finished. He had barely spent a night there. It remains the greatest folly of a preposterous man. The New Delhi of one Anglo–Indian egomaniac.

***

On a golf-free day we rickshawed up to Fort St George, the East India Company's original seventeenth-century trading post, which became the administration centre of the Raj

Madras Presidency. It was wonderful. Nowhere in India is there such a large and intact collection of British-era buildings in such good shape, and they are still used – often for the same purpose for which they were built.

By the early eighteenth century, the British East India Company, from their bases in Bombay, Calcutta and Madras, has secured a significant foothold in the subcontinent. Each of these three 'presidencies' operated independently and reported to the company's directors and shareholders back in London. The Company would forge links with local rulers – often offering them use of the company's military resources to quell local disturbances in return for trade concessions. Increasingly, the British Army was used to further and defend the East India Company's commercial exploitation of the country – thus, a private company, answerable to shareholders, making huge profits for a handful of individuals, had the might of the British Navy and Army at its disposal. Perhaps all that has changed in 300 years is that oil has replaced opium, tea, spices and cotton as the commodity national armies protect.

The Fort St George complex includes a building dating from 1795, which houses the best museum in India for Raj ephemera. An imposing, eight-foot tall white marble statue of Lord Cornwallis, also depicting the surrender of two sons of Tipu Sultan, greets the visitor. On the walls of the ballroom upstairs hang portraits of various lofty Brits including a rather pompous, fat-looking Robert Clive, presumably late in his life. Clive's image has lasted here and elsewhere in India. In Whitehall, Clive's statue commands the most scenic position of all the imperial heroes honoured in stone around Westminster. It stands outside the old India Office at the top of a grand set of steps, and around its base are illustrated bronze plates of his triumphs in India. Despite its impressive look and aspect, Clive's statue is very much tucked away, unlike those of Churchill or Montgomery. There is, perhaps, a sense of shame in its placement, as though we would all be happy if people *didn't* see it.

Clive's most enduring legacy, though, is Adwaita, his pet giant tortoise. This rare animal was presented as a gift to Clive in the early 1770s, presumably as a gesture of respect from a local ruler. These tortoises are very rare and only found in the four island-atoll of Aldabra in the Seychelles. The remarkable thing is that *Adwaita has only just died.* In March 2006 she expired in a Calcutta zoo. There is some dispute about exactly how old she was, and her corpse awaits a full carbon-dating analysis, but it is thought she was around 250 years old. Clive himself – rogue, chancer, social climber, class renegade, general, pirate – was not so long lived; always prone to depression and by then painfully physically ill, he became addicted to opium, faced censure by Parliament for the way he amassed his wealth and committed suicide by stabbing himself with a pen knife at the age of forty-nine.

***

The Madras Gymkhana Club Golf Annexe is a golf course in the middle of the city's famous old racecourse – a tropical Sandown Park with a post-apocalypse visual panorama. There has been horseracing here since 1777, before that the seventy-five acre site was used as a training ground for the East India Company's army. By 1837 the Madras Club was formed to administer the place and the golf club was founded in 1886. After several days lounging around Chennai, unable to play golf due to the weekend, tournaments, Gandhi's birthday and an inability to get up at a decent time, we finally reached the club. I wasn't looking forward to it. The course was uninspiring, and the gloopy migraine-inducing overcast weather had put me in a terrible mood that was entering its third day. But, I reassured myself, this is what I'm here for, all I have to do is knock a golf ball round for a few hours, then I'll be back under the fan and in the cold shower.

I have never enjoyed a round of golf less. We turned into the golf annexe entrance in our little fragile tuk-tuk and were assaulted, even before the rickshaw had stopped, by about fifteen caddies, all of whom were grabbing our golf bags, trying to be the first to pull them out of the vehicle and thus claim us for the round; it was pandemonium. With a dozen voices shouting at us, Shaib, our rickshaw guy, both scared that his treasured tuk-tuk was about to be damaged and slightly less worried that he was going to damage one of the caddies, skidded to an abrupt halt, sending up a candyfloss cloud of dark brown dirt. A dozen faces jabbered at us and our clothes were pulled in the relentless struggle to grab our golf bags. I have been in rock bands were I have felt a tiny sense of the mania of fans; but this is the only time in my life that I have felt anything close to the fear The Beatles must have felt every night as they were mobbed in and out of their cars whenever they arrived at a gig. We couldn't get out of the rickshaw, there were too many bodies blocking us. I felt stupidly claustrophobic. I clutched my bag firmly and said in a calmish voice, 'Please let us get out, I will carry my bag.' Gradually we were able to escape the rickshaw, but not the hands grabbing at the bag and our shirts. We were now surrounded. I needed to do something, so seeing the security guard nearby with his signing-in book, I headed to his table with intent. As I leant over to sign, still the hands were grabbing me and I lost my cool.

'Will you please take your hands off my bag and stop pulling my shirt?' I said. Well, semi-shouted. All right, shouted. There was a hush. Then slowly they backed off. Fuck. I felt stupid. This rubbish city, this crappy golf course and this horrible weather; and I end up shouting at people who will carry my bag on their shoulders for four hours in this horrible climate for a pittance. I felt I'd found my Raj voice, and I was ashamed.

It was my Marabar Caves, *Passage to India* moment. It's the time in India when the heat and the alienation bursts inside a European's head and they see imaginary demons, filtered through centuries of repressed colonial prejudice, and unspoken terrors.

So we carried our own bags the 300 yards to the clubhouse. Not a good look, along with, Pied Piper-like, a trail of caddies sauntering behind us, pretending not to be following us just in case I shouted at them again. There was no one at the clubhouse. Two of the caddies were still nearby and sheepishly told us to just play, we could pay later.

I played terrible golf. I started to hate our caddies, the course was tatty and whenever I looked up in search of a pleasing view to calm my soul I was faced with a *Mad Max* vista of battered and burned-out buildings that circle the racecourse. Worst of all, Tom was playing the best eighteen holes of his life, destroying me at every hole and playing like he just breezed around golf courses, scoring in the mid-eighties, every day. He was fantastic. Which made my own mood even worse. I realized how churlishly competitive I was; I'm wise and post-imperial enough to go through this guilty self-laceration, but to the outside world I probably just seemed a stroppy snob.

The caddies started to skip holes. We had no idea of the course layout – Indian courses rarely follow any sort of logic and are often very badly signposted. There were no scorecards with course maps on either, so we were relying on the caddies to show us the way. We went from the eighth green to the tenth tee. When I asked why we didn't play the ninth, I was told that we were avoiding course congestion; but apart from a few Korean housewives playing their genteel and elegant little shots in scattered corners of the course, it was empty. My caddy also lost interest in looking for my ball if it went into the rough. Even when he did look, he rarely found it, and often was thirty yards or so away from where it had landed. In England, of course, unless you are a tournament player, you never have the luxury of a caddy, so to even feel angry about it felt petulant. But it was one of those days.

By the fifteenth, the caddies were clearly bored sick. 'We play one more then finish,' I was told. There would have been nothing I would have preferred than to escape this nasty golf course there and then. But there was a principle here. 'No, we play all eighteen,' I said. The caddies scowled, muttered some Tamil curses then rolled their heads sulkily in an if-you-say-so sort of way. I hacked my way through the last three holes; Tom gracefully parred the lot and was euphoric. He'd carded 86 – easily his best ever score on any course. I was way over 100 and in a sulk. I stomped off the course, ignoring the caddies' pleas to pay them. My head was throbbing horribly and I felt like munching a whole packet of paracetamol and drinking two litres of water. I was soaked from sweat all over and just wanted to flee. An extra sting was that the round was twice as much as we normally pay – and on this grubby flat wasteland.

In the end, we gave the caddies double their prescribed fee, as normal. If we like our caddies we give them triple. We didn't like these two and they kicked off at us for not tipping them enough.

As we exited the course complex a big Hyundai 4x4 pulled up. It was surrounded by a dozen faces and sets of grabbing hands as its bemused, immaculately dressed Korean couple emerged from inside.

This round of golf had brought out something distasteful in me: an old odour of British snobbery and lack of connection with India. Maybe for all my travels, I was never really leaving the safety of the cantonment, the British

Residency Compound, and when I did, I cried 'rape' like Adela Quested in *A Passage to India,* when nothing of the sort ever happened. It was just India getting to me.

***

One more day to go in Chennai, then we could run. Tom, heading home and leaving me with a final week on my own, had a plane to catch at 4 p.m. the next day so, with little enthusiasm, we set our alarm for 6 a.m. The plan was to play as many holes at the Cosmopolitan Club as we could before 11.30 a.m. and then get Tom to the airport as soon as possible. Somehow we got out of bed; somehow we found a rickshaw. I bought some samosas and bananas in a roadside shack which we munched on Chennai's version of the North Circular, which was already starting to heave and fart with pre rush-hour traffic. I felt sick. My skull pounded. Already it was getting warm. I wanted to be in Bangalore, eating McDonald's and shopping for denim jeans and Nike shoes in designer shops.

We drove to the suburb of Nandanam and reached the Cosmo. The course was built in 1873, but was significantly redesigned by Australian golf champion and India course-design guru Peter Thomson more recently. What we could see of the course as we bumped our precarious way down the long drive lifted us. Firstly, it was very green, this lush impression augmented by the blossom on the trees up the fairways and the handsome tamarinds that seemed to punctuate the holes. I even glimpsed a deer in the bushes near a green. The Gymkhana Club famously has no trees. Not one. At the Cosmo, I realized how much I like them. Perhaps this is a legacy of growing up in Surrey where there are more trees per capita than in any other county in the UK. Perhaps I just like the photosynthesizing vibe. I'm a sucker for chlorophyll.

I took a breath, strolled into the pro shop and met the nicest person in Chennai – the wonderful Mr J. A. Das, who seemed to be pro shop manager, starter and general admin guy.

I recalled the conversation I had with him two days previously when I was trying to blag us a round on a tournament day: 'Hello there, we'd like to play golf please, would that be possible? We are on a golf tour of India, where we are playing all the courses that the British built. We have just come from Delhi, Simla and Kashmir, where we have played on their fine courses, and would be honoured if you let us play at the Cosmo.' The usual patter, now delivered, I thought, almost convincingly. Somewhere we were playing with ancient Raj dynamics; somewhere we were embracing the archetype of the eccentric English Indian-phile sahib; sometimes I'm sure we just came across as a couple of Hugh Grant-like dolts who were taking the piss.

'OK. No problem, it is always a pleasure to welcome foreign visitors to our club,' said Mr Das. 'When would you like to play?'

We looked at him, a little surprised.

'Er . . . now,' I said.

Mr Das looked pained.

'Oh blast,' he said. He seemed in agony. 'I am so sorry, but that is not possible as a tournament has just started; if you had come earlier you could have played, but now, no.'

'Oh. That's a shame . . .' I said, then pulled out my trump card. 'We have brought our own clubs . . .'

Mr Das liked the sound of our golf bags; thank God he didn't look at my battered bag with its broken zips and my raggle-taggle collection of second-hand golf clubs, but he still maintained with regret that we could not play today. Or tomorrow. But Monday might be possible . . . and it was!

Mr Das cheerily welcomed us and fixed us up with two caddies. The early morning sun had just come out, and the course looked tempting, ripe and, above all, very, very green. At 7.45 we teed off, Tom straight down the fairway, me slicing into the deep trees on the left. Lost ball. Never mind, we were on a mission: to do as many holes as we could as quickly as we could, then leave. We had a great few hours; the course is really enjoyable, one of the best maintained in India, and with the most true and inviting greens I have seen in the country. Often the greens, even on the most famous courses, are bumpy, holey, stony and almost impossible to read.

We both played well; while none of the holes are *beautiful* as such, playing at the Cosmo is an enjoyable experience; in fact, a very English golf experience with driving and pitching over several walls/roads/water tanks/rickshaws/schoolchildren/ladies with cows adding to the fun.

We started to skip holes as we felt time was running out, ending up on the eighteenth tee at 11.20. On this 403 yard, dog-leg par four, I hit an average tee shot that gave me a good, straight line into the green. I scuffed my five-iron second shot, leaving me 180 yards or so to the pin. The problem was that the green, lying in front of the clubhouse, was the other side of a road, and was protected by a fence. The sensible shot would have been to lay it up then pitch in . . . but then I'd be looking at a six or worse. What the hell. I was feeling good. All the gyps and self-hatred of yesterday were gone. I grabbed the five-iron again and hit a scorcher – first bounce just on the green side of the road, through the meshed fence and delicately braking to nestle on the tabletop, ten feet from the hole. I was delighted. These quick few holes had made me love golf again and made me feel I could play it a bit. At the Gymkhana Club, I couldn't function as a decent human being, let alone a golfer. I two-putted, of course. But I could at least leave Chennai on a high, after several very trying days.

We said our goodbyes to Mr Das, then in the full heat of

the noonday sun, marched out of the Cosmo, with our golf bags on our backs like two gunslingers quitting town at the end of a movie, job done.

We had to walk for fifteen minutes until we found a rickshaw, passing the drivers of all the Korean ladies and well-to-do old Indian boys who were the other players at the Cosmo that morning. I was certain that I heard chuckles, sniggers, contemptuous voices as we passed, but whenever I turned round there was nothing.

It was like the echo in the Marabar caves. I needed to go somewhere and cool down.

19

Maharajah Macs in Bangalore

As time passed, grief became less about how much I hurt, and more about remembering the wonderful times my father and I had together. From the darkest solipsism to an appreciation of the other. As I travelled across India it became less about me, and more about him; less about despair for what is lost, and more about celebration for what I had. In Hindu ritual, loud public mourning lasts thirteen days, during which time the departed's soul is undergoing reincarnation. Then, once a *kriya* ritual is performed, where, as a show of gratitude, rice and milk are offered to the departed, the mourning is over. Every physical death leads the true soul nearer to the ultimate goal in Hinduism: *sansara,* the constant cycle of birth and death.

By unclasping the fingers around his dead heart a little, perhaps I was releasing his *atman*? One of the films Tony worked on was Michael Powell's masterpiece, *A Matter of*

Life and Death, as a very young junior camera assistant when on leave from the RAF. The most famous scene in the movie – indeed, one of the landmark moments in British film – is the 'stairway to heaven' sequence. A huge 106-step escalator connecting this world with heaven was constructed in Denham Studios, Buckinghamshire, under the supervision of the London Passenger Transport Board. The film's plot at this point has a Hindu sensibility underlying it. The airman hero – played by David Niven – is in limbo between life and death, and is shown the escalator that will take him to 'the other life'. As he is about to ascend, his girlfriend decides to go in his place, and rushes up the staircase ahead of him. But, unable to face existence without him, she turns back. Heaven's jury looks kindly on his case and decides to grant the airman a new lifespan. One of the character says, 'nothing is stronger than the law in the universe, but on Earth, nothing is stronger than love'.

Tony helped film this scene, and though I know he had no realization of its iconic status in film history, he remembered it vividly. He told me that the noise of the escalator machinery was so great that it was impossible to record the soundtrack of the film at the same time as using the staircase. All the dialogue was dubbed in post-production.

Maybe his soul is stuck on that stairway because I'm not letting it go. Unlike Niven's airman, his life was not robbed too soon, he did not perish heroically. He had reached the end of this cycle. He needed to move on to the next. And so do I.

By coming to Bangalore, the heart of the new world order, the future city, I was able to do this. Slowly, day by day, in the most optimistic, forward-looking place on earth, I released my white-fingered grip on the past. On his heart. I stopped clinging to daddy.

I am taken back to early 1976. I am five years old, and am self-awake for the first time, feeling my separateness from my parents, half relishing the independence, the self-empowerment, and half in freefall panic about the loss of an anchor. We are at Edinburgh Waverley station. The previous day, in the grounds of a Peebles hotel, I have played proper golf for the first time – a pitch-and-putt course that they let kids on to. My father showed me how to chip, how to putt, standing behind me, enshrouding me, his huge bony hands on mine, twisting my little fingers gently around the club to form a perfect Vardon grip. I could smell his cigarette and tea breath; he was a giant of a man.

At the station there is a kiosk selling small cuddly toys in kilts. I want one so badly that I cry. My father is bewildered why I am so upset, but buys me the toy anyway. Later, we are high up the top of Arthur's Seat, gazing out across the crazy spires of the city. He holds me in his arms, my head next to his, father and son, forever locked in our mutual love.

I must let him go.

***

Earth has not anything to show more fair:
Dull would he be of soul who could pass by
A sight so touching in its majesty:
This City now doth like a garment wear

The beauty of the morning: silent, bare,
Ships, towers, domes, theatres, and temples lie
Open unto the fields, and to the sky,
All bright and glittering in the smokeless air.

William Wordsworth, from 'Composed upon
Westminster Bridge, September 3, 1802'

I am alone in the centre of the new universe. I am here at

the very moment a new trade economic superpower is in bloom, and it is staggering. Only here do I realize quite how decaying and faded European cities feel. Bangalore's citizens – from captains of industry to hotel porters – *buzz*. The amount of new property development is astonishing. A vast new metro system is about to open. It resembles the Docklands Light Railway but it dwarfs the DLR in scale. Along the city's famous MG Road, a gigantic elevated section of track flies through the air, fifty-feet up, to link the huge half-constructed stations that are blossoming everywhere.

In the city's Dooravani Nagar district, a massive new shopping mall is being built. It is cocooned in bamboo scaffolding and has the appearance of a Mogul palace from Rajasthan. Nearby, across the incredibly noisy, gridlocked Old Madras Road (now called National Highway 4) – imagine London's Euston Road after a major accident, but with everyone jostling for every inch of space, all the time, with horns on full blare – are the pristine Silicon Valley-style offices of Google India. Next to the offices on one side is a McDonald's, home of the 'Chicken Maharajah Mac' (chicken is the only meat used in Indian McDonald's); on the other side is a shack with a corrugated iron roof in front of which smart IT workers are slurping their super-sweet gooey tea in the traditional roadside way.

The cabbies of Bangalore are the proudest bunch I've ever encountered, keen to point out all the new massive building projects that any route through the city takes you past. On one road out, my cabbie pointed in the far distance to a Twin Towers-like edifice that apparently is an apartment complex that will be taller than the massive Petronas Towers in Kuala Lumpur. Bangalore is immense, under construction and ominous.

I flew out of Bangalore in 2006 after doing a BBC News job nearby. I drove to the airport through dusty Karnatakan plains, sparsely populated by farming families – India at its typically impoverished and rural. The airport then was in the centre of the city. It was a small, regional, dilapidated affair. Built in the 1970s, it was already falling to bits. As I waited to check in, the air conditioning started farting out noxious fumes followed by a thick white cloud that filled the whole check-in area, leading all the blinded, spluttering passengers to wish they'd flown from Chennai. The staff crammed us all into a small room that was meant for half the amount of people. I coped with this Black Hole of Bangalore by sitting cross-legged on the floor for three hours, playing Tiger Woods's golf game on my phone. As we huddled on the floor I also chatted to the Minister of Tourism for the Maldives Islands. He told me of the environmental catastrophe that could make his country sink due to global warming; in a few months time the unexpected trauma of the tsunami would hit those beautiful islands with full force.

These days Bangalore has the most beautiful airport in the world. When I arrive, it feels like I am in the Federation launch complex in *Star Trek*. It's an hour's drive out of town, sure, but it's vast, glassy, shimmering, like a six-star hotel spread over 200 acres. I think about how depressed I feel when I arrive at Heathrow off a plane and stagger, tripping with jet-lag through those narrow, dreary 1960s arrivals corridors to passport control and the baggage carousels. My last image of India will be this amazing statement of wealth, investment and global intent; on my return, my first impression of London will be of decline, drudgery and weary, half-hearted, making do. Hey, Bangalore seems to be saying, if this city is going to be at the centre of the new world order, it needs an airport to match these ambitions. It's got it. We in the West can watch in awe.

***

Bangalore Golf Club (BGC) is literally caught between the old and new cities; the British and the future. Founded in 1876 it is the oldest golf course in India that still plays on its original site. The Royal Calcutta Club is much older (founded 1829) but moved its location, and so, even though the course has been remodelled over the years, it is quite a thrill to play on pretty much the same fairways and greens that have been in use for 135 years.

The club couldn't be closer to the city centre. From the KFCs, Costa Coffees and Western-style shopping malls of the MG and Brigade roads, it is a short rickshaw ride to the golf club. The site is a beautifully maintained, lush, semi-tropical oasis amongst the frenzy of the city. And yet it is hard to ignore the road that rings half of the holes. On some tees it feels like the M1 is roaring past you on the other side of the thin fence.

The club has the finest pro shop in India, and you are served by *women.* It is all very slick and customer care-centred. I was told to wait twenty minutes after the Starter had been informed I wanted to play, and that he would contact me when he could squeeze me in. I waited an hour-and-a-half, but didn't mind, as I could watch people teeing off on one of the busiest, most gender-equal and friendly golf courses in India.

As I waited, I glanced at *The Times of India* and saw that Arjun Atwal had just about made the cut but Jeev Milkha Singh had fallen by the wayside in the wonderfully named 'Justin Timberlake Shriner's Hospitals for Children Open Golf Tournament' in Las Vegas.

I felt at the centre of the new golf world in the new India. What I suspected might be happening – that the values, class history and physical aesthetics of golf were becoming a way for India's new rich entrepreneurial class to express itself – seemed to be true. In the centre of the new high-tech world, golf is booming.

The BGC is venerable, but its clientele seemed dynamic, and it is building a new sports and swimming pool complex behind the club house. Located at the heart of Bangalore, its members are the movers and shakers of the new economic success.

The club's rival, the Karnataka Golf Association course near the old airport, opened for business in 1986, helped by a huge donation from the then chief minister of Karnataka state, Shri Ramakrishna Hegde, who was himself a big golf fan.

Then there is the US-style mega golf centre, the Eagleton Golf Village, a ninety-minute drive from the city. Its mission statement on its website is truly terrifying: 'We are proud to introduce ourselves as the pioneers in introducing the concept of leisure with business facilities of high standards. "Eagleton – The Golf Village" is known for presenting a unique capsule for the present day corporate that demands business with pleasure.' This made me want to run a mile. It also states: 'Golf is the future of Indian luxury and leisure.'

There are also the courses at nearby regenerating town Kolar, which I went on to visit.

I went around the BGC in a delightful fourball with some old boys, hacking around with them as dusk fell on the city of tomorrow.

In the 2010 Masters tournament at Augusta, Tiger played the most amazing shot I have ever seen. His whole performance was absolutely compelling. Here was a man, the greatest player in history, who had barely lifted a club in four months; he had been through marital break-up and the most public sexual exposé in sports history; and his legion of sponsors were pulling out of deals every week. Here was a man who should be in the Priory, not on the world's most famous golf course, potentially destroying that image of himself that we have from 1997, when, at just twenty-one, he strode up the eighteenth fairway, eighteen under, having smashed every Masters record in the book, and fully announcing himself to the world.

Yet amazingly he was competing and even challenging for the lead for three of the four days; he wasn't playing great, but even Tiger hacking, slicing and cursing his way round a golf course is still better than most. It was like watching George Best after the glory years; the magic was still there, it's just that the muscle memory wasn't refreshed enough. On the ninth he sliced his drive wildly into some pine trees. He shouted one of his famous Anglo-Saxon expostulations and marched into the trees to find his ball with a look on his face like that of a Viking who has returned from conquest to find his family have been eaten by trolls. The ball was about six feet behind a tree, which completely blocked his view of the green, 200 yards away. Any other golfer on the planet would have chipped out, essentially forfeiting a shot. Tiger took a three-iron, hit it as hard and low as he could, and *bent* the ball from right to left around the tree, finding a line through a criss-crossing avenue of pines out on to the fairway and bouncing several times on to the green. It had the precision of the greatest Beckham free-kick ever combined with the power and arrogance of an Ali punch. He parred.

In Bangalore Golf Club I was in a similar spot. On the twelfth, I had hit a terrible short drive, then sliced my second badly so that I was the other side of a small wood that guarded the green, in light rough that fringed the adjoining fairway. My caddy, Babu, a wise old boy whose opinions I respected, handed me my lob wedge and told me to hit it full and high over the trees and on to the green. I was going to but then I saw that 'Tiger line' from the Masters.

'Give me the three-iron, Babu,' I commanded. 'I can see a way through.'

He gave me that look that good Indian caddies always give you when they know you're going to screw up, but are too polite to say so. I got in the zone, I found my inner Tiger, I came down low and hard on the ball, with side swerve . . . and hit the ball into a tree ten yards in front of me. It ricocheted off to a position behind where I was standing in the first place. Then Babu did something for the first and only time in the round. He said, 'Let me show you, sir.' He put a ball down on the spot where the first one had rested, took my lob wedge, and hit the most beautiful, high-lofted pitch I have ever seen. He hit it so sweetly it was as though the club had not even touched the ball, but merely suggested to the air particles around it that they gracefully ascend it. The ball easily cleared the trees, hit the green, then beautifully backspinned like a deep-screwed cue ball on a snooker table to within three feet of the hole. It was in Bangalore that I understood fully the attitude middle-class Indian hackers have with their usually Dalit caddies: always listen to your caddy; he is always right; just pretend that you aren't listening to him, never look him in the eye and never ever say thank you for a good tip.

***

When I returned to the Hotel Empire after my round with these big cheeses, I found the following story in *The Times of India,* about a horrific ritual that was occurring in another part of southern India:

> More than 700 devotees of a local deity especially girls and women of different age groups, line up to be whipped by the priest and thus cured of their malady at the annual festival at the Achappan Temple in Vellalapatti on Sunday. Two main priests assisted by five others all dressed in traditional attire, hold long frightening whips and lash the 'possessed'. The priest whipped the victims till

> they chose to cry and run away in gnawing pain . . . under the belief that the sprit had been driven away. One of the victims, K. Priya, a Class VIII student and the youngest of them said her parents had advised her to participate in the festival.

Such Stone-Age savagery exists cheek-by-jowl with the most dynamic, ultra-modern economy in the world. In Bangalore I started to see that India's new economic success had not happened recently despite of its ancient religions, but *because* of them, specifically because of Hinduism – the dominant religion in the country (80 percent of the one billion Indians are Hindus).

Hinduism is the ultimate entrepreneurial, free-market religion. There is no pontiff, no holy scriptures sacred to all Hindus, no Vatican, no prayer book, no hierarchical priest class determining liturgy. It is chaos; it is the perfect expression of the madness, imagination, hubbub and spirituality of India. It is the ultimate hybrid, hotchpotch faith; anyone can set themselves up as a guru; if they are followed, their cult survives; some flourish and become the Hindu mainstream, others disappear without trace. Thus has Hinduism operated for 3,000 years; it's a DIY, get on your bike, seize the day, work out what the market wants and give it to them religion. In a way it shares much with the sort of entrepreneurial Thatcherite economics that are creating the Indian economic miracle at the moment. Indians are born entrepreneurs – witness the 24/7 all-hands-on-deck 'corner shop' business model that has enabled some Indian families in the UK to thrive after only thirty or forty years in the UK. A British Indian friend of mine once shocked me with a heavy bit of racism, snarling at how lazy and selfish black (he meant Caribbean) people are in London – they are content to sponge off the state, smoke drugs, not work and generally piss the rest of society off, he said;

somewhere through his wall of inherited prejudice there is a pride about Indian hard work, centred on the success and growth of the family.

Mrs Thatcher famously decentralized government, stripped the City of regulation, created favourable tax breaks for the aspirant southern, suburban, lower middle class and performed her own morally dubious economic miracle. A free market with few restrictive trading practice rules makes for a dynamic entrepreneurial economy. Napoleon Bonaparte famously sneered that 'England is a nation of shopkeepers'; Mrs Thatcher, who herself grew up in Grantham above her father's grocery shop, fully believed that this inundation of new small businesses in Essex and Kent, coupled with an aggressive thrusting City of London and massively quietened unions, would pull Britain into a new prosperous age.

I think the structure of free-market entrepreneurial capitalism and Hinduism share a great deal; and I would suggest that this is partly why Bangalore and most cities of India are booming; creating new creeds around a loose decentralized hub is what Indians do well. There is also a social-Darwinist side to both capitalism and Hinduism. Both believe in the survival of the fittest; weak, poorly managed small businesses that are not giving the market what it wants fail. In Hinduism, not only do unpopular cults fail, but the whole central idea of reincarnation and karma seems curiously evolutionist. Hinduism is surely the most patient religion on earth. Christians are told all they have to do is live seventy or so years of this wretched life and then the pearly gates will swing open and Jesus will give them a hug and a frappuccino. Hindus are playing a much longer game. They believe that your soul is reincarnated over and over again through the centuries, with each new incarnation trying to atone for the bad vibes (karma) that you embraced and embodied in previous lives. Through constant reincarnated struggle and work, your soul can reach a state of grace and achieve perfection. Some survive, some don't. The fittest have the best stab at Paradise.

One of the reasons the British and the Indians tolerated each other as much as they did for 300 years, was their mutual obsessions with trade and class. Indian salesmen have been haggling for thousands of years. Hinduism gave them the structure and mythological representation to justify entrepreneurial business adventure. They were just waiting for the right time and the right industry; with IT, they found it. One of the sole-trader entrepreneurial sectors that first saw the business potential of the internet was astrology. In the early 1990s astrology programmes were among the first software packages written in India. And skilled use of internet marketing has meant that this most ancient of trades, dealing in the mumbo jumbo of hunter-gatherer fear, has thrived in a perfect union of the ancient and very modern India.

Old creeds, new technology. Indians are brilliant at both, and mixing them together; Bangalore is their capital.

Soon it will be capital of the world; Robert Clive's statues in Whitehall, and in Chennai, will seem like that of Percy Bysshe Shelley's *Ozymandias.*

***

The Thirteenth Day

> *O Fire. Accept this dead body. Give it refuge. May your acceptance of the body bring you glory. O God in the garb of fire, burn this body and deliver the person to the abode of righteousness.*
>
> *Atharva-Veda* (*c.*3000 to 1000 BC)

Hinduism prohibits excessive mourning for the dead, as

this can prevent the departed soul reincarnating successfully. My mourning has my father stuck, like David Niven, halfway up that stairway. On the thirteenth day after a death, Hindus perform a fire ceremony – Sraddha – where offerings are made to the gods to ease the soul's passage through the realms as it journeys through reincarnation to its reappearance on Earth. A Sraddha ceremony is performed every year on the anniversary of the death, to continue aiding this journey. There is part of this ritual where the grievers acknowledge that the soul has joined its ancestors, and the gods. It is also, it seems to me, the moment when people admit that this human is dead. Not on the stairway anymore. Even after the death, the corpse, the funeral, seeing the bones lowered into the ground, I had not really accepted that my father was dead.

At the wake I stood at the bar downing pint after pint of Guinness, and generally entertaining the mourners with stories about my father. There was much laughter and I felt a little like Dave Allen or Ronnie Corbett, two of my father's comedy heroes from the 1970s who were experts in the very long, digressive, shaggy-dog tale. Many people commented how moving it was when, to end my funeral address, I read out a lyric about my father's love of cigarettes. I drunkenly turned to one of them and slurred, 'You know what, when I have a moment, I'm going to write down all the stories he told me, and all the stories I know about his life, and do something with them . . . as a tribute to him.' This book, and the dozen or so songs based on his life around which I have created a stage show, are the result. This is my Sraddha. I am at my thirteenth day.

On the thirteenth day, Hindus clean the shrine of the departed. Recently, surprising myself, I have started to visit my father's grave. I water the flowers, trim the grass and pluck out any weeds. Perhaps by doing this I am nudging his soul a step nearer rebirth, and enabling mine to live fully in this life once more. His ashes will not be carried down the Ganges, but his bones will be there under the soil for centuries, beyond a point where his – or my – deeds have any significance. It seems strange to be in a Christian culture that venerates *bones.* Hindus believe in destroying the corpse as quickly as possible so that the soul can be set free. Dying is about bones; *death* immediately becomes something philosophical.

A Sraddha prayer: 'Let the ancestors residing on Earth attain an evolved region. Let the ancestors who are in heaven, that is, at a higher plane of existence, never degrade. Let the ones who are at a medium plane of existence, attain a higher plane. Let the ancestors who symbolize the Truth protect us.'

20

Golf on the Gold Fields

On the final two days of my trip, as I explored the area around Bangalore, I found the Raj. And I found it so intoxicating that I nearly didn't come home.

***

'Beware of croc-o-diles!' read the sign, hand-daubed in splurged red paint on a piece of driftwood and banged into the ground on the banks of the river Chauvery, at the foot of the walls of the ruined city of Seringapatam.

As if the Duke of Wellington's forces – a motley collection of his own third foot regiment, assorted Highlanders and embittered local princes with a grudge against the city's rulers – hadn't enough to deal with as they charged at the walled city in 1799: Tipu Sultan's ruthless warriors were performing a savage defensive action; the British had to scale or destroy thirty-foot high stone walls, the heat was intense and they had to negotiate a difficult river crossing.

The last thing they would have needed was to have to tiptoe over angry crocs.

The crocs are still there, basking motionless in the sun, prehistoric relics of a purely savage time. Tipu Sultan's city is long destroyed. After the British and their allies finally seized it after a siege of several months, they razed it almost to the ground. As a symbol of the military ruthlessness of the East India Company, it did the job. As an act of British Imperial cultural barbarism, it was not atypical.

Thankfully a few wonderful buildings do remain intact as well as many evocative ruins. The Daria Daulat Bagh – the Sultan's summer palace – is a beautiful if very poorly preserved, mostly wooden summerhouse on a scale reminiscent of the Mogul princes. Set in vast, lush grounds the palace was Wellington's (then plain old Arthur Wellesley) headquarters after his victory over Tipu. A mile down the road is the Gumbaz, perhaps the most impressive site here. Much of visiting India is taken up by visiting ever more preposterous tombs. From the *folie de grandeur* Taj Mahal to the exquisite Hanuman's Tomb in Delhi to the immense minimalist bulk of Bijapur's Gol Gumbaz, death is celebrated on a grand scale here. The Gumbaz at Seringapatam is one of the most beautiful mausoleums in India. Small scale and yet still impressive, the chamber is decorated in the stripes of red, gold and brown – tiger colours for the 'Tiger of Mysore', Tipu's self-proclaimed nickname. He actually kept a menagerie of tigers to ram home the point. He is buried, under a tiger skin, of course, next to his father, the even more impressive but less well-known Hyder Ali.

The taking of Seringapatam, which was the climax of the Fourth Mysore War, had great significance far beyond Mysore or even India. The defeat of Tipu and the ceding of his lands enabled the East India Company to open up for trading in southern India. Before 1790 they had been operating almost exclusively north of Bombay only. More significant still was that this campaign was the making of Arthur Wellesley. After the military success, he ruled as governor here until 1805 with distinction – and terror. After the recent loss of America, Britain needed a hero and Wellesley stepped up to the mark. His triumphs here led him to Waterloo, to personal iconhood and to Britain establishing imperial mastery over the French for the rest of the century.

***

The next day I headed east of Bangalore to the Kolar Gold Fields, once India's Johannesburg, now a bleak post-industrial area with big regeneration plans. There was a gold rush here in the late nineteenth century, state of the art mines were established and, at one point, almost 300,000 people worked around the industry in the KGF (as the place is still known) community. For almost a century it boasted the world's deepest mine, Champions Reef, 11,500 feet deep. To transport the enormous mining equipment to the area the first wide gauge railway track in India was built – which is still there and still in use. KGF was also the first city in Asia to get electricity. However, the mines were all but abandoned a decade ago, and the town now acts as a rundown satellite for the Bangalore cyber-city two hours drive away; 3,000 people commute from KGF to Bangalore on the train every day.

British-style cowboy-prospectors flooded KGF, and these Cecil Rhodes rednecks wanted to play golf. So in 1885 they built the Kolar Gold Fields Gymkhana Club, with a twelve-hole golf course attached. It is the most perfectly preserved relic of the Raj in India. It is as though everyone British left in 1947, and the whole place was mothballed, untouched.

Getting there had a touch of cloak-and-dagger about it. I had read an article about KGF by the eminent British golf architect Howard Swann, which had piqued my interest. On the phone from his Essex base he kindly agreed to put me in touch with Mr Chandra Prakash, a big cheese at the Bangalore Golf Club, who would help me. So I waited. Feeling a little like Bill Murray's character in *Lost in Translation,* I started to live a very hotel-based life – wandering out to the pay phone at the sweet shop two roads away (try talking to Essex when the banshee wail of Chennai traffic is all around you. . .), eating too much room service, showering too often, generally just waiting. I was that fidgety. Finally, I reached Mr Chandra Prakash who, as a captain of Bangalore industry, I'm sure had far better things to do than worry about me. He gave me the number of a man in Kolar called Pradeep who could help me. Click. The phone went dead. It took me another day to get hold of Pradeep on his mobile. We agreed to meet by the side of a remote road in the village of Bangarapet, near Kolar, the next day. It was such a major daytrip that I knew there was a chance I could miss my flight back home. I sensed in my guts that it would be worth it. I could smell the Raj, strongly.

Pradeep was there as planned, his small, round body covered in a tight orange polo shirt, tucked into a pair of blue jeans. He was fiftyish, instantly welcoming and passionate about golf. And his wife's cooking.

We drove in convoy to the Gymkhana Club. It is a wonderful place. It also has the air of being shut. Really shut. Shut since 1947 shut. At the rather grand Mogulesque yellow-and-white brick clubhouse we were greeted by the three caretakers of the club. Pradeep gently bossed them around and ordered one of them to fetch him some fags. They followed us around at a discreet and slightly baffled distance for my whole visit, keys jangling, extremely courteous and tacitly quizzical of my motivations.

I was shown into the huge billiard room, where three full-sized tables lay under dust sheets, and cues and rests lay around the walls alongside boards commemorating tournaments from long ago. I thought of the peace I have always found in snooker clubs at home; the dark, the quiet, the click-clack of the balls, the slow, long drinking, the maleness, the focus away from everything. Opposite is the lounge area, unchanged since the Raj and feeling like a village hall in the Kent Weald; a small stage at one end for amateur dramatics, Edwardian chairs grouped round in newspaper-reading clusters, and a mini grand piano that has been in that room for a century. Passing the collected heads of boar and bison nailed to the wall, I came to the Dodge City-like saloon bar, where the last cowboys left many years before. On the wall is a pencil portrait of John Taylor, one of the early gold prospectors who made a fortune and helped found this club. His family still have interests in the area's gold, apparently.

Down a short, open-air pathway, roofed in corrugated iron sheets, I was shown into the gem of the place: the main hall. About the size of a small school sports hall, it is dominated by the badminton court marked out on the floor, with the net still up. Portraits of British denizens of the club – golf captains, chairmen, treasurers, sports teams with trophies – dating back to its foundation decorate the walls. Here, and in the adjoining library room, are rows of glass bookshelves housing volumes on mining, chemical engineering and geology. These publications have titles like *The Periodical of British Chemical and Physiological Abstracity.* As gold-prospecting libraries go, this must be one of the best in India, though slightly out of date, perhaps.

As we walked out of the library I saw a large rusting piece of mining winch equipment, the size of a large elephant. Then Pradeep took me through a small wooden gate and on to the golf course.

I'd never seen a course like it. 'Links' isn't quite the word. It is a course moulded on very dry, very brown earth on a gentle hillside, with desert-feeling trees and bushes dotted here and there. There are browns of pure beach sand instead of greens, which a caddy smoothes over and flattens with a twig brush before every putt. Pradeep and I chipped and putted a few on the ninth green. He showed me how to adjust to chipping on to sand, and how to 'skid' your putt in, like you would on an iced up green. We walked the course and I marvelled at the views over the Karnatakan plain; Pradeep chain-smoked; I perspired.

At one point we were approached by a group of five women and a child. They looked like several generations of the same poor family. Pradeep excused himself and started talking to them. They behaved with considerable deference, and I noticed that they were entreating him in a very subtle way. Having heard their story, Pradeep gave a gentle nod, took his wallet from his pocket and gave the head lady 300 rupees. The average wage for a rural worker in Karnataka is around 60 rupees (about £1) a day. Their gratitude and relief was palpable.

'Come, the next hole,' he said to me, and we strode up the fairway.

After a while I asked, 'Who were those ladies?'

He looked pained that he had to talk about this, but clearly felt duty bound to be polite to a guest. 'They are poor women. They work for us. I am a freemason. They clean our lodge. Their child is sick, and they need money to take him to a doctor and get some medicine. They do not have this money, so I gave it to them.' He cleared his throat, mimed a few clubless practice swings, then said 'OK let's play a hole properly – you versus me. England v India.'

He had told me many times how the course was closed, communicating that there was no chance I was going to get a game today, so don't even think about it. But Pradeep is a man with a golf obsession. And he saw I was similarly afflicted. We had to play. Luckily I'd brought my clubs, just in case, and everyone snapped into action. One of the caretakers caddied for me and one for Pradeep, and we settled ourselves on the ninth tee, a long par-four back to the clubhouse. There was silence. Hell, I felt under pressure. But I drove moderately well, landing in the light rough to the right of the fairway – though actually most of the time it was hard to tell what was rough and what was fairway as it was all roughish. Pradeep landed fifteen yards ahead of me. I played a good, strong, cross-fairway, five-iron second shot to leave a pitch in. Pradeep topped his second, muttered 'Blast!' and swiped the ground with the iron angrily. He played his third to the edge of the green.

I realized how seriously we were both taking this. I really wanted to do well on this hole. I wanted to win it, and already I was in the better position. I took out my pitching wedge and played exactly the same shot that nearly killed some tourists at Kodaikanal: a perfect, full, wonderfully parabolic pitch. This time, though, I'd judged the distance spot on. It landed on the 'brown' and, with no bounce, settled into the sand. 'Good shot!' shouted Pradeep, who chipped on well. We both two-putted, leaving me with a five and him with a six.

'Congratulations, England win – this time. Makes a change, eh?' he said to me, then we both dissolved in hearty chuckles.

Pradeep insisted I lunched with him and his wife. The first rule of India is: never eat with your left hand. The second is: never decline an offer of food. You are being a selfish ungrateful Western git if you do. So we drove to Pradeep's place, and on the way he showed me another course – the Earth Mover Golf Course. This is owned by the BEML corporation, which makes industrial tools and vehicles for the mining industries. This course is for workers' R&R and it is very pleasant, too. We walked round it, then finally reached Pradeep's wife and her lunch.

'If you do not eat everything my wife puts in front of you, I will think she is a bad cook, and a bad wife,' he said. I'm not sure he was joking.

I was hungry, but I was a) acutely conscious that every second I stayed eating this food, I was jeopardizing making that plane home, and b) this lady's food was delicious, but phenomenally hot. My stomach was already in a bad way. I was about to fly twenty hours with this meal inside me, bubbling away like molten lava. Oh God.

I ate and ate. And still there was more. I ate until there was a pain in my diaphragm. Still more food was produced. I had to call a stop. I had to insult the lady. I felt terrible, but I had to get that plane. Pradeep had shown me great kindness. I met his ninety-year-old father who remembered the British in Kolar. We talked golf and Pradeep showed me the trophies he had won. Golf is a state of mind. If you find someone else at the same golf place you are there is connection. There is *home*.

Pradeep is not a wealthy man, not a Bangalorean captain of industry, but he seemed to represent a new type of Indian golfer – middle class and passionate. Howard Swann has a big vision for golf in Kolar – seeing the potential of this underdeveloped moon of the new Eldorado. A golf training centre is being built nearby, and there are plans to redevelop the Gymkhana Club and add a golf academy there. Nothing at the moment can stand in the way of progress and development in this area. It is like being in London in 1840, just as the Empire was hitting its stride. The KGF Gymkhana Club won't for much longer look so cryogenically frozen in 1947. I was grateful to have caught the last days and the final distant echoes of the Raj here.

***

There is a town in the Haute-Vienne region in the middle

of France called Oradour-sur-Glane. On 10 June 1944, the SS massacred 642 of the its inhabitants, then destroyed the town. The French decided after the war not to rebuild the place, but to leave it exactly how it looked in 1944 as a memorial to those who died in the war. To this day nothing has been altered.

KGF Gymkhana Club has the same feeling of history having stopped. As I walked back through the clubhouse I felt the strongest sense, in this place of Raj ghosts, of being with my ancestors, being with my father, being home. This moment of ultimate nostalgia, this finding the core point of my cause-and-effect history, propelled me forward with irresistible force.

In neighbouring Tamil Nadu, they call sleep paralysis '*amuku be*' or 'the ghost that is holding you down'. I made the plane – just. But I had connected myself up again in Kolar, and a part of me stayed there in the forever dead Raj.

21

Brighton

I arrived at my hotel, walked out onto the balcony and immediately smelt the gardeners cooking their curries – the same smell that came from the servants' quarters in my parents' house. The whole of my childhood in Calcutta flashed back to me. I had been searching for my roots in all the wrong places.

Mark Tully, on returning to India
to start his BBC posting (1965)

I am sitting by the fire in the bar of East Brighton golf club, founded in 1893, around the same time that the golf craze hit the Raj. Tom is next to me, texting Claire, like they did throughout the night on those long Indian train rides. We are into our third pints of London Pride ale. I have just played the best nine holes of my life. I am good at golf. I feel elated for the first time in a year. I no longer talk to ghosts.

Apart from Walton, I've always thought of Brighton as my home. It's the place where I feel I can be most me, where I can wear what I want, sit in a café or pub and talk to like-minded people. It's where I can wear shades all the time and not get the looks I do in London. Where most people who pass me in the street are much madder than me. Four times I have tried to live here. Four times I have left. I am about to leave again, in seven days. I do not think I will ever come back.

I am the son of a south coast boy, whose grandfather was a fishmonger in Hastings; whose father joined the Navy and lived in Eastbourne and Polegate; who himself saw the land between the Ashdown Forest and Beachy Head as his homeland. For a while my parents lived in Pevensey Bay, where the Normans first stepped foot on English soil – the last time anyone invaded us, as my father would say (ignoring the Dutch takeover in 1688, which was an invasion in all but name and without bloodshed) – and started the history that led to the Raj.

Once a month we drove to see my grandparents in Polegate. On the way we would take in the Sussex my father grew up in. We holidayed in Bournemouth, Hayling Island, the Isle of Wight, the New Forest. From our home in Surrey it was only an hour's drive to Worthing or Brighton. We would go there on a whim, for a drive, for a day out, for something to do. For some seaside fun. For my father to reconnect with his roots, sitting on shores, looking out to sea. My parents retired to Keyford-on-Sea, a permanent Saga holiday in brick.

For ten years I have kept returning to Brighton, looking for something, a shard of my genetic past from long, long ago. Perhaps now, as I enter what in Hinduism is called *garhasthya* – the second, householder stage of life when a man has responsibilities to his family and community – I can leave this place and re-enter the world. I fled here after my father died. I have been burying him ever since. It is time to stop talking to ghosts, and claim the kingdom.

It is one year exactly after my father died. Tom and I hadn't seen each other since India and we headed to this wonderful course at East Brighton, on the cliffs high above the town. When I first crash-landed in Brighton, I used to go for long, solitary walks in the late afternoon and evening. I would often walk up to the golf course, bordering the horseshoe swoop of Brighton racecourse, and watch the golfers come and go.

We stood on the eighteenth tee half-an-hour ago and absorbed the panorama. It was many months since we'd stood high in the Himalayas on the driving range in Kashmir, drinking in the glory of the place. Now we were home, and this vista touched me more than any. To our left lay the fields of Rottingdean and Falmer, the final undulations of the downs before the sea; Roedean school, a sinister gothic pile, a burning Mandalay edifice amongst them. The marina was ahead, with its hugging-arms sea wall, like a modern Lyme; the masts of 300 yachts and pleasure boats bobbing up and down in the calm of their sheltered moorings. To our right, there was the racecourse and the heathland in its centre, dogs being walked, horses trotting, families exercising, the grandstand large and empty like some phantom of the 1930s. In the valley sat the town of Brighton, looking as small and cut off as it actually is. Hardly Oxford or Prague, no umbrella of spires and domes, no city walls or modern architectural wonders, but a unique town all the same. It takes people a long time to get to Brighton; it takes them even longer to return home.

The sun was starting to set over Worthing in the west, and was already shooting out delicious pink, orange and yellow candyfloss across its sky canvas. This was as splendid as any sunset over the Arabian Sea in Goa, or in the desert in Rajasthan, or amongst the Sundarban swamps, or in the

Himalayan foothills. This was more splendid because it was *mine.* The sunset of my childhood, made more splendid by the toxic refraction of a straining ozone layer. It's my father's sunset, and it is beautiful.

We were about to tee off into it. Despite an eight on the first hole (I was aiming for the wrong green for my first three shots), I knew I had played well. Since the turn, I was dimly aware that I had played really well. I hadn't added up my strokes yet, but I parred the tenth and fifteenth and birdied the thirteenth and sixteenth. I had never birdied two holes in four before. I was utterly in the zone; very occasionally I touched a level of genius; I felt the Tiger within.

So, 474 yards into the setting sun. We both hit good drives, me far right, Tom far left, but both just on the generous fairway. I hit a good five-iron in, and my ball rested near Tom's, whose second shot was equally good. As we walked to our balls, we headed downhill into the sunset, like two cowboys on their way home, with Morricone soundtrack booming, reclaiming the land left to them. We were the last pair out and darkness was gathering behind us, but the red disk of the sun was enough illumination for us to play two beautiful pitches on to the green, and both to two-putt. A pair of par fives. Sometimes golf can be the most perfect expression of a man's mental, emotional and physical contentment.

In the bar I do the math. Because of the hideous eight on the first, and some average ball striking, I went out in forty-nine. But I'd come back to the clubhouse in forty-one. Forty-one! That is astounding. Only four over par. Tiger on a really bad day might get four over on the back nine here. Maybe.

My father is dead. His ghost no longer haunts me. I have pulled myself through by golf, therapy, alcohol, friends and love. And India, which took my character to pieces and reformed it, over and over again, until I found myself. I discovered how I could honour him. This book is my tribute to him, my Sraddha.

The Raj is long gone, too, and good riddance. But through it I came to better understand myself, my father, and what it means to be a sportsman and an Englishman.

Acknowledgements

So many people played roles in making this book come to life, none more than Tom Aldwinckle, who was my near constant companion, golf partner, shoulder to cry on and dangerous-food compadre. In dark times in remote hills and jungles Tom's unflappability, sense of humour and bewildering lack of interest in Indian history kept me calm. I also need to say a profound thank you to other good friends, Mark Ellis, Liz Eyre, Pete Briley, Zoe Byrne and Daphne Harris, all of whom have put me up in turbulent times, and given me places to write and regather. Simon Nicholson and Angela Clerkin have been my writing and publishing gurus throughout this book, always free, generous with their time and up for a moan, as indeed has been Dr Andrew Teverson, who has given me enormous support and valuable literary contexts on the Raj. Also thanks to Ish Kalia for those through-the-night chats on anything Raj or Indian, and to Jari Vlckova.

The Dhaka crew (you know who you are!) were amazing to me in Bangladesh and I thank the great Sakhawat Hossian Sohel for his time and patience. Karoki Lewis has been a valuable subcontinent companion for years, and he and the kind Kunal Batra helped me out of a jam in Chennai . . .

Thanks to the fantastic Howard Swann and Chandra Prakash for helping me reach Kolar, and to Peter Allis for his kind supportive comments and for giving my father so much pleasure throughout his life both as player and commentator. Thank you, Tiger, for your inspirational genius, Ian Poulter, for breaking the mould, and above all thanks to Seve who was my father's hero, a man who consistently made my dad's spirit soar. May they both rest in peace in the nineteenth hole in the sky.

I thank my brilliant agent Lizzie Kremer for sharing the concept and having the faith to push the book through, and all at David Higham Associates who have provided a great support for me. The Society of Authors very kindly gave me a Travel Writing Award that enabled me to finish this book, for which I am incredibly grateful. Also the staff of the British Library's Asian and African Studies Room were extremely helpful when handling my idiosyncratic requests. This book would not exist without the vision of my editor Andreas Campomar, and I am profoundly grateful to him for taking a punt on this high handicap hacker.

Finally I would like to send my love to my godfather Geoff Cooper, who I have played golf with since I was a child, and his wife Joy. And, above all, to my mother Gloria, who has gone through much of this book with me.